relations and indu ... st recent research
looks at the role ... g and developing
corporate strateg ... y people become
personnel directoi ... yee Relations) for
the IPD.

Graham Judge runs JW Business Advisors, a consultancy providing a
bespoke personnel service to organisations which do not employ a
senior personnel professional. He has held a number of personnel and
training posts within printing and packaging, and was a director of the
British Printing Industries Federation. He is also an Associate Lecturer
in Human Resources Management at the University of East London
and an Associate Examiner (Employee Relations) for the IPD.

IƆ

Other titles in the series:

Core Personnel and Development
Mick Marchington and Adrian Wilkinson

Employee Development
Rosemary Harrison

Employee Resourcing
Ted Johns and Stephen Taylor

Employee Reward
Michael Armstrong

Personnel Practice
Malcolm Martin and Tricia Jackson

The Institute of Personnel and Development is the leading publisher of books and reports for personnel and training professionals, students, and all those concerned with the effective management and development of people at work. For details of all our titles, please contact the Publishing Department:
tel. 0181-263 3387
fax 0181-263 3850
e-mail publish@ipd.co.uk
The catalogue of all IPD titles can be viewed on the IPD website:
http://www.ipd.co.uk

PEOPLE AND ORGANISATIONS

Employee Relations

JOHN GENNARD AND GRAHAM JUDGE

INSTITUTE OF PERSONNEL AND DEVELOPMENT

First published in 1997

Reprinted 1998

Design by Curve

Typeset by Fakenham Photosetting Ltd, Fakenham, Norfolk

Printed in Great Britain by
The Cromwell Press, Wiltshire

British Library Cataloguing in Publication Data
A catalogue record of this book is available from the British Library

ISBN 0-85292-654-5

INSTITUTE OF PERSONNEL
AND DEVELOPMENT

IPD House, Camp Road, London SW19 4UX
Tel: 0181 971 9000   Fax: 0181 263 3333
Registered office as above. Registered Charity No. 1038333
A company limited by guarantee. Registered in England No. 2931892

Contents

EDITORS' FOREWORD   VI

ACKNOWLEDGEMENTS   IX

PART 1 INTRODUCTION   1

PART 2 EMPLOYEE RELATIONS: AN OVERVIEW   11
1 Employee relations: an overview   11

PART 3 PARTIES, PROCESSES, OUTCOMES AND
CONTENT   41
2 The corporate environment   41
3 Employee relations institutions   66
4 Employee relations strategies and policies   90
5 Employee involvement and participation   114

PART 4 MANAGING EMPLOYEE RELATIONS   143
6 Negotiating skills   143
7 Handling disciplinary matters   174
8 Grievance-handling   198
9 Bargaining with employees   222
10 Handling redundancy situations   238

PART 5 REVIEW   259
11 Examination questions and advice   259

REFERENCES   267
INDEX   270

Editors' foreword

People hold the key to more productive and efficient organisations. The way in which people are managed and developed at work has major effects upon quality, customer service, organisational flexibility and costs. Personnel and development practitioners can play a major role in creating the framework for this to happen, but ultimately they are dependent upon line managers and other employees for its delivery. It is important that personnel and development specialists gain the commitment of others and pursue professional and ethical practices that will bring about competitive success. There is also a need to evaluate the contribution that personnel and development approaches and processes make for organisational success, and to consider ways of making them more effective. Such an approach is relevant for all types of practitioner – personnel and development generalists and specialists, line managers, consultants and academics.

This is one of a series of books under the title *People and Organisations*. The series provides essential guidance and points of references for all those involved with people in organisations. It aims to provide the main body of knowledge and pointers to the required level of skills for personnel and development practitioners operating at a professional level in all types and sizes of organisation.

The series has been specially written to satisfy new professional standards defined by the Institute of Personnel and Development (IPD) in the United Kingdom and the Republic of Ireland. The series also responds to a special need in the United Kingdom for texts structured to cover the knowledge aspects of new and revised National and Scottish Vocational Qualifications (N/SVQs) in Personnel and Training Development.

Three 'fields' of standards have to be satisfied in order to gain graduate membership of the IPD: (i) core management (ii) core personnel and development and (iii) any four from a range of more than 20 generalist and specialist electives. The three fields can be tackled in any order, or indeed all at the same time. A range of learning routes is available: full or part time educational course, flexible learning methods or direct experience. The standards may be assessed by educational and competence-based methods. The books in the series are suitable for supporting all methods of learning.

The series starts by addressing *core personnel and development* and four generalist electives: employee reward, employee resourcing, employee relations and employee development. Together, these cover the personnel and development knowledge requirements for graduateship of the IPD. These also cover the knowledge aspects of training and development and personnel N/SVQs at Level 4.

Core Personnel and Development by Mick Marchington and Adrian Wilkinson addresses the essential knowledge and understanding required of all personnel and development professionals, whether generalists or specialists. Practitioners need to be aware of the wide range of circumstances in which personnel and development processes take place and consequently the degree to which particular approaches and practices may be appropriate in specific circumstances. In addressing these matters, the book covers the core personnel and development standards of the IPD, as well as providing an essential grounding for human resource management options within business and management studies degrees. The authors are both well-known researchers in the field, working at one of the UK's leading management schools. Professor Marchington is also a chief examiner with the IPD.

Employee Reward by chief examiner Michael Armstrong has been written specially to provide extensive subject coverage for practitioners required by both the IPD's new generalist standards for employee reward and the personnel N/SVQ Level 4 unit covering employee reward. It is the first book on employee reward to be produced specifically for the purposes of aiding practitioners to gain accredited UK qualifications.

Employee Relations, by chief examiner Professor John Gennard and associate examiner Graham Judge, explores the link between the corporate environment and the interests of the buyers and sellers of labour. It also demonstrates how employers (whether or not they recognise unions) can handle the core issues of bargaining, group problem-solving, redundancy, participation, discipline and grievances, and examines how to evaluate the latest management trends.

Employee Development by chief examiner Rosemary Harrison is a major new text, which extends the scope of her immensely popular earlier book of the same name to establish the role of human resource development (HRD) and its direction into the next century. After reviewing the historical roots of HRD, she considers its links with business imperatives, its national and international context, the management of the HRD function, and ways of aligning HRD with the organisation's performance management system. Finally, she provides a framework setting HRD in the context of organisational learning, the key capabilities of an enterprise and the generation of the new knowledge it needs.

Both these books, like Ted Johns and Stephen Taylor's *Employee Resourcing*, are carefully tailored to the new IPD and N/SVQ standards, while Malcolm Martin and Tricia Jackson's *Personnel Practice* is focused on the needs of those studying for CPP. This also gives a thorough grounding in the basics of personnel activities. The authors are experienced practitioners and lead tutors for one of the UK's main providers of IPD flexible learning programmes.

In drawing upon a team of distinguished and experienced writers and practitioners, the People and Organisations series aims to provide a range of up-to-date, practical texts indispensable to those pursuing IPD and N/SVQ qualifications in personnel and development. The books will also prove valuable to those who are taking other human resource management and employment relations courses, or who are simply seeking greater understanding in their work.

Mick Marchington   *Mike Oram*

Acknowledgements

We would like to thank the following individuals for their help and assistance with this book: Mike Oram for his encouragement in the early days of this project, and Geoff Hayward, the associate examiner, for his contribution, and especially for the material on Europe; Mick Marchington and Matthew Reisz, who provided invaluable comment and feedback on many of the drafts; Debbie Campbell, who put together the final document and also did much of the word-processing. Family and friends also made a huge contribution with their encouragement: John would like to thank Anne for her support, while Graham knows that without Kim the book would never have been finished – he now promises to do all the other outstanding jobs!

John Gennard
Graham Judge
March 1997

Part 1

INTRODUCTION

THE INFLUENTIAL MANAGER

If personnel/HR managers, at any level of seniority, are to be pro-active and to have influence in an organisation, they must demonstrate certain abilities (see Figure 1). First they require a successful record of professional competence in the personnel/HR management field and one that is recognised by their managerial colleagues both within and outside the personnel function. Second, they must demonstrate an understanding of the personnel/HR management function as a whole and how its separate components integrate. Third, they must understand the interests of the business or organisation as a whole, and that these take preference over those of any management function as a whole or its component parts. Fourth, they need to develop a network of contacts with managers, both within and outside the personnel/HR management function, in their own organisation and with managers in other organisations, including employers' associations and professional bodies such as the Institute of Personnel and Development (IPD) and the British Institute of Management (BIM). Fifth, they also require to build fruitful relationships with their superiors and to possess excellent inter-personal skills, particularly with respect to communications and team-building. Each of these five abilities is a necessary condition for an effective and influential personnel/HR manager, but each is an insufficient ability on its own.

All people managers regardless of their seniority (personnel assistant, officer, manager, executive, etc) need to understand the nature of the business of the organisation in which they manage in terms of its mission, objectives, strategies and policies. In the private sector the effective and influential personnel/HR manager will know what is the 'bottom line' for the business and be able to contribute constructively, at the appropriate level of decision-making (department, section, management team, working party, etc), to discussions on how the

Figure 1 Necessary conditions for an effective and influential personnel manager

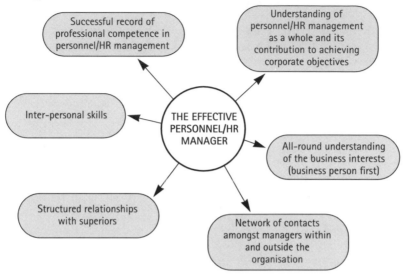

business might be developed and expanded. In the public sector the effective and influential personnel manager will understand the objectives of efficiency, effectiveness, economy, 'value for money' and high quality of service delivery to the customer or client.

Effective personnel/HR managers understand how the people-management function contributes to the achievement of the organisation's commercial and/or social objectives. They are capable of explaining to other managers, particularly outside personnel-HR management, how the function's strategies and policies help the business to develop and grow, 'add value' to the business as a whole, and help provide a higher quality of service to the customer, client and the Council Tax payer. In a nutshell, the personnel/HR manager can explain to the other managers how the activities of the personnel/HR function match with the objectives of the organisation as a whole. This is vertical integration of a management function with the overall business objectives – and this was a key feature to which you were introduced in your core personnel and development studies.

In addition the effective personnel/HR manager can explain how the various components of people management – employee resourcing, training and development, reward and relations – contribute to the achievement of the objectives of the personnel/HR management function. This involves them in understanding fully how the strategies and policies of the components of the personnel function link together to achieve the goals of the function. Such horizontal integration of the personnel/HR management function will not be new to you for it was a central theme in your core personnel and development studies. It is important during your employee relations studies that you understand vertical and horizontal integration since the compulsory case-study question on the employee relations examination papers is designed to assess your ability to integrate personnel/HR management activities (horizontal and vertical) by suggesting solutions to the problems posed in the mini-case-study.

Effective personnel/HR managers in their management teams have a proven competence recognised by their management colleagues in employee relations as well as in employee resourcing, training and development, and pay and reward. It is essential, therefore, if personnel managers are to be effective, that they have an adequate knowledge and understanding of employee relations and have acquired the appropriate skills to apply that knowledge and understanding to solve employee relations problems in order to enable the organisation to achieve its commercial and/or social objectives. One implication of this statement is that it is not only existing, and prospective, personnel managers who need to acquire employee relations knowledge, understanding and skills, but all managers, regardless of their seniority or specialism, who manage people problems.

The personnel/HR manager who lacks professional competence in employee relations will be a less effective manager. The trend in many organisations to devolve their personnel/HRM management function across management teams reinforces this view. Devolution often means that the services of a personnel manager with a specialism will not always be required. However, the activities of the employee relations function (for example, communications policy, handling employee grievances, dealing with disciplinary matters and the adjustment of the size of the workforce) nevertheless must be delivered to the management team. Generalist personnel managers with employee relations skills are essential to any management team. Specialist personnel managers are less attractive to a management team.

This book therefore aims to provide the generalist personnel/HR manager, and any other managers who have to manage people, with the appropriate employee relations knowledge, understanding and skills to apply that knowledge and understanding to solving people-management problems. This in turn will contribute to the organisation's achieving its commercial and/or social objectives. It will have the additional advantage of enhancing the credibility of personnel/HR managers in the eyes of their managerial colleagues both within and outside the personnel/HR management function.

A central theme of the book is that 'Best Practice' in the delivery of the personnel/HR management strategy and policies adds value to the business and thereby contributes to the achievement of the corporate-organisational economic and social objectives. It explains not only what constitutes the best practice (ie acting with just cause and behaving fair and reasonably) but why operating to best practice standards is sound business practice (eg avoidance of falling foul of industrial tribunal decisions by having 'bad' practices exposed, and the financial and image consequences of this). The book also aims to help personnel managers/professionals develop and acquire skills not only to solve people management problems but also to develop and improve their inter-personal skills and thereby the quality of their relationships with superiors.

EMPLOYEE RELATIONS ACTIVITIES

The purpose of employee relations activity is to reconcile the different interests of the buyers of labour services (employers) and the sellers of labour services (employees), and in so doing assist the organisation achieve its business and/or social objectives. This difference of interests revolves around the 'price' (including the quality and quantity) at which labour services are bought and sold. Although there is this difference of interests, both management and employees have a common purpose in reconciling their differing interests. The alternative is mutual destruction of the employing unit. The closure of the enterprise is of no benefit to employers or employees. There is mutual advantage to both employers and employees in resolving their differences as buyers and sellers of labour market services. They accommodate their respective interests by making agreements, rules and regulations by utilising various employee relations processes – collective bargaining, unilateral imposition by management, joint consultation, arbitration, mediation and conciliation, and Parliamentary legislation.

The agreements, rules and regulations express the price at which labour services are bought and sold, and are made at different levels (workplace, company, industry) and have different degrees of authorship. Some are written solely (imposed) by the employer with little or no influence from the employees, whereas others – usually as a result of collective bargaining – are jointly authored by the employer and representatives of their employees.

The agreements, rules and regulations cover two broad ranges of issues. One comprises substantive issues (pay, holidays, hours of work, incentive schemes, pensions, sick pay, maternity leave, family-friendly policies, etc) and the other is procedural issues. Employee relations procedures provide fair and reasonable standards of behaviour to resolve in a peaceful manner issues over which employers and employees have differences. Such procedures normally cover issues such as employee complaints against the behaviour of employers (known as grievances), employer complaints about the behaviour of employees (referred to as disciplinary matters), the need to reduce the size of the workforce (redundancy), employee claims that the responsibilities of their jobs have increased (job-grading), and employee requests for union representation (union recognition procedures).

The content of agreements, rules and regulations, and the employee relations processes used to reach to secure them, reflect the relative balance of bargaining power between employers and employees. This balance is heavily influenced by changes in the corporate environment in which an organisation undertakes its employee relations activity. The major factors shaping the external corporate environment are the economic and legal policies of national governments and European Union political decision-making institutions. In an attempt to enhance their economic interests, both employers and employees, via representative organisations, spend relatively large sums of money on the political lobbying process to persuade the Government to introduce appropriate economic and legal policies. A further factor in the external corporate environment that influences employee relations is the implementation, by employers, of technological change.

The balance of bargaining power is a central concept that needs to be understood by employee relations managers. It helps explain the constraints within which managements can exercise their power. Abuse of power to obtain one's aims is not professional behaviour. It inevitably leads to pressure for legal restraints to be imposed to curb the abuse. Unprofessional behaviour along the lines of 'might is right' will result in employees' behaving in the same way when the balance of bargaining power shifts away from management towards the employees. Professionalism means tackling matters in a systematic and careful manner. The fact that the state of the balance of bargaining power means that management can 'succeed' without behaving systematically and carefully is no excuse for managers not to behave in a professional way. Best practice dictates that they behave in a professional manner, gaining consent by discussion, consultation, negotiation and involvement, not the crude exercise of power.

However, personnel managers/professionals require more than just knowledge and understanding of employee relations parties, processes, agreements, rules and regulations and the external environment in which these activities take place if they are to solve people-management problems effectively. Employee relations problem-solving also requires the development and application of certain skills, of which the most significant are communication (oral and written), interviewing, listening, negotiating, evaluating and analysis.

This book should therefore widen and develop the employee relations knowledge and understanding you acquired in your core personnel and development studies. It provides sufficient knowledge, understanding and skills for personnel managers (and those who manage people in other management functions) to operate as professional people managers in a number of different situations, including both union and non-union environments. The book also aims to introduce you to how important it is that personnel managers/professionals become effective and influential in the organisation by understanding the concepts of best practice and the balance of bargaining power, and that they acquire and develop the general management skills of oral and written communication, interviewing, listening, evaluation and negotiation. Negotiation includes the ability to talk directly with managerial colleagues, with more senior management colleagues and with management colleagues from other management functions, to gain their commitment to proposed courses of action or to the introduction of new policies. It also involves serious discussion with individual employees over their grievances against management behaviour, and with employees and groups over issues such as pay and other employment conditions and redundancy.

THE BOOK'S MAJOR THEMES

There are a number of key themes associated with this book. The major ones are:

- the IPD qualifications are different in perspective from academic qualifications

- employee relations are just as relevant in non-union environments as unionised ones

- the unforeseen impact of changes in the corporate environment on the balance of bargaining power between the buyers and sellers of labour services and on the employee relations policy and arrangements of organisations

- how important it is that management behaves in a fair and reasonable manner

- the need to evaluate whether new employment practices introduced into one organisation can be successfully transplanted into another organisation

- the day-to-day grind of intra- and inter-management negotiations.

The IPD Graduate Professional Qualification is not an academic qualification. It indicates to employers that its holders can be reasonably expected to be aware of and to understand prevailing trends, topics and management techniques deployed in employee relations, and can display an acceptable level of proficiency in terms of operational skills. An IPD qualification indicates the competence of personnel managers to solve people-management problems by the application of their acquired knowledge and understanding using appropriate management skills. Knowledge and understanding is essential, but limited, if managers lack the practical skills to apply it. Holders of an IPD professional qualification should be capable of entering a personnel department and operating without causing mayhem when asked to undertake tasks with little or no supervision.

University degree/diploma qualifications should have a curricular balance between the theoretical and vocational needs of students different from that of the IPD graduate professional qualification. University degrees require students to be aware of the plurality of perspectives on issues and themes. IPD professional qualifications are management qualifications, and students seeking IPD qualifications should be taught from a management perspective. IPD graduates must be capable of demonstrating an ability to identify, define and explain the significance of employee relations managers' possessing (or not possessing) specific skills to solve people-management problems. This book is written solely from a professional management perspective. It explains why personnel managers require specific skills. It is a 'how to do it' book in which the importance of proceeding on the basis of best practice is to the fore.

It is an acute misunderstanding to believe employee relations is a relevant management activity only if the organisation deals with trade unions. In non-union environments, as in a unionised one, collective relationships exist. In non-union firms there are employee representative bodies (eg employee councils, works councils, joint consultative committees) and, just as in unionised environments, employee grievances have to be resolved, disciplinary matters processed, and procedures devised, implemented, operated and monitored. In addition, in non-unionised situations as well as in unionised ones, the support and loyalty of management colleagues, at all levels of seniority, has to be gained by using negotiating, interviewing and communication skills *inter alia*. Employee relations knowledge, understanding and skills acquisition is just as relevant to non-union environments as to unionised environments.

As we have seen, an important employee relations concept is the relative balance of bargaining power between the buyers and sellers of labour services; we have also seen that important determinants of this relationship are external to the organisation – for example, Government economic and legislative policies. One result of this is that the key employee relations policies and practices could be rendered irrelevant, illegal or more expensive to operate if the UK Government were to pass a law giving employees the right to be represented in grievance and disciplinary procedures by a trade union representative. In such a case, companies who did not recognise trade unions would nonetheless then be obliged to do so: if the UK Government made trade union recognition compulsory, non-union firms would have to comply. Professional personnel managers have to be capable of offering advice on how their organisations might deal with such situations that stem from decision-making sources over which companies have no direct control. This book is designed to help in this regard.

Changes in the corporate environment that influence the balance of bargaining power help to explain changes over time (eg the 1990s relative to the 1970s) in the employee relations behaviour of employees and employers in terms of processes used, the rules, regulations and agreements, and their authorship. In the 1970s, when the corporate environment was very different from today's, trade unions grew steadily, strike action was more frequent, and higher wage increases were gained by employees from their employers. In the corporate environment of the 1990s, trade union membership has fallen, strike action has fallen to historically low levels, employers are able to decide the rules, regulations and agreements unilaterally, and wage increases are much smaller. Personnel managers/professionals require an understanding of the impact of changes in the corporate environment on management-employee relations strategy, of policies and agreements in order to predict the impact of possible external changes on the organisation's employee relations, and of how they might seek to mitigate these.

In conducting their employee relations activities, professional managers should behave in a fair and reasonable manner. This means acting with just cause (for example, having a genuine reason to dismiss a worker or for selecting an employee for redundancy) and behaving in procedural terms via a series of stages throughout which behaviour is compatible with the standards of natural justice (eg, following a statement of complaint against an individual, a proper investigation is undertaken; the accused is given the opportunity to cross-examine witnesses; sufficient time is made available for the accused to prepare a defence; and an appeals procedure exists, and different individuals are involved at the different stages in the operation of that procedure).

By behaving to these standards a management is operating 'best practice' and can minimise the possibility of falling foul of an adverse industrial tribunal decision.

It is not illegal for employers to dismiss employees – but if they do so without just cause and without acting reasonably towards the dismissed individual, the individual concerned can seek redress via an industrial tribunal. But, there may be circumstances where it may be in the best interests of the business not to behave fairly and reasonably, and instead to dismiss an employee arbitrarily. It is important that personnel managers appreciate that the underlying principle of employee relations procedures is that they establish standards of behaviour which will pass the tests of *reasonableness*. Personnel managers must, however, not only appreciate what constitutes fair and reasonable behaviour but why such best practice is essential to protecting and advancing management's interests – viz the avoidance of adverse financial consequences through the payment of compensation to individuals wronged by such action and damaging the organisation's labour market image in the eyes of the sellers of labour services. As we have already indicated, by behaving in a fair and reasonable (best practice) manner managers help to add value to the business. This is a key theme of the book.

Change and innovation in employee relations policies and practices to gain a competitive advantage or to deliver a service at a higher quality is essential in a modern competitive-based economy. New and developing management practices (eg performance-related pay, single union-no strike agreements) of the 1980s have been successfully introduced into organisations. However, personnel managers cannot assume that such practices can automatically be transferred successfully to their own organisations which may be operating in very different environments. They need to be able to evaluate whether practices successfully introduced in one organisation can be successfully transplanted into their own. Organisations cannot change policies and practices constantly without any reference to organisational needs or existing practices. A further assumption of this book is that new fads in management practice have to be evaluated very carefully indeed in relation to whether they can be introduced with equal success into another organisation.

A further theme of this book is that it is vital for personnel managers to understand why negotiating skills are necessary for the effective solution of people-management problems. They need to be able to identify the different negotiating situations (grievance-handling, bargaining, group problem-solving) in which managers may find themselves, and to appreciate the various stages through which a set of negotiations progresses and the skills required in different negotiation situations. Managers are constantly negotiating with their managerial colleagues – for example, to gain their support for proposed courses of action, and/or to gain the necessary resources to introduce new policies and arrangements. Intra- and inter-management negotiations are the most common negotiating situations in which managers will find themselves. Negotiating skills are therefore required by all managers. It is an activity in which managers are involved on a daily basis with their managerial colleagues, less frequently with employees in handling employee grievances and much less frequently in the case of bargaining with the workforce and/or its representatives. Negotiation is not an activity which occurs solely between the managed and the managers, and only then if there is a union presence. It is a daily activity between managers. Because managers are constantly engaged in the negotiating process, they must acquire and develop the necessary skills to conduct this daily managerial task in a competent manner.

THE BOOK AND THE IPD SYLLABUS

The indicative content of the Professional Qualification Scheme covers five areas:

• employee relations management in context

• the parties in employee relations

• employee relations processes

• employee relations outcomes

• employee relations skills.

The Employee Relations Management in Context covers the corporate environment in which organisations undertake their internal employee relations activities. A growing and important part of this external environment is the evolution of the 'social' dimension (social chapter, social policy agreement, social charter) of the European Union. This section of the syllabus also covers the role of the national government as an economic manager and as a lawmaker, as well as state agencies such as the Advisory, Conciliation, and Arbitration Service (ACAS) and the industrial tribunal system. The Employee Relations Management in Context part of this syllabus is covered by Chapters 1 (Employee Relations: An Overview) and 2 (the Corporate Environment) of this book.

The Parties in Employee Relations section of the syllabus deals with management objectives and styles, employee relations strategies, gaining employee commitment and participation, and managing with or without unions. It also covers the changing role and functions of employers' associations (such as the Confederation of British Industry and the Engineering Employers' Federation) and management associations organised at the level of the European Union. The Parties section of the syllabus is covered in Chapters 3 (Employee Relations' Institutions) and 4 (Employee Relations: Management Strategy and Policies; Management Style; Output and Outcomes) of this book. The Parties component also covers employee organisations (trade unions, professional associations, staff/employee associations, etc) and the role of the state as a 'model' employer.

Employers have a wide choice of employee relations processes from which to choose. These include joint consultation, unilateral imposition by management, task-related participation and involvement schemes (quality circles, team-briefing, etc), third party intervention (arbitration and conciliation), collective bargaining, industrial sanctions (lock-outs, suspensions, collective dismissals) and Parliamentary legislation. The Employee Relations Processes part of the syllabus is covered by Chapters 4 and 5 (Employee Involvement and Participation).

The Employee Relations Outcomes component of the syllabus covers the various dimensions of agreements (both collective and individual), their types (substantive and procedural), their authorship (joint or single by employer), the levels at which they are concluded, and their scope (the subjects covered by agreements, rules and regulations). This section of the syllabus is dealt with in Chapter 4.

The Employer Relations Skills section of the syllabus covers the definition of negotiations, the different types of negotiating situations and the various stages involved in the negotiating process. It also covers the skills required by managers in preparing for and conducting bargaining, in presenting claims/offers and counter-offers, in searching for the common ground, in concluding the negotiations and in writing up the agreement. The syllabus also covers the skills required by a manager (or management team) in handling employee complaints against management behaviour (commonly referred to as grievances), in handling disciplinary proceedings and in managing a redundancy situation. It also covers the management skills, knowledge and understanding required in devising, reviewing and monitoring procedures arrangements. Chapter 6 deals with negotiations in general terms (ie its definition, its different types and its component stages) and Chapter 7 deals with handling disciplinary proceedings, including how important it is that of management behaves in a fair and reasonable manner (good practice), and with the preparation of evidence to defend management's behaviour before an industrial tribunal. Chapter 8 deals with grievance-handling, while Chapter 9 covers bargaining collectively with the workforce. Both these chapters stress the skills required of management in the preparation stages, in grievance-handling and bargaining and in particular in identifying the common ground with the other party via the use of techniques like 'if and then' and the Aspiration Grid. Chapter 10 centres on managing redundancy situations and the devising, reviewing and monitoring of redundancy procedures.

Chapter 11, the concluding chapter, offers help and advice to students who are preparing for the Professional Qualification Scheme Employee Relations examination. Some specimen case-studies and questions are discussed.

We hope you enjoy reading this book. If you can acquire and develop a deep understanding and appreciation of its contents you have an excellent chance of gaining an IPD professional qualification.

Part 2

EMPLOYEE RELATIONS: AN OVERVIEW

1 Employee relations: an overview

Some people view employee relations as being about trade union behaviour, collective bargaining, industrial disputes and UK Government–trade union relationships. This perspective of employee relations is regarded as of little relevance to modern management because the trade unions, together with collective bargaining procedures and arrangements, strikes and tripartism, have declined steadily over the last two decades. They have been replaced by a greater focus on the individual employee rather than on employees as a collective body, and this has been reflected in management-led changes in communication methods (for example, team-briefing), in work organisation (quality circles, teamworking and single-status), and changes in payment systems (eg performance-related pay).

On the other hand, there are those who view 'employee relations' as the management practice of interacting with employees both as individuals and as a collective group – as a study of the regulation of the employment relationship. In some cases, such relations are on an individual basis, with the employer apprehended as determining employment conditions with little or no influence from the employees and/or their representatives. In other cases, the employment relationship is recognised as being managed jointly by management and trade unions.

Both views are right to some degree. Employee relations does concern itself with the players in employee relations activities – for example, individual employers, individual employees, trade unions, employers' associations, private companies, public bodies, and the UK Government in its role as a major employer of labour services. These players operate in a labour market in which they attempt to protect and advance their economic interests which are quite different. Sellers in the labour market have different interests from those of buyers, but both have an interest in finding each other. So the interests of employers and employees are an important component of employee relations.

The buyers and sellers of labour services use different processes to reconcile their different labour market interests, and the circumstances in which management can use these mechanisms – unilateral imposition by the employer, collective bargaining, etc – is of central interest to employee relations managers. The use of these processes results in agreements, rules and regulations which cover the employment conditions. These are the conditions upon which employers are prepared to purchase supplies of labour and the employees are prepared to make their services available to employers. Agreements, rules and regulations are thus another central component of employee relations.

However, the process of selling and buying labour services does not take place in a vacuum. The UK Government through its economic and legislative policies sets parameters within which the behaviour of the buyers and sellers of labour services is acceptable. Legislative policies set out the redress one party can seek from the other if it steps outside these limits. At the macro-level the UK Government's economic and legal policies also influence the relative bargaining power of the buyers and sellers of labour services, which in turn influences the outcome of employee relations activities. If the UK Government's economic and legal policies are closer to the interests of employees, this will be reflected in the content of the agreements, rules and regulations which the parties make. The external environment in which employee relations activity takes place is another key area of employee relations interest. In addition to the relative balance of bargaining power at the macro-level, it is essential to investigate why some work groups still retain power and influence relative to the employer even in times of depressed economic activity. This is the issue of relative bargaining power at the micro-level, analysis of which involves examination of such factors as the strategic position of workers in the production process and the existence of an alternative workforce. If a group of workers can inflict significant costs on the organisation's activity, are willing to exercise that power, and have exercised it successfully in the past, they will have a greater bargaining power than their employer and the contents of agreements between the work group and the employer will be closer to the ideal of the former than to those of the latter.

This chapter therefore examines the different and common interests of employers (the purchasers of labour services) and employees (sellers of labour services), the processes whereby their different interests are reconciled, and the terms of that reconciliation as expressed in agreements, rules and regulations. It also considers the concept of the relative balance of bargaining power and how this influences management's employee relations policies and practices. By the end of this chapter you will be able to

- identify the different labour market interests of the buyers and sellers of labour services

- explain the common interests in the labour market of the buyers and sellers in reconciling their different interests to mutual advantage

- identify the institutions the buyers and sellers of labour market services establish to protect and enhance their interests in the labour market

- describe the main processes whereby the buyers and sellers of labour services accommodate (reconcile) their different interests

- explain the output of employee relations activities in terms of agreements, rules and regulations which establish the conditions under which labour services are to be bought and sold

- understand the concept of the balance of bargaining power.

The main components of employee relations are shown in Figure 2. For employers, the purpose of employee relations activity is to reconcile their conflicting interests, as buyers of labour services, with those of the sellers of labour services (employees) and in so doing assist the organisation achieve its business objectives. Both management and their employees have a common interest in reconciling their differing interests. This is achieved by the use of employee relations processes (employee involvement, collective bargaining, etc) which result in agreements, rules and regulations. These can have varying degrees of authorship. Some are authored by the employer with little influence from employees. Others are authored jointly by the employer and their employees. The content of these agreements and the processes used to reach them reflect the relative balance of bargaining power between employers and employees. At the macro-level, this balance is influenced heavily by the economic and legal policies of governments and the implementation by employers of technological change. At the micro-level, the relative balance is heavily influenced by the ability of a work group to inflict costs on the organisation, the willingness of the group to exercise its power, the previous use of its power by the group, and the outcome of the use of that power.

Figure 2 **Employee relations: reconciliation of interests**

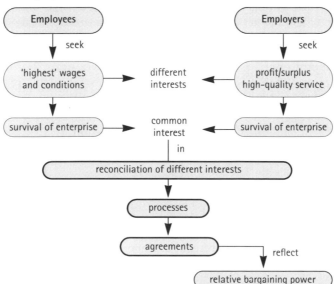

EMPLOYERS' INTERESTS IN THE LABOUR MARKET

Relative to employee interests

The rationale for employee relations is to solve the problem that in a labour market the buyers (employers) and sellers (employees) have an endemic conflict of interests over the 'prices' at which they wish to exchange their services. Employee relations is thus a management problem-solving activity designed to reconcile the problem of the 'price' at which labour market services may be exchanged. The word 'price' is in quotation marks because it involves both monetary and non-monetary aspects of supplying and buying labour.

The monetary considerations of an employer when purchasing labour services include the obvious ones of pay, hours of work, paid holidays, sick pay schemes, incentive schemes, pension arrangements and the provision of family-friendly policies such as child-care facilities. The non-monetary aspects include such matters as job security, the ease with which labour services can be hired and released back into the labour market, the deployment of labour between tasks (flexibility), the shortages or surpluses of the type of labour in the market place, and the quality of the labour in terms of qualifications, training received or required to be received, its attitude, aptitude and previous experience. In purchasing labour services the employer will seek to gain the best possible 'price' in terms of a package of monetary and non-monetary conditions of employing people.

In recruiting labour services, the employer will trade-off the items in the package of conditions. A management, for example, which would like to hire labour services as and when required and then release them back out to the labour market when they are not, may be willing to give potential employees a higher financial reward to compensate for the decreased job security. Employers who would ideally like to deploy any labour services they purchase flexibly between various tasks are likely to be willing to offer a higher package of financial rewards to attract such flexible employees to come and work for them. If the employer has a policy of only purchasing labour services of the highest quality in terms of skills, attitude, etc, he or she will be willing to offer a more advantageous package of financial rewards than employers who are happy to purchase labour services at a lower price. Ford Motor Company and Marks & Spencer have always invested in better employment conditions than those of their competitors on the grounds that they will only employ labour of a higher quality than that purchased by their competitors. The argument is that the higher financial rewards to the employees are offset by the increased productivity, lower labour turnover, greater motivation, etc, that results from ensuring higher-quality labour services.

In purchasing labour services, the employer cannot ignore the longer-term interests of the organisation. To do so will ultimately put the survival of the whole enterprise at risk. The package offered, and accepted, by the suppliers of labour services may be minimal in that it consists of low wages, long hours of work, little or no opportunities to acquire and develop skills, and little employment security. The suppliers of labour services may be prepared to accept such a package because the costs of *not* doing so may be much greater (in that the alternative is unemployment). However, suppliers of labour services working under such an employment package are likely to have low morale, perform at standards below which they are capable, and feel no commitment or loyalty to the purchaser of their labour services. Low morale, low commitment, etc, could have adverse consequences for the organisation's economic performance and/or quality of service offered to customers. So although employers can, and do, purchase their labour services at the least possible package of monetary and non-monetary conditions, they may only be gaining a short-term advantage. In the longer term, the poor quality of the labour services employed will increase the organisation's costs, reduce its competitiveness in the product market and put at risk its very survival.

In purchasing labour services, the package of conditions that the buyers of those services will have to offer is influenced by the relative balance of bargaining power between the buyers and sellers of such services. If the relative bargaining power favours the buyers, they will be able to purchase labour services for a lesser package of conditions than would be the case if the power relationship were reversed. Should, however, the buyers of labour services abuse this market power by offering unacceptably low wages and conditions, then not only will the costs mentioned in the previous paragraph arise but pressures will develop for the state to intervene to restrain – by means of the law – such use of their market power. Such restraint might include the imposition by the UK Government of a national minimum wage which must be paid to all those in employment. So in purchasing labour services employers need to have regard to longer-term considerations and not merely to what can 'be got away with' in the present.

The buyers of labour services seek to maintain and enhance their interests by organising themselves into companies or enterprises, of which there are four main types:

- private businesses

- public organisations

- public services

- voluntary bodies.

Private businesses in the UK employ some 18 million people. Although there are large numbers of small incorporated businesses, the most common form of organisation is the registered company. A major feature of the corporate sector is the concentration of output into a small number of very large private limited companies (many of which have production and/or service capacity in more than one country) alongside a substantial but growing number of much smaller private firms. This concentration of output into fewer enterprises is the result of corporate mergers.

In the ownership of large private-sector businesses, there is a divorce of ownership by individual and institutional shareholders, such as banks and pension fund managers, from management control, which lies with a team of professional managers who are accountable to the

Table 1 Public-sector employment 1979–92

	1979 (million)	1992 (million)	Percentage change
Total public-sector employment	7.4	5.8	−22
Nationalised industries and public corporations	1.8	0.9	−50
Central UK Government	0.9	0.8	−11
National Health Service	1.2	1.2	−
Local authorities	1.3	1.3	−
Education	1.5	1.4	−7
Police	0.28	0.3	+11
Armed forces	0.31	0.29	−6

Source: Central Statistical Office (1993)

owners for the performance of the company. The top professional managers are the board of directors who determine corporate strategy and policy and appoint senior, junior and middle managers to implement the agreed policies. In private corporations, the chain of command in authority is from the top downwards through management structures.

Public-sector organisation can be divided into public corporations and public services. The latter, which include organisations such as the Royal Mail, employed some 900,000 people in 1992 (see Table 1). The capital of public corporations is publicly owned; their revenue is gained from sales, their capital expenditure is raised by borrowing from the Treasury (as well as from the general public) and their boards are appointed by the appropriate Secretary of State. The main public services are central Government (the civil service), the National Health Service and local authority services. Together they employ some 6 million people. Their income comes from National Insurance contributions and receipts from income and property taxes (for example, the Council Tax). Voluntary bodies are usually small, privately-owned organisations with social rather than economic objectives. The voluntary sector also contains worker or producer co-operatives which are owned and controlled by their members.

Between management
There are differences of interests within management at the workplace. Management is not, as is sometimes thought, a united whole working to a common end. Managers have differences which, like those between the buyers and sellers of labour services, have to be accommodated if different management interests are to be reconciled and corporate objectives achieved. In large organisations, it is not uncommon to find management activities divided into different functions – for example, marketing, production-operations, personnel and finance. Although these management groups have a common interest (namely the survival and growth of the business by ensuring the product-service reaches the marketplace at the right time, at the right price and at the right quality), they can, and do, have competing interests.

The main aims of the production-operations management functions are usually perceived as the achievement of production targets, and to this end they may consider the company's interests are best served by employment policies which permit freely the hire and fire of labour and the buying-off of employee demands to prevent production-service disruptions. This management approach conflicts with the main aims of the people-management function, which is likely to see the organisation's interests best served by employees' being recruited, selected and dismissed in accordance with good personnel practices so as to protect the organisation from legal claims from its employees. The people-management function is also likely to perceive the organisation's interests as being best served by employees' being rewarded on some rational basis (eg performance) rather than the short-term consideration that production-output targets must be met, regardless of longer-term cost, to satisfy customers.

Differences between interest groups within management are resolved by negotiation between themselves or by arbitration by a more senior manager (or some other third party). By use of argument and making constructive compromises, managers gain the commitment of their managerial colleagues within and between the different management functions to proposed policies to which there is initial opposition from colleagues. Should managers at the same level of seniority be unable to settle their differences by negotiation, a senior manager will arbitrate and decide the appropriate course of action to be taken.

Employee relations managers cannot take it for granted that what they propose will not be opposed by other managers. However, differences between managers have to be reconciled in a constructive, not a destructive, manner. Most management differences over how to solve problems are resolved quickly. As an employee relations manager you will find yourself frequently negotiating with your management colleagues (at the same, a lesser or a higher level of seniority) to resolve differences over what constitutes the 'best' employee relations policies and practices to be operated if the organisation is to achieve its objectives.

> When did you last have a difference with a colleague over how a problem should be resolved? What was the problem about? What were the differences between you? What was the resolution of the difference? Why was there a difference in the first place?

Relative to employers' interests
In the labour market, the sellers of labour services seek from the buyers of their services (employers) the best possible available package of monetary and non-monetary employment conditions. The monetary aspects of the package include those issues that buyers of labour services also have to consider (wages, hours of work, etc). The non-monetary elements will comprise such items as job security; the opportunity to work with good colleagues; the potential for advancement; being treated as a human being, not merely a

commodity; access to training; and the existence of family-friendly employment policies (for example, child-care facilities) which enable a balance to be achieved between being a family person and the need to provide for that family. Like the buyers of labour services, the sellers will also give different weight to the items in the package of employment conditions at which they are willing to sell their services. They may, for example, be prepared to work for lower wages if this is compensated by greater employment security. The importance employees attach to the components of their desired package of employment conditions will also depend on factors such as age and family circumstances. Nevertheless, employees, like any seller in a marketplace, will seek the best possible package of monetary and non-monetary employment conditions.

> What is your monetary and non-monetary package of employment conditions? Which are the most important to you, and why?

Employees attempt to strengthen and enhance their interests in the labour market by presenting a collective face to the employer (the buyer). In an attempt to even up their influence relative to employers, workers have traditionally formed organisations to determine, on their behalf, the minimum conditions on which they will supply their labour services to employers. The most common employee labour market organisations are

• professional associations

• trade unions

• staff associations.

In enterprises where such organisations do not exist, employers often create a collective employee organisation (sometimes called an employee council, a works council, a representative committee, etc) so they can obtain a collective and representative voice from their employees. It is only in very small firms that a truly individual and personal relationship can exist between an employer and the employees. Once an organisation grows, in numbers of those employed, beyond a critical size, the views of the employees are best collected (in terms of time and efficiency) through some representative collective organisation. It becomes too time-consuming to talk to each separate employee. Employers' interests can therefore be enhanced by their employees' having a representative body. However, employer attitudes vary over what form of collective employee organisation best serves the organisation's interests.

Professional bodies usually control the education and training of new members to the profession by acting as 'qualifying associations'. They also establish, maintain and review professional and ethical standards for their members. However, some professional associations, especially those whose members are mainly employed in the public sector, also protect and promote their members' employment interests in pay bargaining. In the health service, for example, there are groups of professional employees, such as nurses and midwives, who use their professional bodies in the dual capacity of an executive and a negotiating body.

Staff associations are in some cases the creation of employers who wish to keep their business non-union. The majority are trade unions in all but name – for example, the bank staff associations. Nevertheless, most staff associations are characterised by weak finances and a narrow membership base confined to a single employer. Larger staff associations tend to acquire their own staff and premises and rely less on the employer for services and facilities. In 1995, the Certification Officer's list of employee organisations contained 62 staff associations concentrated mainly in the financial sector, of which 30 were recognised to be independent of employer influence and domination.

Trade unions are the best-known type of employee organisation. They were formed to protect and advance the interests of their members against employers and members of other trade unions. In the UK, trade unions have different recruitment strategies. Craft and occupational unions (eg AEEU, GPMU) focus on recruiting employees who perform certain jobs. Some unions confine their recruitment to all grades of employees employed in a particular industry: these are referred to as industrial unions. General unions, such as the T&GWU and GMB, organise workers across the boundaries within and between industries. They will take any workers into membership, regardless of the job they do and the industry in which they do it.

In the UK, trade union organisation is characterised by a large number of small unions co-existing with a very small number of large trade unions. In 1995, 75 per cent (224) of the total number of trade unions registered with the Certification Officer had memberships of less than 5,000. On the other hand, 7 per cent (20) of the unions had memberships in excess of 100,000. Unions thus represent different interests in terms of jobs, types of workers, industries, services, and public and private sectors of the economy. They also have different interests within them (skilled, unskilled, non-manual workers, etc) but these are accommodated through their decision-making procedures which are based on the principle of representative democracy.

The Trades Union Congress (TUC) is the national centre for UK unions. Unions join on a voluntary basis. In 1995, it comprised 68 unions representing a total membership of 7.2 million. The TUC is the largest pressure group in British society. In addition to making representations to the UK Government, it provides its affiliate unions with high-quality information, research, and education programmes to assist policy development and aid the recruitment and retention of members.

Between employees

Just as there is a plurality of interests within, and between, groups of managers, so there is within groups of employees and their organisations. In a workplace, different types of employees (white-collar, craft manual, semi-skilled, unskilled, etc) are employed and have interests different from each other. Non-manual employees usually seek to maintain employment conditions differentials over manual workers. Craft manual workers perceive their interests relative to lesser-skilled workers as best served by pay differentials expressed in percentage terms. Should this percentage figure be reduced, craft workers usually demand improvements in pay to re-establish accepted percentage differentials.

Lesser-skilled manual workers view their interests relative to craft manual workers as best served by pay differentials expressed in monetary terms, and they oppose percentage increases in pay on the grounds that such increases widen monetary differentials. This was demonstrated during the so-called 'winter of discontent' in 1978–79 when low-paid lesser-skilled workers in the public sector undertook industrial action against their employers who were offering them pay increases of 5 per cent in line with the then UK Government's incomes restraint policy. They argued that to accept 5 per cent would widen pay differentials relative to skilled manual workers, would give the largest money increases to those who needed it the least and would give the least increase to those who needed it the most (ie the low-paid).

EMPLOYER–EMPLOYEE COMMON INTERESTS

Although as buyers and sellers of labour services, employers and employees have different interests, they have in the longer term a common interest in ensuring that their different interests are accommodated. To do so provides mutual advantages. There are strong economic pressures on employers and employees to accommodate each other's interests rather than to perpetuate their differences. If employers fail to reconcile their different interests with their employees, a number of costs arise:

• The employer has no goods/services to sell in the marketplace.

• The employer cannot make a profit or provide services at value for money.

• Goods and services cannot be supplied to the marketplace at the right price, at the right time and at the right quality.

• Customer needs cannot be satisfied.

• Plants, shops, etc, lie idle.

• Customers take their business to competitor firms.

• Plants, offices and shops close.

The problems for employees of failing to resolve their different interests from the employers' are equally obvious. They do not gain employment, they do not receive a steady income stream, they have no power as consumers, they cannot enter into long-term financial commitments (eg mortgages, bank loans, hire-purchase contracts, etc) and the continuity of employment service upon which legal employment rights and some company employment conditions (eg paid holidays and sick pay entitlement) are based is effected adversely.

If workers gain no income from employment they become dependent on the state for a minimum level of income to satisfy their basic needs of housing, heating, lighting, food, etc.

Employers and employees have a common, enlightened self-interest in ensuring that their differing interests are reconciled. There is mutual gain. Employers secure the survival of their enterprises, gain profit or provide services at value for money, and satisfy the needs of their customers. On the other hand, employees obtain job security, income security, consumer power and status from being employed. In the long run, both employers and employees have an overriding common interest in ensuring that companies/enterprises, etc, are successful. However, in the short run this common interest might not seem very common to employees who are told that they are to be made redundant so that cost cuts will help to ensure the future of the enterprise.

One of the methods by which the different labour market interests of employers and employees are accommodated is the process of negotiation, which involves the coming together of two parties (employers and employees) to make an accommodation (agreement) by purposeful persuasion (through the use of rational argument) and by making constructive compromises towards (identifying the common ground in) each other's position. There are different types of negotiating situations, but the most usual that involve employers and employees are:

• grievance-handling to resolve a complaint by an employee against management behaviour

• bargaining during which employers and employees trade-off items within a list of demands they have made of each other

• group problem-solving in which the employer settles the details upon which the employees will co-operate with a request from management to assist in obtaining information to help solve a problem of mutual concern.

Why do you think it is essential for employees and employers to reconcile their differences?

There are, however, other ways in which the conflict of interest may be resolved. In many cases, individual employees who find that their ambitions – for example, for promotion or for higher pay – cannot be realised with their present employer, resign their employment and go and work for another where their interests can be, or are more likely to be, better accommodated. Although voluntary labour turnover represents a peaceful method of resolving the basic differences of interest between employers and employees as players in the labour market, management still has to keep such cases to manageable proportions because labour turnover is not cost-free to the employer.

In other cases, however, the accommodation is achieved not by labour

Table 2 Individual conciliation cases received by ACAS (1987–95)

Date	Unfair dismissal cases	Total conciliation cases (Individual)
1987	34,572	40,817
1988	36,340	44,443
1989	37,324	48,817
1990	37,654	52,071
1991	39,234	60,605
1992	44,034	72,166
1993	46,854	75,181
1994	45,824	79,332
1995	40,815	91,568

Source: ACAS annual reports

turnover but by the dismissal of the employee by the employer. In such circumstances, the employer says that it is not in the interests of the company to continue to employ the individual concerned. The employee, however, holds the opposite view and sees his or her interest as best served by continuing in employment with that employer. These differing interests cannot be resolved, so the employer forces the issue by dismissing the employee, who is then likely to respond by complaining to an industrial tribunal about having been dismissed unfairly. The tribunal then makes a decision in favour of either the employer or the employee, which may be a directive for reinstatement, re-engagement or financial compensation. At the end of the day, then, it is the tribunal which resolves the differences of interest between the employer and the employee. The number of complaints by individuals of an unfair resolution of the differing interests of employers and employees over nine years is shown above in Table 2.

So we have seen that although employers and employees have a constitutional conflict over the 'price' of labour services, they have an overriding common interest that these differences be reconciled to mutual advantage. However, in the short-term – for example, in the case of redundancy – we have also seen that those employed who are then dismissed may not see this overriding interest as common to them. Employers and the employees prefer to accommodate each other's interests and to have a long-term stable relationship rather than to be in permanent conflict which can only end in the mutual destruction of the enterprise that is providing the employment. The priority of the common interest over the differing interests explains why buyers and sellers of labour services make concessions to each other. It enables, *inter alia*, the employing unit to survive to the mutual advantage of both employers and employees. However, the accommodation of the interests of employers and employees does not produce the package of employment conditions at which they would ideally like to have exchanged their services. The actual package is influenced by the relative bargaining power of the buyers and sellers of labour services. This power relationship (see below) results in an employment package of conditions that is inevitably more favourable to one party than to the other. Nevertheless, the accommodation brings a package of employment conditions that are 'acceptable' to the employer and the employee, and gives benefit to each, relative to the costs of *failing* to make an agreement: eg loss of income, loss of employment, closure of the enterprise.

EMPLOYEE RELATIONS PROCESSES

Accommodation of the interests of employers and employees is achieved by the use of employee relations processes, of which the most important are:

- unilateral action
- joint consultation
- collective bargaining
- third-party intervention
- industrial sanctions.

In addition to these processes, the state can interfere with the buying and selling of labour services by establishing minimum terms that the buyers must offer the sellers. This is effected by the legal enactment process. Unlike the other processes listed above, management has no control over this process. Any influence it may have is through lobbying the UK Government of the day.

The factors that determine an employer's choice of process from this menu are discussed in Chapter 4. Here we concentrate on defining the different employee relations processes and the extent to which they are, or have been, used.

Unilateral action
Unilateral action is a form of employee relations by which the employer is the sole author of the agreement which the employees accept by continuing to work in accordance with its terms. This is particularly the case in the UK where non-union companies make greater use of programmes of consultation and communication to resolve the differences of interests with their employees. However, even in highly unionised organisations – eg commercial television companies and the NHS Trusts – unilateral changes by management to employment conditions of employees do take place. In the extreme, by imposing unilateral changes to their employees' employment conditions unscrupulous managers take the line 'accept these new terms or consider yourself dismissed'.

It is difficult to know how frequently and how seriously management-imposed changes are made to the employment conditions of employees since there is no source of such information. The general impression is, however, that in the 1980s and 1990s the use of unilateral action by employers has increased. One of the reasons for this view is that in the past 15 years the number of establishments that recognise trade unions has declined. The Workplace Industrial Relations Survey

(WIRS)of 1984 showed that 66 per cent of establishments recognised unions. By 1990, the figure was 53 per cent. In making a unilateral change to the employment contract, employers risk being sued for breach of contract or constructive dismissal. However, they have frequently got away with such behaviour because for the last 15 years the relative bargaining power has been in favour of the employer.

Joint consultation

Joint consultation is the means by which management seeks the views, feelings and ideas of employees and/or their representatives prior to making a decision. Although the process may involve discussion of mutual problems and is a form of employee participation, management makes the final decision. There is no commitment on the part of the employer to act upon the employees' views and opinions.

Workplace Industrial Relations Surveys (WIRS) provide information on the use of joint consultative arrangements in establishments employing 25 or more employees. The 1990 WIRS showed that 23 per cent of private manufacturing workplaces had joint consultation committees, compared with 36 per cent in 1980. The proportion of employees covered by joint consultation arrangements fell from 43 per cent to 30 per cent over the same period. These trends are an indication not of employers' rejecting joint consultation but of a fall in the number of large employing units where such committees had traditionally existed. Joint consultation is supplemented in many organisations by employee involvement schemes which take the form of two-way communications on company matters, problem-solving groups, financial participation (employee share-ownership schemes, etc) and the harmonisation of terms and conditions of employment. Such schemes are tailored to foster trust and a shared commitment by employees to the organisation's objectives.

Collective bargaining

Collective bargaining is a method of determining the 'price' at which employee services are bought and sold, a system of industrial governance whereby unions and employers jointly reach decisions on matters concerning the employment relationship, and which involves employee participation in management decision-making and unions in the management of the enterprise. In practice, the outcome of collective bargaining is not confined to union members. Unionised companies apply collectively-bargained terms and conditions to their non-union employees as well as their union ones. Non-unionised companies need to have regard to collectively-bargained rates in their industry or comparator firms when deciding on their own employees' employment conditions. Many non-unionised companies seek to retain union-free workplaces by paying above-union-negotiated pay and other employment conditions. Over the period 1984–90 inclusive, the coverage of workers by collective bargaining declined. The 1990 WIRS revealed that the overall proportion of employees covered by collective bargaining fell from 71 per cent in 1984 to 54 per cent in 1990.

> What are the main processes used to determine employment conditions in your organisation? Why are these processes, rather than others, used?

Third-party intervention

In situations where the employer and employees are unable to resolve their collective differences, they may agree voluntarily to seek the assistance, in resolving such differences, of an independent third party. Third-party intervention can take one of three forms:

• conciliation

• mediation

• arbitration.

In the case of disputes between an employer and an individual employee over the fairness of a dismissal from employment, the law requires conciliation to be undertaken before the case can proceed to be heard by an industrial tribunal.

In conciliation, the role of the third party is to keep the two sides talking and assist them to reach their own agreement. The conciliator acts as a link between the disputing parties by passing information the parties will not pass directly to each other from one side to the other until either a common position is established or both parties agree there is no common ground. Conciliation permits each side to continually reassess its situation. The conciliator plays a passive role and does not impose any action or decision on either party.

Listening to the argument of the two sides, a mediator makes recommendations on how their differences might be resolved. The parties are free to accept or reject these recommendations.

Arbitration removes all control from employers and employees over the settlement of their differences. The arbitrator hears both sides' cases and decides the solution to the parties' differences by making an award. Both parties, having voluntarily agreed to arbitration, are morally, but not legally, obliged to accept the arbitrator's award. Pendulum arbitration is a specific form of arbitration which limits the third party to making an award which accepts fully either the claims of the union or the final offer of the employer. It reduces arbitration to an all-or-nothing, win-or-lose, outcome. By creating an all-or-nothing expectation, pendulum arbitration is said to encourage bargainers to moderate their final positions and reach a voluntary agreement.

Table 3 shows that since 1979 the use of third-party intervention has fallen significantly. The number of completed collective conciliation cases handled by ACAS fell from 2,284 in 1979 to 1,299 in 1995. Mediation is rarely used. In 1990 there were 10 mediation hearings reported by ACAS, eight in 1994 and five in 1995. Throughout the 1990s the number of arbitration hearings arranged by ACAS has fallen. In 1990 there were 190 such hearings but in 1995 the number was 136. Over the period 1990–95 inclusive, ACAS statistics show some two-thirds of voluntary arbitration and mediation cases were over job-grading claims, dismissals and discipline, all of which are individual rather than collective concerns, were small but important issues to those involved, and were situations where the cost of 'losing' to the

Table 3 The use of third–party intervention in industrial disputes

Date	Competed collective conciliation	Mediation	Number of arbitration hearings
1979	2,284	32	394
1980	1,910	31	281
1981	1,716	12	245
1982	1,634	16	235
1983	1,621	20	187
1984	1,448	14	188
1985	1,337	12	150
1986	1,323	10	174
1987	1,147	12	133
1988	1,053	9	129
1989	1,070	17	150
1990	1,140	10	190
1991	1,226	12	144
1992	1,140	7	155
1993	1,118	7	156
1994	1,162	8	148
1995	1,299	5	136

Source: ACAS, annual reports, 1979–95

employer was relatively low and where the chances of adverse publicity from the issuing of any award was virtually zero.

Industrial sanctions

The use of industrial sanctions is generally a last resort because it is costly to both sides to impose them on each other. The main sanctions available to the employer are the locking-out of the workforce, closing the factory, office, or shop and re-locating operations to another site, and the dismissal of employees participating in industrial action. The main industrial sanctions that may be imposed on employers are bans on overtime working, a work-to-rule, the imposition of a selective strike, and the undertaking by the workforce (or sections of the workforce) of an all-out strike. The threat of the imposition of industrial sanctions is important in bringing about a reconciliation of the differing interests of employers and employees. The threat that one side might impose industrial sanctions, with their ensuing costs falling on the other, may be just as important as sanctions actually being imposed. It is the effect of this threat that makes the parties adjust their position and negotiate a peaceful settlement. Both parties are reluctant to impose industrial sanctions because of the associated costs. However, their existence means the parties have to have regard to them and adjust their behaviour accordingly. Without their existence there would be no restraint on the behaviour of the parties. There would be no incentive for the parties to settle their differences peacefully.

Employers have to think carefully before imposing or threatening to impose industrial sanctions. There is little to be gained in imposing industrial actions if they are unlikely to be successful, given that economic pressures may quickly mount as the employers' product market competitors take advantage of the industrial problems to poach their customers. It is pointless to re-locate operations to another site unless an alternative competent workforce can be recruited to work at the new site. To impose sanctions that fail to bring any further concession from the other party undermines the credibility of the threat to use them at a future date.

In the UK, official statistics on the use of industrial sanctions relate only to strikes. They measure three dimensions of strike activity – their number (frequency), their size (the number of workers involved) and their duration (the number of working days lost). This last measure is often distorted by a few big strikes. For example, in 1979 an engineering-industry-wide strike accounted for 55 per cent of all working days lost in that year. In 1995, the number of stoppages of work in the UK was 205, the lowest in any year since records began in 1891. In 1979, the corresponding figure was 2,125. However, disputes still happen. There was, for example a series of one-day stoppages in 1996 in the Royal Mail service over the employers' attempt to introduce major changes in working practices to remain competitive in the light of the growth of alternative communication systems such as faxes and e-mail.

Although dispute levels have declined in the 1990s (see Table 4), there are signs that some managers have been performing inadequately in

Table 4 Industrial stoppages in the UK 1979–95

Year	Number of stoppages in progress	Number of workers involved (000s)	Number of working days lost (000s)
1979	2,125	4,608	29,474[1]
1980	1,348	834	11,964[2]
1981	1,344	1,513	4,266
1982	1,538	2,103	5,313
1983	1,364	574	3,754
1984	1,221	1,464	27,135[3]
1985	903	791	6,402[4]
1986	1,074	720	1,920
1987	1,016	887	3,546
1988	781	790	3,702
1989	701	727	4,128[5]
1990	630	298	1,903
1991	369	176	761
1992	253	148	528
1993	211	385	649
1994	275	107	278
1995	205	173	415

[1] 54 per cent of total accounted for by a strike of engineering workers.
[2] 74 per cent of total accounted for by a national steel dispute.
[3] 83 per cent of total accounted for by a coal mining strike.
[4] 63 per cent of total accounted for by the continuing miners' strike.
[5] 49 per cent of total accounted for by a strike of council workers.

Source: Annual Report on Labour Disputes in Department of Employment *Gazette* and *Labour Market Trends*

managing their employee relations in that there has been a dramatic growth in the number of complaints against employers by employees to industrial tribunals. Whereas cases reported to ACAS averaged about 45,000 in the 1980s and fluctuated very little year by year, the number has climbed every year since 1990 from 52,000 to nearly 92,000 in 1995 (see Table 2). The IPD statement on employment relations in July 1996 reported a rising sense of grievance amongst people at work, a declining level of employee confidence in top management's handling of employee relations, and a feeling on the part of employees of being less involved in decisions that mattered to them.

Legal enactment

The processes described above are private means whereby the common purpose of employers and employees to accommodate their differences of interest is given effect. Employers have some control over their use. However, on occasions, the state interferes in these private relationships to determine minimum employment conditions that employers must provide for their employees. The employers have no control over Parliamentary legislation and have to regard such legal imposition as part of the corporate environment in which they must operate.

Over the past 15 years, UK Governments have removed from the labour market some significant minimum protection legislation for employees. For example, in 1994 wages councils, which set minimum wages and conditions for employees in certain industries, were abolished. In addition, the UK Government has since then increased the minimum period of continuous service with an employee to qualify for employment rights from 26 weeks to 104 weeks.

Although the UK Government has removed some employee protections from the labour market, the European Union is committed to establishing a 'level playing-field' of social regulation in its Single European Market in which goods, capital, people and services can move freely. Employers, are therefore likely to face increasing legal enactment from the European Union despite the UK Government's opt-out from the Agreement on Social Policy contained in the Social Protocol in the Maastricht Treaty of European Union (see Chapter 2). Although the UK Government is likely to be granted some leeway from the implementation date of November 1996 for the European Working Time Directive it will eventually have to introduce national legislation to comply with this Directive. This establishes minimum standards in the area of working patterns. It imposes for all workers a maximum number of hours they can be made to work, sets a maximum length of eight hours for a night shift, establishes a minimum break period of rest between finishing and restarting work, and provides for a minimum period of paid annual leave for employees.

AGREEMENTS, RULES AND REGULATIONS

The outcome of the use of employee relations processes is an agreement which establishes the package of conditions upon which labour services are bought and sold. These agreements may relate to a group of employees, in which case they are referred to as a collective agreement. On the other hand, the agreement may be between an employer and an individual employee, in which case it is referred to as a personal contract. All contracts are personal in that they relate to individual employees. The distinguishing characteristic of a personal contract is that none of its terms has been negotiated by collective bargaining. The employee alone has negotiated the terms and conditions of employment with the employer as an individual. In practice, personal contracts are not individualised in any genuine sense. At British Telecom, for instance, all terms and conditions for senior managerial staff are standard across all personal contracts. The only difference is that pay is determined 'individually' with no published rates or transparency in the criteria by which pay increases are determined.

It is traditional to divide agreements into two broad types. First, substantive agreements cover monetary aspects of employment conditions (pay, hours of work, paid holidays, etc). Second, procedural agreements lay out set standards of conduct to be met by employers and employees in peacefully resolving their differences over particular issues. They provide tests by which reasonable behaviour (acting with due cause, and treating employees fairly and consistently) by employers can be judged – for example, by outside institutions such as industrial tribunals – and their procedures also provide quick and informal methods for resolving differences between employers and employees. In practice, employers in their enterprises have a wide range of procedural arrangements and agreements covering such issues as disputes, employee grievances, dismissal and discipline, redundancy, union recognition, job-grading and evaluation, health and safety, promotion and staff development, and career review. The 1990 WIRS reported that 65 per cent of UK establishments had procedural arrangements to deal with pay and conditions issues, 90 per cent to deal with discipline and dismissal, 87 per cent to deal with individual employee grievances, and the same percentage to cope with health and safety issues.

> Select three procedures which operate in your organisation. Explain how they demonstrate that management behaves fairly and reasonably in operating these procedures.

Collective agreements have a unique status in the UK in that they are not legally binding on the parties who have signed them. If either the union or management act contrary to the agreement, the other party cannot enforce it through the courts. Collective agreements are binding in honour only. In almost every other democratic society, collective agreements between unions and employers are legally binding and enforceable through the courts.

A consequence of collective agreements' not being legally binding is they are also not comprehensive and their wording can be relatively imprecise. This reinforces the requirement for employers to have a disputes procedure to resolve differences with their employees over whether the agreement is being applied properly. The style of UK collective agreements also reflects the fact that they are normally subject to review and renegotiation on an annual basis.

The scope (ie the subjects covered) of both collective agreements and individual contracts varies widely, but they normally cover some, or all, of the following:

• pay levels and structure

• overtime and shift payments

• incentive (bonus/performance-related pay) payments

• hours of work and paid holidays

• working arrangements and productivity

• training and re-training opportunities

• the means of resolving disputes, individual grievances, etc.

It is traditional for pay rates and working arrangements to be reviewed and amended annually by the signatories to a collective agreement. Hours of work and paid annual holidays are normally reviewed and changed at less frequent intervals. Procedural arrangements can remain unchanged for many years.

Agreements can also be analysed in terms of their formality. Some collective agreements have their contents written down but there are some which do not exist in written form. These are referred to as 'custom and practice'. The employees (or employers) have operated the working practice for many years; management (or employees) have gone along with this behaviour although they have never formally agreed it with their employees (or the employer); the practice has become accepted, and if management (or employees) were to try to change it, the employees (or the management) are likely to expect something in return. In your core personnel and development studies you were introduced to the idea of custom and practice. If you are not sure, you should read again pages 250–55 of Marchington and Wilkinson's *Core Personnel and Development* textbook (London, IPD 1996).

Agreements are concluded at different levels. Some apply only to the place where those covered by it work; others (referred to as company agreements) apply to all workers in the company, such as is seen at the Ford Motor Company and ICI. Some agreements cover a group of workers in an enterprise, while others relate to all workers (or certain grades of worker) in an industry and these are commonly referred to as national or industry-wide agreements. Many employers have in recent years withdrawn from national agreements, preferring to bargain collectively (especially over pay) with their employees at a more de-centralised level; they consider this necessary to recruit, motivate, retain and reward the right calibre of employees if the success of the business is to be secured.

Collective agreements can also be analysed in terms of the number and size of groups of workers they cover. This aspect of agreements is referred to as the size of the bargaining unit. In some organisations, management operates by concluding separate agreements with separate trade unions representing different groups of employees, and thus has a multiplicity of bargaining units and collective agreements. This is the classic multi-union situation. However, other companies prefer to have a single agreement covering all relevant groups, and thus have one bargaining unit covering significant numbers of employees and possibly a different number of trade unions. This is referred to as single-table bargaining, in which all recognised trade unions sit at the same table with the employer. Yet other managements may see the business objectives as more likely to be achieved if they have one bargaining unit in which all employees are represented by a single union (a single-union agreement situation).

THE BALANCE OF BARGAINING POWER

Whether the contents of the agreement are closer to satisfying the interests of the employers or the employees is influenced heavily by the relative balance of bargaining power between them. Issues relating to the relative balance of bargaining power are relevant to employers who bargain individually with their employees as well to those who bargain collectively with their workforce. The balance of bargaining power is a key employee relations concept which influences the selection by the employer of the appropriate employee relations processes, the subject matter of agreements between employers and their employees, whether agreements are jointly authored by employers and employees or solely written by one of the parties, and whether an agreement is closer to the ideal interests of employers or those of the employees. The concept also helps to explain changes in the employee relations system over time – for example, the 1990s relative to the 1970s. This is dealt with in more detail in Chapter 3.

The dictionary gives 23 definitions of *power*, but in the context of employee relations these can be reduced to two. First, power is the ability to control or impose – that is, to direct or regulate a situation or person(s) despite any desire or attempt to influence on the part of another individual or group. Second, power means the ability to influence and thereby secure some modification in another party's decision or action. This might be subdivided into (a) the ability to force a change in the other party's decision, usually after it has been made, by the explicit expression or threat to express that power; and (b) the ability to generate an implicit influence which forms an integral part of the environment, and which has to be taken into account by other parties in the decision-making process. However, whatever definition of power is adopted, it can only have value if those against whom it is employed actually perceive that it exists. So in a unionised environment, management could perceive the union had power and the union could equally perceive that management had power, although the reality could be very different. The balance is determined by assessing which party holds the advantage at a given point in time. In a non-union environment, it is not that a balance of bargaining does not exist, but that it usually swings in favour of the employer because of the inability of individuals acting alone to tilt the relative balance of power between them and the employer. Occasionally, individual employees in non-union establishments do secure the advantage, but this usually only happens in special circumstances – eg when there is a skill shortage in a particular area.

The macro-level
The factors that influence the relative balance of bargaining power between employers and employees are:

• the economic environment

• the legal environment

• the technological environment.

The Government's economic and legal policies have major implications for the outcome of employee relations activities. If economic policies are directed towards the creation of full employment and the maximising of economic growth, this weakens the relative bargaining power of the employer but strengthens that of the employee. Such policies create a demand for goods and services from which a demand for labour to produce/provide those goods and services is derived (a derived demand for labour). The employers' demand for labour services increases, thereby pushing up the 'price' at which those services are bought and sold. If, on the other hand, Government economic policies centre on reducing inflation by lowering household and corporate spending and reducing public expenditure, then demand (spending power) in the economy will fall as will the derived demand for labour. The effect will be an increase in unemployment. The supply of labour services will exceed the demand for those services, causing a downward pressure on the 'price' of labour services. The relative balance of power of employers will be strengthened and that of the employees weakened. The 'price' of labour services will either fall or fewer will be employed at existing prices.

If the Government of the day introduces legislation favourable to employers' interests – for example, by narrowing the circumstances in which trade unions can call on their members to undertake industrial action without those affected adversely by the action's being able to resort to the courts for some redress (eg compensation to cover economic losses) – then the bargaining power of employers relative to employees is strengthened. This is what Conservative Governments over the period 1980–97 inclusive did by nine pieces of Parliamentary legislation (see Chapter 2). If a Government introduces legislation favourable to the interests of employees and trade unions, the bargaining power of employees relative to employers is strengthened. Legislation by setting standards (eg the right not to be unfairly dismissed) regulating the relationship between an individual employee and the employer also influences the relative balance of power between employers and individual employees.

One reason why at the macro-level the outcomes and processes used in employee relations activity in the UK since 1979 has been more favourable to employers than in the 1960s and earlier 1970s is that

Conservative Governments implemented economic and legal policies designed to weaken the bargaining power of trade unions and individual employees relative to employers. They also gave greater encouragement to employers to treat their employees as individuals rather than as collective groups. At the macro-level, this enhanced relative employer bargaining power has been witnessed in

- an increased number of incidents in which an employer has withdrawn recognition from a trade union. Particular examples are to be found in newspaper production, publishing, shipping, port transport and hotels and catering

- a fall in trade union membership from 12 million in 1979 to 6.5 million in 1996

- significant changes in working practices (task function flexibility) relative to previous periods. Such changes have included greater flexibility between craft grades and, as in the general printing industry, the acceptance by the craft employees, in machine rooms, of undertaking the duties of lesser-skilled employees as well as their own

- a decline in strike action (see Table 4)

- a growth in employee involvement techniques (see Chapter 5)

- more unilateral decision-making by management

- the emergence of new management techniques such as just-in-time management, quality circles, continuous improvement, bench-marking, teamworking, and the reduction of supervisory levels by giving workgroups the responsibility for achieving their own quality and output targets

- greater emphasis on involving employees by opening direct lines of communications with the workforce instead of relying on workplace trade union representatives such as shop stewards.

The implementation of new technology also impacts on the macro-level of relative bargaining power between employers and employees. Technological developments, based on computers, lasers and telecommunications, have in some sectors of the economy destroyed jobs – for example, those of compositors (typesetters) in the printing industry – de-skilled jobs, blurred demarcation lines between existing jobs and industries, and created for employers an alternative workforce. These impacts all help to increase the bargaining power of the employer relative to the employee. Developments in telecommunications have produced global product markets (for example, the financial sector) thereby increasing product market competition, leading to a downward pressure on the price of labour services and a shift in the relative bargaining power towards the employer. Many jobs have been lost in the banking industry by developments such as Switch cards, which enable the employee at the checkout of a retail food store to transfer funds from the bank account of the customer to that of the food store, thereby eliminating the need for bank employees to undertake this task. However, in other sectors of the economy, by creating new jobs, new skills and making some industries more capital-intensive, the implementation of technological change has strengthened the relative bargaining power of employees and weakened that of the employer.

The economic and legal environment influencing the relative bargaining power between employers and employees at the macro-level is determined by the policies of the UK Government and will be increasingly so also by the European Union political decision-making bodies. This means that employers and employees must participate in the political lobbying process to persuade governments to introduce economic and legal policies favourable to their interests. Employer and employee organisations spend large sums of money each year in lobbying political decision-makers. Trade unions lobby the UK Government via the Trades Union Congress (TUC) and the employers through their national centre bodies of the Confederation of British Industry (CBI) and the Institute of Directors (IOD). European Union political institutions are lobbied in the case of employers by the Union of Industrial and Employers' Confederations of Europe (UNICE) and in the case of employees by the European Trades Union Confederation (ETUC).

The micro-level
So far we have been looking at the relative bargaining power of the buyers and sellers of labour services on the macro-level. But the macro-level relativity cannot explain why some groups of employees retain their bargaining power vis-à-vis the employer despite recession and high unemployment, or why some employers are in a relatively weak bargaining position despite expanding economic activity. In many respects what matters for the employers is their bargaining power relative to particular groups of workers with whom they deal. This is the relative bargaining power at the micro-level. In assessing the relative bargaining power of groups of employees, Marchington (1982) points out that management needs to consider the answers to four questions. First, does the group have the capacity to inflict substantial costs on the organisation (power capacity)? Second, is the group aware that it has that capacity (power realisation)? Third, has the group, at any time in the past, exercised the threat of those costs against the organisation (power testing)? Fourth, what was the outcome of the use of that bargaining power (power outcome)? The factors that influence the relative balance of bargaining power at the micro-level are shown in Figure 3.

In assessing the potential relative bargaining power of a group of its employees, management has to consider how crucial the group is to the production/service supply process. The more central the group is to workflow, the greater is its potential power within the organisation. In many organisations computer staff, for example, are now in strategic positions to disrupt workflow. However, a strategic position in the workflow process is not sufficient in itself to give the group relatively strong bargaining power. Management has to assess the extent to which there is organisation, cohesiveness and solidarity amongst the group. This means considering aspects like the ability of the group to close a plant down completely. If it can, the next question is, how quickly can the group bring about this situation? The quicker a group

Figure 3 Factors determining the bargaining power of a group of workers relative to their employer

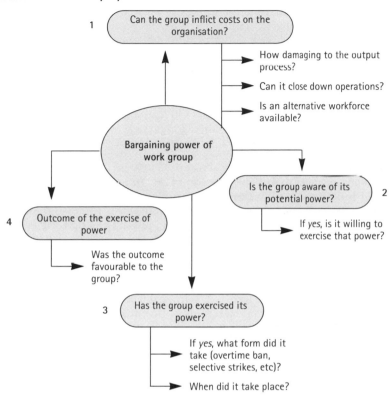

Based on Marchington, *Managing Industrial Relations*, McGraw-Hill, 1982

can bring about a complete cessation of the operations of the organisation, the greater is its bargaining power vis-à-vis the employer.

However, the potential relative bargaining power of a group of employees is also determined by its ability to prevent other people from being able to do its work. Its power relative to the employer is increased if there is a lack of an appropriate alternative workforce available to undertake the group's work on an individual or a departmental basis. In short, a group of workers difficult to substitute has greater bargaining power relative to the employer than one whose services are easily replaceable. A further factor is the extent to which substitute products or services for those produced by the group are available to the organisation's customers. If consumers do not have access to an alternative source of the product or service (ie product market competition is low), the relative bargaining power of the group is increased. The reverse is likely to be the case in highly competitive product markets.

If management assesses that a work group(s) with whom it deals has potential bargaining power to disrupt the organisation, its next step is to make an evaluation of whether the group realises it has the power, and if it does, whether it is willing to exercise that power. If a group is cohesive and aware of its potential bargaining power, it may nonetheless not be willing to press home its advantage. The group of employees may have values and beliefs such that it is reluctant to challenge management's authority. Some groups of workers are unwilling to exercise their potential power because to do so is seen as threatening to human life and contrary to their professional values. Nurses are generally most unwilling to undertake any industrial action that will seriously endanger their patients. Teachers also have been reluctant to exercise their power because of the possible adverse impact on the development of their pupils. On the other hand, some groups are less restrained about using their bargaining power relative to the employer.

A further important consideration for management in assessing whether a group of workers has the advantage in relative bargaining power is the quality of leadership within the group. Management must make a judgement about how representative the leadership of the group is, and the extent of its influence and respect amongst the group. The higher the quality of the leadership of the group, the less likely it is that management will want to see the employees exercise their perceived superior bargaining power. A high quality of leadership amongst the group can, however, be advantageous to management in that the leadership can also exert its influence over the group by restraining the group from exercising its potential power.

The next step for a management in evaluating its bargaining power relative to a group of its employees is to check whether the employees have imposed industrial sanctions against the organisation in the past and, if so, what form the sanctions took (eg overtime ban, work-to-rule, a strike) and what was the result. In short, management examines whether the group has tested its potential power and if so, whether it selected the right sanctions, whether it deliberately selected a particular moment (eg the point of peak demand for the product or service produced by the group) and what was the outcome of the action (eg whether it confirmed the group's power). If industrial sanctions have been imposed in the past, management asks itself what can it learn from the episode. Is there anything it can learn and implement so that industrial action is not called again in the future? And if industrial action is the outcome, might it next time be different? If management concludes that the group has the relatively greater power, realises this fact, is willing to use its power and has used it successfully, then management is likely to be more willing to comply with the work group's demands. Thus we can now explain why some of the most powerful groups of workers, even in times of economic depression, rarely resort to strike action – the threat to do so is sufficient for management to modify its position to one which is closer to that desired by the group. On the other hand, if the group has exercised its power and the outcome has been unsatisfactory, it will be reluctant to impose industrial action in the future, and the relative balance of bargaining power between the employer and that particular group of workers will swing back towards the former.

The best example of this is the experiences of the National Union of Mineworkers in its 1984–85 dispute with British Coal. The union imposed an industry-wide strike which lasted for over 12 months but brought no concessions from the employer. Coal miners returned to work without any agreement. They had failed to inflict the expected damage on other industries resulting from an anticipated closure of steel production and electricity supply. British Coal's customers – for example, electricity-generating companies – continued to obtain supplies of coal which ensured the uninterrupted generation of electricity. British industry continued to function. However, the latent power of the union was exposed as ineffective and the union has not called a national strike since.

If management's analysis of the relative bargaining power shows that it lies with the employees or a group of employees, then it will need to devise strategies to redress the power balance. Management can seek to reduce its dependency on the group by, for example, pursuing policies to ensure that there is an alternative supply of labour available (either within or outside the organisation), that if sanctions are imposed the customer can still be satisfied, and that the outcome of any strike action is unfavourable to the group. This need of management to assess its bargaining power relative to the work groups with which it deals is raised again when we consider management behaviour during a bargaining situation.

Consider the work groups in your organisation. Which have the most potential power to disrupt the organisation? What is the basis of the power? Do they realise they have this power? If not, why not? Do you think they would be willing to use their power?

BARGAINING POWER AND MANAGEMENT BEHAVIOUR

When management has a relatively greater bargaining power than employees, it is important that power is used responsibly. Because the balance of bargaining power favours management, it may achieve its objective despite adopting a management style that is unprofessional and based on an attitude of 'take it or leave it', 'go and work for somebody else', and 'there are plenty of other people who would be only too willing to work here'. The workforce complies not because it is committed to the management decision but because it has little alternative. The employees are cowed, have no respect for management and store up grievances that will come to the surface with a vengeance when the relative balance of bargaining power turns in favour of themselves.

Such management behaviour is an irresponsible exercise of power which may be successful in the shorter term but is not sustainable in the longer term. It is a right to manage based on a crude use (abuse) of power and which will have long-term detrimental effects on the success of the business via a higher labour turnover, lower employee morale and commitment, and depressed productivity rates. A professional management acts on the basis of systematic preparation of its case, proceeds on the basis of just cause, consults and discusses with its employees, and treats them in a fair, reasonable and consistent manner. Managing on the basis of consultation and discussion, regardless of the relative balance of bargaining between employers and employees, normally gains the respect of the latter even though management invariably gains what it wants.

To have a favourable relative balance of bargaining power does not justify management's behaving in an unprofessional manner. If management behaves unprofessionally in exercising power, then when the relative balance changes, the employees and their representatives will behave in like manner. Management can act without just cause and fail to comply with the appropriate procedural arrangements because at the end of the day it can enforce its will. However, a management that adopts this style cannot complain if its employees and their representatives also ignore procedural arrangements and agreements when the swing of the pendulum passes the relative balance of power to the employees. In short, if management behaves unprofessionally when the relative balance of bargaining power is in its favour, then employees and trade unions will respond in like manner when the relative balance of power moves towards the employees.

The possession of power carries the obligation to exercise it responsibly. Should power be abused by management, or be perceived as being misused, the employees and wider society will demand that management's power be curbed. Parliament will intervene to limit the circumstances in which power can be exercised without those who are affected adversely by it having access to law for redress. During the last 15 years, a small minority of employers have abused their relative bargaining power by paying very low wages, by introducing 'zero-hour contracts' (which require a person to be available for work but to be paid wages only when he or she actually works) and by dismissing employees just before they qualify via length of service for unfair dismissal and redundancy rights. This behaviour has led the TUC to demand that a Labour Government introduce a statutory minimum wage, that all workers have employment protection rights from day one of employment with an employer, and that all employees have the right to union representation in their dealing with management.

By the same token, it was the perceived abuse of power by trade unions in the late 1970s that enabled the Conservative Governments of the 1980s and 1990s, justified on the grounds of redressing the balance of power, to introduce legislation to restrain certain types of trade union behaviour (eg strikes, compulsory unionism, picketing). Employers who behave unprofessionally and exercise their power irresponsibly are helping to justify future governments' introducing legislation designed to redress this perceived misuse of power. All employers will have to suffer because of the unacceptable behaviour of a minority of unscrupulous employers.

EMPLOYEE RELATIONS SKILLS

Employee relations managers need knowledge and understanding, and the necessary skills to apply that knowledge and understanding, to solve employee relations problems. These skills will be described in more detail in the appropriate chapters hereafter. Explanations will be given on why management must be competent in these skills. The more important skills required of an employee relations manager are:

Communication skills of note-taking, letter and report writing, and public speaking – Managers do not always communicate effectively yet they rely heavily upon the spoken word in making notes (often in small-group discussion), in writing reports to colleagues and senior managers (ie putting ideas and possible policies onto paper against tight deadlines), in sending letters, and in making presentations to other managers and to employers. Communicating well is a skill. To perform effectively, managers must acquire and develop its techniques.

Interviewing skills – Managers spend time gaining appropriate information to deal with complaints by employees against management behaviour (employee grievances), and with complaints by the employer about employee behaviour (discipline). In negotiation situations, management requires information to confirm its expected areas of agreement and/or whether they need to be reassessed in the light of information received from the employees' representatives. In all these situations, management has to obtain the relevant information to solve problems by word of mouth from interested parties. A competent manager will have excellent interviewing skills.

Listening skills – Management cannot operate by issuing instructions. Managing people requires contact with them. A major source of information for management, even more important than reading reports, is listening to what individuals are saying. Listening is a skill and involves concentrating on what is being said. The ability to listen is often taken for granted, but effective listening skills have to be acquired and developed: they require attention (watching for body language, etc), comprehension ('thinking ahead of the speaker') and absorption (making notes of what you hear). The effective manager will have competency in listening skills. A failure to listen to what one is being told carries a high risk of missing an important piece of information.

Negotiating skills – Managers are frequently meeting with other management colleagues, employees and employee representatives to solve problems by agreement, by purposeful persuasion, and by constructive compromise. Negotiation requires a number of skills – for example information-gathering and analysis, communication, interviewing, listening, anticipating how the other party might react to arguments and proposals, interpreting body language and judgemental skills (ie judging whether a solution is the best that can be reached in the circumstances). The effective manager will be excellent in negotiating skills.

Evaluation skills – Managers are frequently approached by a line manager and asked why a management practice that is reported to have been successfully introduced into one organisation should not be adopted in their company or organisation. It is important the employee relations managers can evaluate why the practice has been successful in one organisation and whether it could or could not be transplanted successfully into their organisation. Evaluation skills are also crucial if employee relations managers are successfully to monitor, review and amend the working of existing management policies, practices and procedures. The competent employee relations manager will possess effective evaluation skills.

It is therefore crucial that employee relations managers acquire knowledge and understanding and the skills necessary to apply such knowledge and understanding successfully to resolving employee relations problems.

FURTHER READING

BEARDWELL I. (ed.) *Contemporary Industrial Relations*. Oxford, Oxford University Press, 1996; chapters 1, 3 and 7.

KESSLER S. *and* BAYLISS F. *Contemporary British Industrial Relations*. 2nd ed. London, Macmillan, 1995; chapters 7, 8 and 9.

KESSLER S. *and* BAYLISS F. 'The changing face of industrial relations'. *Personnel Management*. May 1992, pp34–38.

FARNHAM D. *and* PIMLOTT J. *Understanding Industrial Relations*. 5th ed. London, Cassell, 1995; chapters 2, 3, 6 and 8.

Part 3

PARTIES, PROCESSES, OUTCOMES AND CONTENT

2 The corporate environment

INTRODUCTION

In its 1996 Statement on Employment Relations the IPD drew attention to the need for every organisation to continually improve its performance. Whether the challenge came from an increasingly competitive marketplace or as a consequence of the tight spending controls which continue to characterise the public sector, the pressure is much the same for all organisations and it is unlikely, in the short term, to reduce (IPD, 1996).

The most important thing to note about the IPD statement is that the pressure referred to is external. In this chapter we will be concerned with examining the factors which, when taken together, combine to give us the external corporate environment in which all organisations have to operate. It matters not whether that organisation is a large multinational like the Ford Motor Company, a National Health Service Trust or a medium-sized service company, people issues – and thus employee relations – are influenced and shaped by the way in which those external pressures impact on the workplace.

In Chapter 1 we said that the corporate environment consisted of three elements: the economic context, the political/legal context, and the technological context. These three elements are of immense importance to our understanding of employee relations, and why organisations choose to adopt particular policies, and how such policies might change over time.

The business environment in which employee relations practitioners have to operate is constantly changing, and this means it is important to be aware not only of specific shifts in employee relations policies resulting from such changes, but of the importance of monitoring the environment to identify possible further changes and developments. Employee relations policies in this context have both a reactive and pro-active role – a strategic role that is central to the organisation's growth and survival.

Although each of the elements is crucial in determining the employee relations practices of individual employers, the response of each to the impact on their own business or organisation may well be different. For example, a traditional non-union company such as Marks & Spencer is unlikely to have responded in the same way to the legislative changes introduced during the 1980s as a company that was traditionally heavily unionised. Organisations such as News International used these changes in employment law as an opportunity to make radical alterations to existing working practices in their newspaper plants. Printing trade unions had always been seen as being very powerful within the newspaper industry and had used this power to restrict employment opportunities, to resist changes in working practices and to raise wages to very high levels. Changes to the laws on strikes, picketing and closed shops opened the door to employers who wanted to force through change. The consequences for News International were that they became involved in a very violent and acrimonious dispute with the print unions that lasted for over 12 months.

Employers have their own objectives, their own styles of employee relations and their own structures of organisations and associations. These structures have changed in recent times, and the employee relations specialist needs to keep up to date with these trends and developments. For example, the role, and some would say the importance, of employers' organisations has declined in recent years in response to moves to de-centralise the levels at which collective bargaining takes place. Organisational structure has changed in both the public and private sector. The growth of individual NHS Trusts is but one example. Changes have occurred too in respect of employees and their organisations. As we shall see later in this chapter, UK Government economic policy and changes in legislation have altered the relative balance of bargaining power between employers and employees. This contributed to a decline in the membership of unions which caused individual unions to devise and implement strategies designed to secure their future survival. These included merging with other unions (eg UNISON), creating in their wake a number of 'super-unions'. These issues are discussed in greater detail in Chapter 3.

The role of the state has also changed. Because it is a major employer in its own right, the post-war expectation was that the state would be a 'model employer', encouraging collective bargaining, ensuring that its employees' pay was in line with that of the private sector and encouraging the use of arbitration to resolve disputes. But in recent times this concept has changed. The whole nature of public-sector employment has been altered: former civil servants now work for quasi-private-sector employers such as Training and Enterprise Councils. The growth of executive agencies, the outsourcing of local authority services through the imposition of compulsory competitive tendering and the spread of privatisation has further diluted the concept of the public servant. Most of this change has resulted from the determination of successive Conservative administrations to de-centralise the role of the UK Government. They saw the role of the UK Government as staying outside the employee relations arena. However, although the state remains a large employer, it no longer sees collective bargaining, pay comparability and arbitration as central to its employee relations policies. These have been replaced by an active discouragement of collective bargaining, the relating of pay increases to improvements in performance, and the ending of arbitration as the basis of conflict resolution.

All these changes have impacted on the nature and style of employee relations processes. As the impact of collective bargaining, and thus collective agreements, has declined, we have seen a growth in the use of other employee relations processes. Joint consultation, which while not a new concept has undergone a resurgence, and employee participation and involvement schemes have become much more important.

In Chapter 1 the concept of the balance of bargaining power and how important it is to the selection, by the employer, of appropriate employee relations processes was introduced. This balance is conditioned by changes in the economic, political and technological elements which taken together make up the corporate environment. In this chapter the concept is examined in much greater detail and linked directly to the economic, legal and technical environment in which organisations exist and compete. The concept of the balance of power is also significant in that it helps explain changes in the employee relations system over time – for example, why employee relations behaviour in the 1990s is different from that of the 1970s. When you have completed this chapter you should be able to

- describe how the UK Government in its role as economic manager influences employee relations

- explain the two principal economic theories that have been applied to the management of the economy since World War II

- explain how the legislative system, including laws emanating from Europe, influences employee relations

- explain how the corporate environment affects the relative balance of bargaining power

- explain what impact new technology has on the working environment.

ECONOMIC MANAGEMENT

The economic environment is influenced by the macro-economic policies a particular UK Government chooses to implement. UK Government policies regarding the levels of employment, inflation, taxation and interest rates have a direct effect on employee relations because they have an impact on the price of labour and on the relative balance of bargaining power between the buyers and sellers of labour services. However, it would be a mistake for the employee relations specialist to assume that UK Governments have a completely free hand when deciding economic policies. Like businesses, they are also affected by external events. For example, the effective devaluation of sterling in 1992, which was caused by the UK's withdrawal from the European Exchange Rate Mechanism, had severe repercussions for the economy as a whole. During the next two to three years from now UK macro-economic policy will, inevitably, be affected by any decisions made by the UK Government regarding the proposals on European Monetary Union. Irrespective of whether the UK joins or stays out of a new system, employee relations practices and policies will not be immune from its economic impact. For example, multinational organisations such as Toyota have indicated that future investment decisions may have to be reconsidered if Britain were to operate outside of a system of monetary union.

However, whatever the degree of outside influence, the UK Government has the role of economic manager. While different political parties have different ideologies and policies, the role of economic manager remains, whichever party is in power. It is important for the employee relations specialist to understand that the economic policies of a Conservative Government are likely to differ from those of a Labour Government, and that these distinctions in policy could have differing impacts on the relative balance of bargaining power. There are some politicians who believe Britain should follow a policy of full employment and that the achievement of this goal justifies a degree of direct UK Government intervention into the affairs of public and private enterprises. When this approach has been adopted, the outcome has been to give organised labour a clear advantage in the balance of relative bargaining power. But by far the most important issue of economic policy surrounds public expenditure. All UK Governments seek to keep public borrowing under some sort of control because of its impact on inflation – and in October 1996 the International Monetary Fund (IMF) warned that financial market confidence and long-term interest rates could be adversely affected if attention were not paid to the failure of the public-sector borrowing requirement to shrink sufficiently. Translated into employee relations terms, there is, amongst private-sector employers, always a great deal of concern over the possibility of a Labour Government since it is perceived as likely to take a softer line on public-sector pay than a Conservative Government. If this proves to be the case, it will almost certainly have a knock-on effect in the private sector. That is why one of the most important skills the employee relations manager/professional can develop is the art of scanning the political and environmental landscape to establish the extent to which policy shifts may have an impact on employee relations in the future. If a UK Government is successful in reducing the numbers of unemployed, one of the effects is likely to be a swing in the balance of power towards trade unions and employees and away from employers. Pressure on wage rates will increase as unemployment decreases, particularly if skill shortages increase.

What occupational types, either within your own organisation or externally, could be in short supply in such circumstances? Do you think your organisation has planned sufficiently far ahead in respect of its manpower requirements?

There is evidence that many organisations have, over time, failed to invest sufficiently in training. Once the pool of available labour reduces, its 'price' goes up. Clearly these and other effects are not necessarily the immediate results of a change of UK Government, but over time the needs of economic management changes and shifts. The strategic employee relations manager requires the ability to monitor and to anticipate such changes, to support and inform the organisation's plans and objectives.

In economic terms, a further impact on employee relations comes from the growth in multinational companies and the expansion of the global marketplace. In this world of multinationals, the intricacies of international and multinational finance have effects on employee relations at the local level. Indeed, they can influence the location of new employment opportunities and, in some cases, the underlying culture of employee relations practices. Multinationals see wage rates, expansion and investment in the context of the global market, in much the same way that a national company can make decisions after taking into account subsidies from enterprise areas, development corporations, and so on. International competition has an effect on employee relations in other ways. Firms from the United States and Japan who set up in the UK look for such qualities as flexibility and adaptability. This has caused some of the traditional demarcation lines in industry to become blurred or removed to a great extent. The negotiation of such methods of working makes them important in the area of employee relations.

What changes in working practices have taken place in your organisation? Where there have been changes why were they introduced? Have any traditional demarcation lines been removed as a consequence of such changes?

To understand how the UK Government's role of economic manager can have an effect on employee relations and on the relative balance of bargaining power between employers and employees, it is important to review and understand the changes that have taken place over the last 20 years – not least because a reversal of the economic policies that have been employed during this period could see a return to a high-wage high-inflation economy. This could then herald a return to some form of prices and incomes policy.

The full employment/economic growth era
For nearly 30 years after World War II, successive UK Governments regardless of their political complexion were committed to a policy of

full employment. This led to economic growth, increased public provision (in such areas as housing, education and the National Health Service) and personal prosperity for the majority of households. From the perspective of trade unions, full employment also provided them with increased bargaining power which, in many instances, led employers to concede inflationary wage settlements. Many of the craft unions (eg printers, engineers) also followed policies which aimed to restrict the number of new entrants to their particular craft or were designed to limit change (eg the introduction of new working methods or technology). This type of behaviour created labour shortages in certain occupations or, in others, led to over-staffing, and attempts to resolve this problem led to some organisational conflict. The fact that management seemed unable to implement effective policies to counteract many of these restrictions led, inevitably, to a worsening of management and union relationships.

However, notwithstanding the apparent increase in the overall standard of living, the general level of performance of the British economy was one of slower economic growth compared to our major competitors. As Pettigrew and Whipp report: 'In the three decades after World War II, the British economy showed the lowest rate of growth (an average of two and a half per cent per annum) of the major industrialised countries' (1993, p64). This relative economic under-performance had many downside effects, of which less than constructive industrial relations was certainly one. By the latter part of the 1960s the effect of high wage settlements, together with union restrictive practices and poor management, caused many commentators to take the view that this deterioration in competitiveness was a direct consequence of poor workplace industrial relations (Nolan and Walsh, 1995). This opinion was supported by many of the conclusions of the Royal Commission on Trade Unions and Employers' Associations (the Donovan Commission). The Commission will be discussed more fully in Chapter 3, but because such an authoritative body was prepared to accept that poor industrial performance was a consequence of poor workplace industrial relations it became a widely accepted view. Thus, reform of workplace industrial relations was seen as a major priority, particularly by politicians and employers' organisations. Opinions on the type of reform, and how best to implement it, did of course differ, but the need for reform was very rarely questioned.

By the beginning of the 1960s the concerns about the prevailing system of employee relations and the impact that it was having on competitiveness had become part of the political agenda, and the Labour Government under Harold Wilson, which was elected in 1964, decided that the situation could not continue. The economy was suffering from one of its periodic bouts of inflationary pressure and in its role as economic manager the new UK Government decided to interfere directly in employee relations through a productivity, prices and incomes policy. At the start of the 1960s, UK economic management was heavily influenced by the ideas of the economist John Maynard Keynes, some of whose basic ideas were that

- the general level of employment in an economy is determined by the level of spending power in the economy

- the overall spending power in the economy depends upon the amount of consumption and investment undertaken by individual households and employing units as well as UK Government expenditure

- full employment is achieved by the UK Government's regulating overall spending power in the economy through its tax and public expenditure policies

- if unemployment rises, due to a lack of overall spending power in the economy, the UK Government may inject spending power by reducing taxes and/or increasing its own expenditure.

The principal contribution that Keynes made to economic management was his conclusion that economies could not remain unregulated – that if full employment were to be achieved, UK Governments would have to intervene in order to create the necessary levels of demand. As we shall discuss later, this view – that an economy could not be left to follow its own course – was completely opposed by those who helped to shape the monetarist policies to be followed by successive Conservative Governments throughout the 1980s and 1990s (Donaldson and Farquhar, 1991).

For the followers of Keynesian economics, incomes policies were seen as a necessary additional weapon in the battle against inflation. Because wage costs account for such a large proportion of employers' overall costs, excessive rises in wage levels significantly affect the inflation spiral. As inflation rises, economic policymakers are tempted to put the brakes on by stifling demand. This, in turn, can lead to rises in unemployment. Creating the means (income policies) to moderate wage claims would make it easier to reach the goal of full employment. Initially the policy experienced some short-term success, but by the 1970s such policies were to prove politically explosive. Not surprisingly, such an attempt to limit wage settlements was seen as a deliberate attempt to shift the balance of bargaining power more towards the interests of employers, and was resisted by the unions to the point of industrial disputes (eg the miners' strike of 1972 and 1973–74).

Nor were managements always impressed by the arbitrary imposition of UK Government pay norms; indeed, they were often happy to work with their employees to find ways round them. Private-sector employers were more interested in continuation of production and some were prepared to pay higher wages to avoid industrial action. While we now live in a highly competitive world economy, where maintaining some form of competitive advantage is the holy grail for most businesses, this was not always the case in the three decades after the war. During that period a much greater proportion of an organisation's customer base was static, relative to today, and they therefore had a much greater ability to pass on increased wage costs in the form of increased prices. In the case of the public sector, there was no serious long-term attempt to limit the growth in public expenditure, and companies and enterprises therefore learned to live with high inflation and its consequent impact on wages and prices.

The inability to manage employee relations effectively was a major contributor to Britain's increasing uncompetitiveness. Circumventing pay norms was but one example of a wider malaise. By the beginning of the 1960s the balance of power was firmly with the trade unions and was increasingly being exercised by shop stewards at plant level. These individuals were not prepared to subject themselves to control by union leaders, particularly those national trade union leaders who were prepared to co-operate with some form of pay restraint. Many shop stewards had their own agendas which tended to be very parochial and which, in the opinion of many employers, were based on political and not industrial objectives. Many employers also questioned whether shop stewards' behaviour truly represented the wishes of all their members. Such a view of the democracy of the decision-making process was given credence when many industrial actions were based on voting at mass meetings rather than by a secret ballot of those being asked to become involved.

The post-war consensus on macro-economic objectives was a significant factor in the growth of the union movement. One common theme of the 1960s and 1970s was the perception – partly based on strike statistics, but also based on the trade unions' links with the Labour Party and therefore Labour Governments – that trade union leaders of the period were more powerful than UK Government ministers. We saw, above, that poor workplace industrial relations were judged to be having a negative impact on economic performance. This made it easy to identify unions and union power as major contributors to the UK's economic problems. If businesses were not investing sufficiently, this, it was claimed, was the fault of the unions. If new technology was not embraced sufficiently quickly, again the unions were seen as the basis of the problem. If inflation was out of control, it was the fault of the unions. Although any examination of industrial relations during this period demonstrates that the unions have to accept a large part of the blame, weak management performance during the period was also a contributory factor. There was insufficient investment in training and development, and then, as now, insufficient investment in innovation and research. The debate about skill levels within UK organisations relative to our international competitors is still taking place. Despite the investment in Training and Enterprise Councils, National Vocational Qualifications, the national curriculum, there is still concern that some employers have failed to see the value of investing in people (Nolan and Walsh, 1995).

By 1978–79 an increasing number of people felt the pendulum had swung too far and the power of unions had to be curtailed if the UK were to regain competitiveness. This anti-union backlash had been given momentum by what is now known as the 'winter of discontent'. In 1975 the Labour Government again introduced an incomes policy as response to an unregulated bargaining period during 1974–75 which had produced accelerating inflation and concern about irresponsible union action (Keegan, 1984). Wage restraint during 1975, 1976 and

1977 was broadly accepted by the trade unions, but in 1978 the UK Government decided to opt for a wage norm of 5 per cent – half of what many considered to be the going rate! The unions refused to accept the 5 per cent norm and this led to a series of damaging public sector strikes during the winter of 1978–79 (the winter of discontent). The image of trade unions was now at an all-time low, and there were clear signs that the public mood was in favour of reducing their influence. This, in the view of many public policymakers, meant changing the rules of the game and demolishing the cosy post-war consensus that had been built around Keynesian economics and which was seen as a prime contributor to the UK's relative economic decline.

If the organisation you work in is, or was, unionised, what sort of collective relationship existed during the 1970s?

The New Right and monetarism

The 1978–79 winter of discontent coincided with the end of the five-year electoral cycle, and the incumbent Labour Government knew that they would have to hold a general election sometime during 1979. Although they sought to postpone this for as long as possible, an election was duly held in May 1979. The Conservative Party fought the election on their traditional battleground of the economy, promising lower taxes and less UK Government expenditure, but with additional promises to ensure that trade unions acted responsibly. Throughout their period in opposition (1974–79), a growing faction within the Conservative Party had begun to question the wisdom of Keynesian economics and whether they could ever be effective in managing the economy. Instead, the people Keegan (1984, p66) refers to as the 'economic evangelicalists' began to embrace the concept of monetarism as the means to control inflation and improve competitiveness. While monetarism can mean different things to different people its basic ideas are:

- If the general level of purchasing power in the economy as a whole grows quicker than the increase in the general level of goods and services produced in the economy as a whole, then firms and households will have more money than there are goods and services available in the economy to purchase.

- This situation of 'too much money chasing too few goods and services' results in a general rise in price levels.

- Increasing inflation increases expectations of future inflation, resulting in (a) higher wage demands and settlements, and (b) an ensuing wages-prices inflationary spiral, in turn resulting in an increase in the general level of unemployment as the competitiveness of firms declines and workers 'price themselves out of jobs'.

- To prevent inflation, the increase in the overall level of purchasing power in the economy as a whole must match the rate of increase in the general output of goods and services in the economy as a whole.

- If the increase in the economy-wide level of purchasing power exceeds the increase in the general level of the supply of goods and services in the economy as a whole, spending power (demand) must be decreased by interest rate increases and reducing the level of UK Government (public) expenditure.

For monetarists, unemployment will only fall, in the longer term, if the productive capacity of the economy is increased. Measures to achieve such an increase are usually referred to as 'supply-side' economics. This views the key to reducing unemployment and controlling inflation as enhancing the ability of the economy to supply goods and services to the market efficiently and cost-effectively by

- creating an economic environment conducive to private enterprise and free markets
- creating incentives for individuals to work and for firms to invest, produce goods and services, and employ workers
- liberalising product markets
- reducing taxation
- deregulating labour markets.

The Conservatives duly won the 1979 election, and under the leadership of Margaret Thatcher began the process of applying monetarist policies to the management of the UK economy. These policies have now been applied in one way or another for the past 18 years and there is no doubt that the make-up of our economy has changed radically during that period. It is certainly true that labour markets have been deregulated and direct taxation reduced but, in the opinion of many people, there has been a high price to pay for the various reforms. The reforms to the labour market have seen a move from employment in manufacturing to employment in the service industry which has accounted for an increase in non-manual jobs at the expense of manual ones. Part-time employment has increased while full-time employment has decreased. The rise in part-time employment, when converted to full-time equivalents, does not compensate for this downturn in full-time work. While it would be an over-simplification to blame all the changes in the labour market on monetarist policies, those policies were the engine by which the reforms were driven. Higher unemployment relative to the 1960s and 1970s has had a major impact on employee relations. While trade union influence is certainly lower and industrial disputes have declined, there has been a growth in employee insecurity and, if the number of cases being dealt with by ACAS and industrial tribunals is any guide, a rise in the number of workplace grievances. High levels of employee insecurity are not helpful if, as we said at the beginning of the chapter, organisations need to continually improve their performance.

The feelings of insecurity expressed by many employees are a major concern to employers and thus employee relations specialists. In your organisation have you identified a rise in grievances, individual or collective, as a consequence of such insecurity? If insecurity exists but grievances have not risen, how does the concern over insecurity manifest itself?

The state as an employer

In this section and the sections that follow, we look at some of the policy initiatives of the past 18 years and how they have contributed to the change in employment relationships. During the post-war period, the state always sought to give a lead to the private sector as a model and good employer in a number of ways. Collective bargaining was considered a good and desirable activity. Union membership was encouraged and led to high levels of unionisation in the public sector and to the growth of white-collar unions. Nine out of ten white-collar trade unionists were employed in the public sector. When industries were taken into public ownership both after World War II and in the 1970s, there was an obligation on the public corporation created to recognise and negotiate with trade unions. The state sought to ensure that its public-sector staff received pay and conditions comparable to those doing the same or similar work in the private sector. Comparability was thus the basis of wage claims and adjustments. For example, in the civil service the civil servants were given a Pay Research Unit to look at rates of pay, to compare pay with private-sector employees, and to provide information to the negotiators.

Conservative Governments from 1979 onwards have had a different approach to economic management and pursued a twin-track policy to achieve their objectives. They eschewed the prevailing post-war consensus in such areas as the welfare state, UK Government intervention in industry, incomes policy, tripartite discussions and keeping unemployment in check even at the risk of rising inflation. Instead they made clear their intention of letting the market decide. Monetarist policies were introduced as a means of reducing inflation, which meant increases in interest rates, increases in indirect taxes, and cuts in public expenditure. Their effect was large increases in unemployment, especially in the country's more traditional industries such as shipbuilding and coal mining. By allowing unemployment to rise, the UK Government was able to drive home its message that radical measures needed to be taken if the British economy was to become competitive. In addition, Conservative Governments sought the encouragement of an enterprise culture by the deregulation of product and labour markets, the privatisation of nationalised industries and the curbing of trade unions' industrial activities. As Blyton and Turnbull (1994, p145) saw it: 'The objectives of UK Government policy in the 1980s can be simply stated: namely to encourage enterprise through the deregulation of markets, especially the labour market.' They noted that the foundations of what is described as Thatcherism (the shorthand way of describing the application of monetarism) can be found in the writings of free-market economists such as Milton Friedman and in particular Friedrich Hayek. Of the UK economists who subscribe to the monetarist philosophy, the work of Patrick Minford is a good indicator of why the policy agenda has been developed as it has. Minford argues that trade unions use their power to raise wages above the market rate, which then cause price inflation, which in turn causes further rises in unemployment. This process, he argues, reduces both the efficiency of individual firms and the economy as a whole through the imposition of restrictive practices, demarcation and the like. With such views as these prevailing, it is not hard to see why the focus on trade union power and influence has been so important to successive Conservative administrations since 1979.

The restriction on trade union behaviour was to be two-pronged. Firstly, the UK Government made it clear that it was no longer prepared to fulfil its traditional role as 'model employer'. The idea that the state should be a model to the private sector remained, but the notion of what constituted a 'model employer' changed. In 1981 the Thatcher Government ended the civil service comparability agreement which had operated since 1951. This led to industrial action in the security services, which in turn resulted in the UK Government's ending union recognition at its highly secret communications headquarters (GCHQ). The UK Government became less favourably disposed to collective bargaining and instead argued that employees should be rewarded as individuals. They sought to act against the collective voice, because they subscribed to the view that it led to higher-priced jobs and, consequently, unemployment. The state did not encourage people to become members of trade unions or to take part in collective bargaining. Conversely, it also discouraged the traditional role of employers' federations in national wage bargaining. Comparability of pay for public sector employees was terminated because it was thought that pay increases should be related to the ability to pay and the availability of labour resources. The pay of an occupational group should thus not necessarily be the same in different parts of the country. Differentials should reflect the scarcity of labour. Thus, wage negotiation at operating unit levels, where the ability-to-pay and scarcity-of-labour factors could more easily be taken account of, were encouraged and the traditional 'going-rate' argument was discouraged.

> Have any of these arguments been incorporated into the reward structure within your organisation? If so, what has been the impact on employee relations?

The UK Government argued that inflation was the result of the money supply's increasing faster than the increase in output of goods and services in the economy. Money supply is the total spending power in the economy as a whole, but a major component in this is public expenditure. Given that the UK Government is responsible directly or indirectly for the wages of one third of the employees in the country, and given that pay is an important part of public-sector expenditure, the UK Government could not adopt a neutral stance on pay settlements. Therefore, although the UK Government made it clear that a formal incomes policy with norms and enforcement agencies was not on its agenda, it was prepared to ensure effective controls over pay rises for public-sector employees by the simple expedient of limiting the rise in public expenditure. This approach brought the UK Government into conflict with a number of public-sector unions – for example schoolteachers, who had their collective bargaining rights removed by Act of Parliament.

Further radical measures in the reform of the labour market over the last 18 years have seen a progressive diminution of the welfare safety net for unemployed workers. The UK Government has argued that over-generous welfare provision means that people have less incentive to work and therefore remain unemployed for longer than is necessary. This so-called dependency culture has been tackled by changing the basis on which an individual is eligible for unemployment benefit and by reducing the length of time over which such benefit is payable. Taken together with the fear of unemployment, such changes in the welfare system mean that employees become less resistant to employer control and are less likely to seek reviews of their terms and conditions of employment.

THE STATE AS LAW-MAKER

Otto Kahn-Freund in his classic book *Labour and the Law* (1977) outlined three functions of the law in regulating employee relations. They were:

- the auxiliary function – where the law is designed to promote collective bargaining as well as the making and observance of collective agreements

- the regulatory function – where the law restricts the power of management relative to its employees and the powers of the trade unions relative to their members: this is the area of individual employment rights and the rights of individual trade union members

- the restrictive function – where the law establishes the 'rules of the game' when employers and employees are in the process of making agreements: this type of legislation effectively lays down the circumstances in which employers and trade unions can impose industrial sanctions on each other without the parties having redress to the legal system.

The idea that the law should be used to promote collective bargaining was anathema to Margaret Thatcher and many of her ministerial colleagues, and the auxiliary function of the law as described by Kahn-Freund was unlikely to figure highly in their legislative programme. However, they made no secret that the second part of their two-pronged restriction on trade union behaviour would be to use the law in regulating the behaviour of the unions towards its members and in restricting the scope of a union's lawful activities.

The regulatory function of the law

Statutory rights for individual employees relative to their employer began to emerge in the early 1960s. Parliament justified such rights on the grounds that private arrangements (for example, by collective agreement) had failed to provide an adequate minimum acceptable level of protection to individual employees against certain behaviour by their employers. At the same time it sent a clear message to employers that they must act with just cause and be 'fair and reasonable' in the treatment of their employees on those matters where statutory minimum standards were being established for their employees. Individual employees enforce these rights relative to their employer via industrial tribunals (ITs) which are independent judicial bodies set up to deal with claims quickly, informally and cheaply. They have a legally qualified chair who sits with two other members, each of whom is drawn from panels appointed by the Secretary of State, one after consultation with employee organisations, the other after consultation with employers' organisations. The floor of legal rights was created by UK Governments sympathetic to the view that there should be a basic level of employment protection below which no employee should be permitted to fall. These minimum levels can be enhanced by private agreements – for example, via collective bargaining. However, Conservative Governments post-1979, although accepting the principle of employment protection, have argued that the minimum standards are too high and can be a disincentive for employers, particularly small and new firms, to recruit labour. Conversely, the Labour Party has argued for minimum standards to be increased by lowering the qualifying period of employment that is needed to accrue individual rights.

If employees had the right to claim unfair dismissal from day one of employment, what impact would this have on your organisation? Do you think your existing policies and procedures are capable of coping with such a change?

A statutory floor of rights for trade union members relative to their trade union has been considerably extended under the post-1979 Conservative Governments. This has been justified on the grounds that trade unions needed to be more democratic, more accountable to their members, and to exercise their power more responsibly. The UK Government believed that trade union leaders were, without collecting the views of their members, coercing them to undertake labour market activities (for example, undertaking industrial action) harmful to their employment security.

This has resulted in the enactment of a series of measures to provide positive rights for union members to participate in, or restrain, union decision-making on specific issues. The main trade union member rights are:

• to participate in regular secret post ballots at least once every 10 years to decide on whether or not the union should undertake political activity, through union political funds and the political levy

- to elect all voting members of the union's executive (including its president and general secretary) by secret postal ballot at least once every five years

- to participate in a secret ballot before a union takes organised industrial action against an employer

- not to be called upon to participate in industrial action not supported by a properly conducted secret ballot

- not to be disciplined unjustifiably by the union

- to inspect the union's accounting records.

If your organisation is unionised and participates in 'check-off' arrangements with recognised unions, what happened the last time there was a ballot on whether this should continue? How big was the majority in favour of continuing the arrangement, assuming there was a yes vote? What do you think will happen next time there is a ballot?

As a means of helping individual union members enforce their rights, the Commissioner for the Rights of Trade Union Members (CROTUM) was created under the Employment Act (1988) and has two sets of powers. The first is to grant assistance to union members who are considering or taking legal action against a union arising out of an alleged or threatened breach of a member's statutory union membership rights. The second is to give assistance when a union member claims his or her union has failed to observe the requirements of its own rule book. The Commissioner also acts as the Commissioner for Protection against Unlawful Industrial Action and can help third-party individuals who wish to challenge the lawfulness of industrial action.

The restrictive function of the law

Ever since 1871 trade unions have – except when they were undermined by the Taff Vale decision in 1901 – enjoyed immunity from actions for civil damages. The basic immunity framework was contained in the Trade Disputes Act (1906) and this remained in force until 1971 when the Conservative Government introduced the Industrial Relations Act. This limited trade union immunity by the introduction of the concept of 'unfair industrial practices' which, if unions committed them, gave those affected by such actions the right to sue for damages. The Trade Unions and Labour Relations Act (1974) repealed the Industrial Relations Act (1971) and re-established the trade unions' immunities position as that provided by the Trades Disputes Act (1906) once more. The Trade Unions and Labour Relations (Amendment) Act (1976) extended trade union immunity to the breach of all contracts for which trade unions were responsible when they called their members out on industrial action. This gave trade unions licence to persuade their members to take secondary industrial action. Secondary action is that taken against an employer with whom the trade union has no dispute, but who might, for example, be a key customer of an employer with whom they currently do have an industrial dispute. By taking this type of industrial action the union hopes that the secondary employer will put pressure on the employer involved in the main dispute to settle the dispute on terms which are favourable to the union.

By 1976 trade unions had a very wide immunity from legal action in the case of industrial disputes. They could call, without legal liability, for industrial action in connection with any kind of industrial dispute, no matter how remote those taking the action were from the original dispute. Nobody seriously challenged this union legislative benefit until 1979, when things began to change. As we have discussed above, there was clearly a public mood that something had to be done to restrain the behaviour of trade unions. Firstly, there was the question of internal trade union democracy. Images of large factory-gate meetings at which dissenters were either ignored or too frightened to oppose elected officials, especially shop stewards, were commonplace. Secondly, there was the issue of the closed shop by which individuals were forced to join trade unions, often against their will and with no right of redress if they were dismissed from their job for their non-conformity. Thirdly, there was the question of trade union immunity and what was seen as a lack of responsibility for the trade unions' actions. Businesses were demanding their own rights to counteract what they saw as an unlevel playing-field. The UK Government response was to bring the law into employee relations more intrusively than had ever been the case in the consensual post-war years.

Legislation came at regular intervals, and between 1980 and 1993 there were seven Acts of Parliament designed to restrict trade union activity and behaviour. The Employment Act (1980) removed the unions' immunity if their members engaged in picketing premises other than their own place of work; if they took industrial action to compel an individual to become a union member, or if they took certain secondary action. The Employment Act (1982) went even further in reducing or removing immunities. Among the principal clauses in the Act was a narrowing of the definition of a trade dispute, an outlawing of the practice of pressurising employers not to include non-union firms on tender lists, and the enabling of employers to sue trade unions for an injunction or damages where they were responsible for unlawful industrial action. The Trade Union Act (1984) was probably one of the most significant pieces of legislation in that it introduced the principle of pre-strike ballots. It would be fair to say that most commentators are of the opinion that this Act has certainly helped improve employee relations. The Employment Act (1988) took the reforms one step further by effectively outlawing the closed shop. The Employment Act (1990) then removed the unions' immunity if they organised any type of secondary action or if they organised industrial action in support of an individual dismissed for taking unlawful action. In 1992 the Trade Union and Labour Relations (Consolidation) Act brought together, in one piece of legislation, much of the law relating to collective provision. And one year later, the

Trade Union Reform and Employment Rights Act (1993) made some amendments to existing requirements, most particularly in relation to ballots for industrial action.

These pieces of legislation have substantially increased the grounds on which legal action can be taken against a union by an employer. The circumstances in which unions can claim immunity from civil action have been more tightly defined, now involving provisions which require full-time officials to repudiate the actions of lay officials if they take actions contrary to the legislation. If immunity is to be maintained, such repudiation has to be meaningful, and the courts can require unions to present evidence as to the steps they have taken to bring their members within the law.

There is now little argument that the reforms were both necessary and timely. Requiring unions to hold a pre-strike ballot of their members prior to taking industrial action is not seriously questioned any more. Nor is the requirement that full-time officials should be subject to periodic re-election.

The role of the European Union
It is important to the work of employee relations specialists that they understand the purpose and function of the European Union (EU) in respect of its law-making role. There are four major institutions which govern the EU: the Commission, the Council of Ministers, the Parliament and the Court of Justice. The Commission initiates all EU legislation and has the power to bring legal action against member states deemed to have violated EU laws. It acts only in the interests of the EU as a whole. The Parliament is a representative assembly of 624 directly-elected members, but it has no legislative powers. It participates in the legislative process by giving its opinion on Commission proposals and suggesting amendments. The Court of Justice is the final arbiter in disputes over interpretation of treaties or the failure to implement EU law. The Court can be, and has been, used by UK individuals, groups and organisations to challenge UK employment legislation on the grounds that it contravenes EU law. Examples include discrimination in pensions and retirement ages, equal pay, and questions relating to the transfer of undertakings. The Council of Ministers is a forum of representatives – normally Government ministers – from the member states. It creates legislation by responding to the Commission's proposals and has the ultimate power to adopt or reject them. The Council is the main decision-making body in the EU.

> Which of the EU institutions is likely to have the greatest impact on the work of a professional employee relations specialist, and why?

In proposing, considering or drafting legislation, the Commission and the Council need to consult with the 'social partners', namely the Union of Industrial and Employers' Confederations of Europe (UNICE), the European Trades Union Confederation (ETUC) and the European Centre of Enterprises with Public Participation (CEEP).

They also consult via the Economic and Social Committee (ECOSOC) made up of representatives of employers, employees, consumers, small firms and professionals. From an employee relations perspective these social partner discussions are very important. Although neither the Commission nor the Council can be bound by the views of the social partners, the EU-wide employer and trade union bodies provide a conduit through which the impact of EU legislation on different industry sectors can be evaluated. For example, UNICE recognises the International Confederation for the Printing and Allied Industries (INTERGRAF) as the body who can provide a view on proposals as they are likely to affect that industry sector.

In the field of employment and social matters there are three methods which can be used to get legislation adopted: consultation, co-operation and co-determination. The first is used for matters that require a unanimous vote of the member states; the second is used for dealing with matters that can be decided by qualified majority voting; the third is for those proposals over which the Parliament has a right of veto on final proposals (eg free movement of labour).

For example, proposals relating to employment rights brought under the Social Chapter of the Treaty of Rome (1957), such as consultation procedures in respect of redundancies, require a unanimous vote, while proposals brought under the Social Chapter on Health and Safety are decided by qualified majority voting in which 62 out of a possible total of 87 must be cast in favour. All member states have a number of votes weighted according to population size. The big member states – the UK, Germany, France, Italy – have 10 votes each; 26 votes are required to block a proposal. Qualified majority voting was introduced by the Single Market Act (1987). It was the route used in respect of the proposals on working time, and was opposed by the UK Government who argued that restrictions on working time were employment, not health and safety, matters.

However, the Social Protocol of the Treaty of the European Union (1993), agreed at Maastricht, introduces a further legislation process for the introduction of employment legislation in all member states – except the UK. Before submitting proposals in the social field the Commission consults UNICE and ETUC and asks for their opinion or recommendation on the proposed initiatives. The 'social partners' may then choose to negotiate for up to nine months with a view to reaching a collective agreement on the issue. Any agreement reached can either be implemented by non-binding collective agreements at lower levels or form the basis for legislation adopted by the member states and subsequently enacted in their national law.

What impact on your workplace will the directive on working time have? Will it have an impact on either your suppliers or your customers?

There are four types of EU legislation that stem from the procedures:

* regulations, which are binding on all member states without the need for domestic legislation

* decisions, which are binding with immediate effect on those to whom they are addressed (member states, enterprises or individuals)

* recommendations and opinions, which are not binding

* directives, which are binding on all member states, but each member state can decide how it will implement the provision of the directive (eg by domestic legislation). Directives always contain a deadline by which member states must comply with their conditions.

EU-wide legislation takes preference over national (member state) legislation. Most EU employment law comes in the form of a directive, and in the UK directives have been implemented through the national legislative system. For example, the Acquired Rights Directive was implemented as the Transfer of Undertakings (Protection of Employment) Regulations (TUPE), and the Equal Pay and Equal Treatment Directives were incorporated into the Equal Pay Act and the Sex Discrimination Act respectively. From the perspective of the employee relations specialist, the most significant aspect of our membership of the EU is the social dimension, via the social charter or, to give it its correct title, the Community Charter of the Fundamental Social Rights of Workers, the Social Chapter, and the Agreement on Social Policy contained in the Social Protocol of the Maastricht Treaty. The charter, which proclaims that a floor of basic common employment rights and objectives should be established across all member states, is a political declaration signed in 1989 by all member states except the UK. It has no legal force in itself, but the application of its principles in the UK is the cause of massive political debate. Its floor of basic rights include the rights to be paid a sufficient wage, to adequate social security provision, to join or not to join a trade union, to negotiate collective agreements, to take collective action including strike actions, to access to vocational training, to be informed and consulted, and to health and safety provision. The Social Chapter is contained in the Treaty of Rome (1957). It sets out a clear commitment to the harmonisation of social conditions between member states so that free trade amongst member states takes place on the basis of a level playing-field of minimum employment conditions. The Social Chapter requires member states to ensure and maintain the application of the principle that men and women should have equal pay for equal work. All employment conditions to be introduced under the Social Chapter, except for health and safety, must have the unanimous support of all member states.

During the Maastricht negotiations it was proposed that the social issues under the Social Chapter which could be introduced under the qualified majority voting procedure be increased. The UK government rejected this proposal. All the other member states nonetheless decided to adopt the proposal extensions to the Social Chapter as a separate Social Policy Agreement contained in the Social Protocol attached to the Maastricht Treaty (1993). This Agreement permits all member states other than the UK to harmonise their employment laws by qualified majority voting in five areas: health and safety, working conditions, information to and consultation of workers, equal treatment and equal opportunities for men and women, and the integration of persons excluded from the labour market. It also allows them to harmonise their laws by unanimous agreement in five other areas, including representation and collective defence of the interests of workers and employers, social security, and the protection of workers where employment contracts are terminated. The first proposal under the Social Policy Agreement was the Directive on European Works Councils.

For the employee relations specialist, the EU is an important consideration when developing policies and procedures. It is therefore important that the operation of the EU institutions is understood and monitored.

THE IMPACT OF TECHNOLOGY

A traditional view of technology is that it is a dominating force within an organisation. All organisations operate within certain technological constraints which influence its size and structure. In turn, the size and structure of an organisation undoubtedly have an influence on its culture. Because culture affects relationships between people, it can be seen that technology and technological development are important factors in employee relations.

It is important that employee relations specialists understand the term *technology*. If it merely implies some form of process or engineering, does it have any relevance outside manufacturing? The answer is that technology is more than an engineering process: from the perspective of an organisation it is the application of skills and knowledge. It is therefore both relevant and necessary to understand it.

It is possible to identify three perspectives from which to view the impact of new technology on employee relations. First, new technology, because of its impact on traditional skills, acts as both a de-skilling agent and a creator of unemployment. The second perspective is that new technology is a positive force in that it creates new opportunities for employees who have the chance to learn new skills. The third perspective is also positive: new technology is seen as the means whereby previously unpleasant or repetitive tasks can be eliminated. For example, the introduction of robotics into the car industry has removed the need for employees to carry out mundane operations with, some would argue, a consequent improvement in the climate of employee relations in an industry previously dogged by labour problems. Each of these three perspectives is, to some degree, correct, but the impact of new technology varies from industry to industry and from organisation to organisation.

Most people acknowledge that, in general terms, technological development has reduced the demand for unskilled labour. This has created a consequent rise in unemployment among this group made worse by the non-availability of appropriate training opportunities. The extent to which technological developments have contributed to the decline in trade union membership is much more difficult to quantify. Many unskilled jobs in the manufacturing sector of the economy were lost as a result of national uncompetitiveness. Equally, emerging technologies have created new jobs in the service sector, but many of these are low- or semi-skilled – the difference being that manufacturing has traditionally had high levels of unionisation while the service sector has had very low levels of union density.

A view commonly held about the impact of technological change is that it creates problems, particularly where trade unions are represented in the workplace, and is often resisted. Such a view is given added credence by the way in which the media report such issues. The News International dispute at Wapping in the 1980s is famous for the attempts by the print unions to resist the takeover of their jobs by their fellow trade unionists, the electricians. It provided a useful opportunity to present old craft unions (printers) as resistant to change and 'reformist' unions like the electricians as the acceptable face of collectivism. There was no real attempt by the media to address the real employee relations issues that the dispute raised. When change is on the agenda, both trade unions and employees generally will have fears over job losses, de-skilling and increased management control. The skill of the employee relations specialist lies in understanding these concerns and seeking ways of mitigating them. Personnel specialists should have a vested interest in the *management* of change, not just the imposition of change. One industry that has had to understand this more than most is the car industry. The Rover New Deal is one example of a management seeking to take its employees with it when change is required. Another company example is Ford Motors. At the beginning of the 1980s Ford had more than 80,000 workers in the UK; by the end of the 1990s that figure will be under 30,000. Yet during the whole period Ford have been able to manage the changes that were required to boost the efficiency of its plants and have suffered very little employee relations disruption.

> Some commentators argue that the pace of technological change must inevitably slow down. Do you think this is a fair statement? If not, where do you see change happening, and how is it likely to impact on your organisation?

Whenever the subject of technology is discussed, the question of de-skilling is raised. The debate concerning the long-term impact on skill levels caused by technological change has raged for decades, much of it being conducted by means of case-study investigations. One investigation, the Social Change and Economic Life Initiative (SCELI), provided the first systematic survey data with which to assess the nature of skill change in Britain. As Ashton and Felstead report, the information collected was gathered from interviews with over 6,000 individuals in six areas. Those interviewed were asked to compare their current jobs with what they were doing five years earlier, in terms of the level of skill and responsibility required. Over the period, 52 per cent experienced an increase in the skills that they required, compared to only 9 per cent who saw their skills decline. This common experience of upskilling was true for all occupational categories, but was more prevalent among those already in highly skilled occupations. A further survey, 'Employment in Britain', indicated that the trends identified by the SCELI investigation have continued into the 1990s. Again this survey, conducted during 1992, demonstrated that higher-level qualifications are now required for jobs which some years earlier were not rated so highly (Ashton and Felstead, 1995).

While these surveys have a clear relationship with employee development issues, the employee relations specialist needs to recognise that changes in the balance of skills that are required will have a significant impact on his or her work. In some organisations the effect of de-skilling will outweigh any upgrading that may be required. This in turn may lead on to negotiations about redundancy or reduced pay levels. In other organisations there may well be difficulties in recruiting sufficient skilled labour, with the consequent pressure that this can bring, particularly in respect of unit labour costs. Overall it is important to remember that new technology varies in its impact. This is based on a number of variables including the nature of the product or service, the type of organisation involved, the management strategy employed and the attitude of trade unions (where they are represented) and employees. And, while employees are bound to be concerned about technology, a 1987 survey by Daniel concluded that the reaction of most workers to change was favourable. This manifested itself through the optimism about better jobs and higher wages generated by positive decisions about investment.

THE BALANCE OF BARGAINING POWER

The net result of the changes in economic management that we have discussed in this chapter has been a diminution in the importance and influence of trade unions. When the changes in economic management are combined with the political, legislative and technological change that we have seen since 1979, it is not surprising that the relative balance of bargaining power has changed during that time. Successive Conservative Governments have taken the view that eradicating inflation from the British economy was a crucial step to improved economic performance, and that if the result was high levels of unemployment, it was a necessary short-term penalty. The effect on the balance of bargaining power of such economic policies was probably greater than the changes in legislation. A key issue in employee relations is conflict resolution, and the question we need to ask is Has conflict disappeared? The answer is No. That there has been a change in the balance of bargaining power is unquestionable. When people feel insecure in their employment, and they are unable to see other job opportunities opening up, they are much more likely to be passive. This does not mean that conflict has disappeared, merely that it has submerged. While it is submerged it is much easier for organisations to plan and implement change safe in the knowledge that the legal system can – as we discuss in Chapter 4 – offer them greater protection against employee resistance than it did 20 years ago. Then, introducing change was hampered by the fact that the balance of bargaining power was in the employees' favour.

Wherever the relative balance of bargaining power lies at any one time, it is important to understand that, if the bargaining pendulum can swing one way, it can swing back. The balance of bargaining power has altered over the past years because of the policies of the economic managers. If those policies are changed, a number of variables may be affected. For example, suppose the under-investment in training continues and skill shortages become more prevalent? Suppose the UK and world economy picks up significantly, such that demand for goods and services exceeds supply? Suppose there is direct interference in employee relations through a statutory minimum wage or an incomes policy? The relative balance of bargaining power may change because employers might not be prepared to maintain some of the rigorous bargaining positions that they have adopted in recent times. While it is unlikely that a Labour Government would wish to see inflation rise, ideologically they tend to take a much more sympathetic approach to the problems of unemployment and this is likely to be reflected in their economic policies. Irrespective of whether the relationship between 'New Labour' and the trade unions is different in the 1990s compared to the 1970s, unions are more likely to look forward to a Labour Government as they would perceive that the balance of bargaining power would swing back to them.

As a never-ending procession of statistics shows, there are both fewer unions and fewer union members than there were 20 years ago. This has further influenced the relative balance of bargaining power. However, it is important to recognise that assessments about bargaining power are much more complex than is often apparent. A simple reference to the union membership and density statistics, or to the apparent weakness of trade unions as a result of economic change, needs to have a large caveat attached. There is some evidence that individuals see trade unions as less influential than they were 30 years ago, and this may make them less inclined to be members – but where unionisation exists within an organisation there is very little evidence of employees deserting the union or of employers considering de-recognition. We will be examining the issue of union de-recognition, and examining research on the extent to which this has happened, in Chapter 4.

The difficulty with a concept such as the balance of bargaining power is that it has different impacts on the behaviour of the employee relations players at different levels. At the national level, there is no doubt that the overall balance of bargaining power has moved in favour of the employer. At the level of the workplace, the balance of bargaining power can be totally different. No matter how much trade unions may have been weakened overall, if they have maintained 100 per cent membership within a particular workplace their influence and power can still be very great. The extent to which this influence and power can be exercised depends very much on the organisation and the nature of its business. As the miners found out in the early 1980s, a strong workplace organisation does not guarantee that the balance of bargaining power will be in the union's favour. The UK

Government and the then National Coal Board ensured that contrary to the situation in the 1970s, sufficient stockpiles of coal would be available in the event of a trade dispute. Lack of coal supplies during the 1970s mining dispute had led to the imposition of a damaging three-day week on British industry. Furthermore, individuals who were disillusioned with the National Union of Mineworkers (NUM), were encouraged to use legislative procedures to limit the activities of their union.

On the other hand, if you work in a business where the product or process has a limited shelf-life, a trade dispute could have an immediate and costly effect on customer confidence or income generation. In such circumstances a well organised union could see the relative balance of bargaining power as being very much in its favour. This situation can be made even worse if the management of the business has no clear employee relations strategy, or policies and procedures are non-existent or out of date.

> Where does the relative balance of bargaining power lie in your organisation? Do you see this balance as static, or is there potential for a significant shift in power?

SUMMARY

This chapter has examined the role of the UK Government as an economic manager in terms of the objectives of macro-economic policy, and how employee relations is affected by the way in which that policy is implemented. In particular we examined the contrast between the Keynesian and monetarist approaches to economic management and the impact that the change to monetarism has had on the UK economy since 1979. We have looked at the role that the state, and the EU, play in developing the legal framework in which employee relations has to operate, and how the combination of a changed economic system and reforms to labour law have caused trade union power and strike activity to decline. These changes have clearly had a marked effect on the balance of bargaining power, insofar as they have made employers more confident and given them back the 'right to manage'. The confidence that managers now have stems from a number of factors, but one of them is a growing realisation among trade unions that industrial action is not necessarily in the best interests of their members – that change, in one form or another, is inevitable if employment opportunities are to be protected. It therefore makes more sense for that change to be negotiated. However, it is important for the employee relations specialist to appreciate that the wheel can turn full circle. Although it is widely acknowledged that requiring trade unions to ballot their members before taking industrial action is a positive step forward, it can be a double-edged sword. The legitimacy that such a ballot provides can actually give the union more bargaining power, not less. The public sector strikes in the Post Office and London Underground during 1996 provided clear evidence that trade unions have certainly not gone away. Notwithstanding this, most employers would say that the legislation is supportive and has helped to tilt the balance of bargaining power in their favour.

We have looked at the role of the UK Government as an employer, and discussed the way in which the concept of the UK Government as a 'model employer' has changed over time. In the immediate post-war years there was encouragement of collective bargaining and an attempt to ensure comparability of pay between the public and private sectors. From 1979 the emphasis was on a more individual approach to the employment relationship, with a clear discouragement of national pay bargaining.

Finally we looked at the impact of technological change on the corporate environment, and acknowledged that it influences employee relations in a number of ways. It can create unemployment, it can provide the opportunity for employees to learn new skills, and it can generally improve the working environment.

From whatever perspective you view the corporate environment, there is no doubt that over the last 18 years there has been a radical change in our system of employee relations. This change has manifested itself in changes to working practices, and changes in the employment relationship with an increase in part-time and temporary working. Reward systems have also changed, so that issues like performance-related pay, reward for teams and profit-related pay have become more prevalent. The common theme running through all these changes is the need for them to be negotiated. Negotiation, as we discuss in Chapter 6, is one of the key employee relations skills, and is an absolute necessity for any employee relations specialist who is going to operate in a constantly evolving corporate environment.

FURTHER READING

FARNHAM D. *The Corporate Environment*. London, Institute of Personnel and Development, 1995.

INSTITUTE OF PERSONNEL AND DEVELOPMENT. *European Update*. Monthly publication from the Institute of Personnel and Development.

INSTITUTE OF PERSONNEL AND DEVELOPMENT. *European Employment Law: The State of Play Checklist*. Quarterly publication available with *European Update* from the Institute of Personnel and Development.

INSTITUTE OF PERSONNEL AND DEVELOPMENT. *Personnel and Europe: Executive Brief*. London, 1996.

LEWIS, D. *Essentials of Employment Law*. 5th ed. London, Institute of Personnel and Development, 1997.

3 Employee relations institutions

INTRODUCTION

This chapter is concerned with the institutions of employee relations – employers' associations or federations, trade unions and staff associations, umbrella organisations such as the Confederation of British Industry (CBI) and the Trades Union Congress (TUC), their international and European equivalents, and finally, state organisations such as the Advisory, Conciliation, and Arbitration Service (ACAS) and the Central Arbitration Committee (CAC). The foregoing list demonstrates that both employers and employees have a range of options open to them in relation to external organisations about which they have to make choices. For example, do employers join their trade association or federation? Do they join umbrella organisations such as the CBI or the Institute of Directors (IoD)? If they decide to join their industry or sector organisation, do they – assuming that the organisation they are considering joining is one which gets involved in collective bargaining in the first place – allow that organisation to bargain on their behalf? Does becoming a member bind them to particular courses of action? Even if the reasons for contemplating membership are nothing to do with collective bargaining, what sort of services are available to employers, and how will they be paid for? On the other side of the coin we need to examine trade unions and trade union behaviour. We need to look at the way trade unions organise themselves, why people join or do not join trade unions in the first place, and what opportunities and rights individual members have to influence their union.

It is also important to explore the role of the state in the context of external organisations. We know from Chapter 2 that the state has a very influential role in employee relations, but in this chapter we shall be examining its interventionist activities in respect of such third-party organisations as ACAS and the CAC. When you have completed this chapter you should be able to

- explain why some organisations join employers' associations and some do not

- explain why some employers see a collectivist approach as being in their best interests while others see collectivism as contrary to management's interests

- explain the role of national bodies like the Confederation of British Industry and the Trades Union Congress

- understand what is meant by union structure and trade union organisation

- explain why the ideology of UK trade unions is industrially-based rather than politically-based

- explain the role of state institutions such as the Advisory, Conciliation, and Arbitration Service

- explain why some organisations are prepared to use third-party intervention and others are not.

EMPLOYERS' ORGANISATIONS

Employers' associations are voluntary private bodies which exist to provide information and co-ordination in areas of common interest. There are many different associations, covering overlapping areas of geographic spread, industrial sector, and groupings of larger or smaller organisations. The 1996 *Directory of Associations and Professional Bodies* in the United Kingdom lists 3,780 organisations. These range in size and influence from the very small with no full-time staff to large influential organisations like the Building Employers' Confederation with 140 employees. In both the public and private sector employers' associations are still – despite the views of those who see them as a declining force – of sufficient importance in employee relations to make it necessary to understand something of their history and the type of role they currently fulfil.

The origins of employers' associations

Associations primarily came into being as defensive mechanisms against the trade unions in the eighteenth and nineteenth centuries, and tended to become active for the duration of an industrial relations problem only. 'As with trade unions, early organisation was often informal and ephemeral, or spasmodic' (Clegg, 1979; p63), and activities tended to be limited to a geographical basis. By the end of the nineteenth century these local, geographical associations were beginning to come together and create national federations of employers whose interests lay in one particular industry. The Engineering Employers' Federation, the Building Trades Federation and the Shipbuilding Federation were just some that were formed in this period. This bias towards a federated approach was, in many respects, a response to the growing power and influence of trade unions, and by the early part of the twentieth century a move had begun towards a system of industry-wide bargaining. Interestingly, despite very high levels of unemployment in the inter-war years and a relative decline in trade union influence, employers did not try to modify the then prevailing system of industry bargaining. Compare this with the almost feverish desire during the 1970s and 1980s to limit the influence and extent of collective bargaining. This may have been because Britain's employers had, by the end of World War II, 'secured a system of collective bargaining which suited them' (Clegg, 1979; p70). In the years following the war, the main activity of employers' associations was in the determination of pay and conditions for their particular industry. However, in the post-war push for full employment it became more and more difficult to maintain the pre-war style of binding industry agreements, particularly as some industries were beginning to experience skill shortages. Consequently, individual companies who had to compete for the skills that were available began to negotiate additional rates of pay at local level. This in turn led to an increasingly complex package of rewards. Such a shift from total national determination of pay and conditions to a mix of national and local bargaining was helped by the fact that the relative balance of bargaining power was in favour of the employee. It was also a factor in the decision of many organisations to opt out of their association in order that they could determine all conditions locally.

Definition of an employers' association

The current legal definition of an employers' association is contained in section 122 of the Trade Unions and Labour Relations (Consolidation) Act (1992). The principal part of the definition is that employers' associations are organisations 'which consist wholly or mainly of employers or individual owners of undertakings of one or more descriptions and whose principal purposes include the regulation of relations between employers of that description or those descriptions and workers or trade unions'.

The definition is phrased in this way so that it covers those organisations which wish to deal exclusively with industrial relations issues, and those – like the builders' federation and the printers' federation – which deal with both industrial relations and commercial matters. This latter group is by far the most common type, and it would be difficult to identify any employers' association today that concentrates solely on industrial relations. Competition and commercial imperatives have caused them to take a much more pragmatic view of their activities.

In common with trade unions, employers' associations who wish to have their legal status confirmed must be registered on a list kept by the Certification Officer. We will examine the role of the Certification Officer in more detail later in the chapter, but suffice to say that many of the obligations that are placed on trade unions apply to employers' associations.

The activities of employers' associations

All employers' bodies both in the public and in the private sector, organise themselves in different ways. The priority that each of them gives to employee relations, as opposed to trade matters, differs according to tradition, the nature of the industry it represents and the degree of unionisation in its particular sector. Generally it remains true that those associations which are most concerned with employee relations are those which comprise companies using semi-skilled and skilled labour in areas where there is a high concentration of a single industry, such as engineering or printing.

There are three types of employers' associations: national federations to which local employers' associations are affiliated – eg the Engineering Employers' Federation (EEF), which is a federation of 15 autonomous organisations; single national bodies, such as the British Printing Industries Federation (BPIF), which is divided into six regions for administrative and representational purposes (until 1982 this was a federated body like the engineers, but a serious national dispute in 1980 caused it to re-invent itself); and single associations with a national membership, like the British Ceramic Confederation. Although organisations of employers have been around for a very long time, there are those who believe that 'in recent times their prominence and influence over employment issues has ... declined' (Marchington and Wilkinson, 1996; p48). Although it may be possible to demonstrate a decline in the number of industry-wide collective agreements, there are still many employers' associations which continue to negotiate agreements at national level. In the private sector national agreements still exist in electrical contracting, construction and general printing. In the public sector national pay arrangements still exist for doctors and nurses, and the National Association of Health Authorities and Trusts – an employers' body – provides evidence to the appropriate pay review body. Nevertheless, we must acknowledge that national agreements are becoming less important in many industries. But where an industry is made up of many small companies which are very competitive with each other – eg in the baking and printing industries – the national agreement is important to members because it is seen as having the ability to take labour costs out of competition – an argument used by many of those in favour of a minimum wage.

While it has become fashionable for commentators and academics to write employers' associations off, the associations can still exert tremendous influence in respect of employee relations policy and practice. The 1996 annual review of the Engineering Employers' Federation (EEF) records how it 'provides member companies with practical advice about the issues they should consider when reviewing their employee relations policies'. In 1995 the EEF also published a guidance document 'Developing Employee Relations'. Given that the EEF has around 5,000 establishments in membership employing in excess of half a million people, it would be foolish to pretend that, even without a national agreement, they are without significant influence.

Employers' associations consist of companies of varying sizes, from the very small to the very large, the largest of them organised into autonomous local associations (like the engineers) or non-autonomous district associations (like the printers). Some of them have an organisational structure similar to the trade unions with the ultimate decision-making authority: a national council of some sort. Representation on such a national council differs from association to association, but apart from those with local autonomy, local and regional committees tend to be more for consultative purposes than for decision-making.

Marchington and Wilkinson (1996) identified four major sets of services that employers' organisations have traditionally offered to their members:

• collective bargaining with trade unions

• assisting in the resolution of disputes

• providing general advice to members

• representing members' views.

The first of these services – collective bargaining – has clearly declined, even within those industries which maintain some form of national agreement. In spite of what we said above about the continuing influence of employers' organisations, it is important to recognise some of the difficulties that they face. Recruitment and retention of members is becoming more and more difficult as the rationale for national agreements decreases, and there is considerable evidence that they are becoming increasingly unattractive to larger employers. When membership meant buying into a national agreement, persuading employers to join was not so difficult. Now, the membership fee is subject to the same scrutiny as any other item of expenditure, and it can be very hard to persuade large businesses to spend 'thousands of pounds' for a very intangible product, particularly if it ties them into a collective agreement that they find difficulty in endorsing. During the 1980s these factors caused a number of companies, particularly large ones, to pull out of those employers' associations of which the primary purpose was the negotiation of national terms and conditions. Their preference was to negotiate their own arrangements. They were much more likely to have had their own personnel specialists in-house and considered that with these resources they could achieve better results than could be achieved nationally. One reason that they adopted this position is because of the way that many national agreements are structured. They can consist of a number of enabling clauses, particularly in the area of productivity improvements, which set out, in broad terms, that certain things must happen as a consequence of an increase in pay or the provision of other benefit. For example, there may be a clause allowing for full flexibility of labour with no demarcation lines. The difficulty with such clauses is the problem of finding appropriate words to fit the circumstances of every employer, and this can lead to a less than favourable endorsement of the principle of national bargaining. As the chief executive of one of Britain's largest printing companies said, 'We may pay a larger cash increase at local level than at national level, but the difference is that the productivity clauses we negotiate mean our agreement pays for itself. With the national agreement we get a cash settlement supported by clauses "enabling" us to introduce productivity measures to pay for it. The problem with enabling clauses is that we pay the union the money and then start negotiations at local level in order to make those clauses effective. If we have to negotiate something locally, we may as well do it all.'

The difficulties posed by national collective bargaining have been considered by most associations at one time or another, including the EEF in 1989. They found that as the nature of national negotiations and business policies and practices changed during the 1970s and 1980s the relevance of national agreements declined. By 1989 only minimum rates of pay and working time remained live issues at national level, and the EEF took the decision to withdraw from national collective bargaining on terms and conditions of employment with the unions representing blue-collar employees (EEF *Guide*, 1995). In making this change the EEF were reflecting the needs of their members, who can continue to enjoy the advantages of strength in numbers but are not obliged to follow nationally agreed terms and conditions. The Printers' Federation tried to introduce a similar concept, but this was not acceptable to its predominantly small membership, who continue to see distinct advantages in nationally agreed wage rates.

Some organisations have left, or resisted joining, employers' associations because of their policy on trade unions. They may have a policy of non-recognition, or they may have used the 'change in the balance of bargaining power' to opt out of nationally agreed pay rises and marginalise their union at the same time.

A further reason that national agreements are not popular with some employers is that the organisations that negotiate them have little power or sanctions that they can impose against members who do not conform to them. After all, one of the purposes of a national agreement is to create some form of level playing-field in respect of wages and conditions. The constitution of many associations might allow for expulsion for bringing the organisation into disrepute, but we can find no evidence that this has ever happened in any of the organisations we have examined.

Furthermore, if an association becomes involved in a dispute with one or more trade unions, it tends to have even more problems than the trade unions in retaining solidarity among its members. The pressures of competition between the members of an employers' association may cause the breaking of ranks. We noted above that the British Printing Industries Federation (BPIF) had to reconstitute itself in 1980 following a dispute with the National Graphical Association (NGA). At that time the BPIF was a federated organisation, similar to the EEF, with autonomous regional alliances. The dispute followed the breakdown of national negotiations and resulted in the pursuit by the union of individual companies, under the threat of industrial action, to settle on the basis of the union's national claim. It proved impossible for the BPIF to maintain any sort of collective stance, and the union gradually achieved their demands. (For a more detailed account of the BPIF–NGA dispute in 1980 and its effect on the workings of the employers' association, see Gennard, 1990; p409.) A similar occurrence in 1993 caused much the same problems, and the BPIF found it necessary to consult its members on the advisability of continuing with national wage bargaining. In the same way, the claim for a shorter working week in the engineering industry was pursued by the trade unions against individual companies, which could not withstand the sanctions imposed on them and remain competitive.

But what of the other three services identified by Marchington and Wilkinson – assisting in dispute resolution, general advice to members, and the representation of members views? The issue of dispute resolution has links with national bargaining arrangements, and many national agreements provide access to an established dispute procedure. Such procedures tend to define a number of stages through which a dispute should be processed. Stage one may include the involvement of a local employers' association representative, a union branch secretary, lay union officials from within the organisation in dispute, and the organisation's management. If the dispute is not resolved at this stage it may, depending on the employers' association and union involved, move up to a district or regional level. Some of the players will stay the same, but the full-time officials will probably differ. The third stage will involve national officials of the two organisations and, if there is still no resolution, many procedures provide for the involvement of an independent third party whose decision will be binding. Organisations who use such dispute procedures will find that they usually contain provisions that state 'no hostile action' is to be taken by either side, and that the status quo must prevail while the dispute is going through its various stages.

We said above that many organisations were having to consider the issue of membership recruitment and retention, and many of them have had to react to the problems caused to their membership base by a diminishing reliance on collective bargaining. During the post-war years, with national collective bargaining in the ascendancy, many employers' organisations became very bureaucratic and unimaginative. They tended to have a very captive audience, which meant that they had to pay very little attention to membership retention, or to the range of services that they offered. All this changed as organisations began to alter their bargaining arrangements. As a consequence, they began to examine what else they were receiving from their associations in return for not insignificant subscriptions – for subscriptions for larger employers can run into several thousands of pounds, and although the cost to smaller organisations is less, everything is relative. The better organisations quickly realised that to stay in business, they needed to provide a package of benefits to their members which could be seen to 'add value'. In the context of employee relations this meant widening their existing advisory services on issues such as disciplinary, dismissal and redundancy procedures. Their ability to market services in these areas was helped by the growth, particularly in the 1970s, of employment legislation that added to people's 'rights' at work. Unfair dismissal, health and safety, and equal pay are three examples. If you look at the membership sales literature of any of the larger employers' associations you will note the stress they place on employment advice and support. For example, the Building Employers' Confederation (BEF) offers its members advice and support on wage rates and conditions of employment, disciplinary procedures, redundancy procedures, representation at industrial tribunals, and a regular bulletin with articles and relevant developments in employment law. Most employers' organisations can provide data about pay rates, and some – like the printers and engineers – conduct regular surveys on wages and conditions which their members can use as a means of aiding local negotiations. Such surveys can be very problematic because the associations tend not to have any means of enforcing individual returns, but provided that an employee relations specialist recognises the limitations in such surveys, they can be a valuable tool.

> Does the sector in which you work have any sort of employers' organisation? What benefits could it provide that would assist in the process of employee relations? How would you place a value on its advice?

A major growth-area of activity for many is the representation of members' views to a range of other organisations, which can include political lobbying. Representational activities can be of particular interest to the large company whose inclination might be to leave an association if its only purpose was the negotiation of a national agreement. Now that many large organisations are operating in a European and world market, they know that their only means of influencing UK Government or European policy is through some sort of collective voice. In its 1996 review the EEF reports on its representations to the major political parties to try and ensure that the employment policies they develop meet the needs of the engineering industry (EEF *Annual Review*, 1996). Despite their lack of warmth towards employers' organisations during the past two decades, UK Governments have found them to be useful in obtaining employers' comments on a range of consultative documents. Examples include reform of the industrial tribunal system, statutory sick pay (SSP) and collective redundancies and business transfers. The opportunity to be involved in such consultative exercises, particularly where significant costs can be involved, as in SSP, can often contribute to the decision of an individual company on whether to join their organisation or not.

For some companies, however, employers' associations are too restrictive, and they take the view that by being a member it is less easy to be independent and innovative. They consider innovation to be an essential managerial activity in today's economic climate, whether in operational matters or in people issues such as employee relations. They therefore feel that they need to be responsible for, and co-ordinate, their own negotiations. Yet it is important to remember that even those companies which negotiate unilaterally or independently of the appropriate employers' association must still take account of what is negotiated in their industries at national level. An important part of the employee relations function is to take account of other wage settlements, particularly within the sector in which its own organisation operates. Not being aware of such settlements, many of which affect its competitors, could seriously weaken its own bargaining position and impact on its competitiveness.

There are businesses which, despite their feelings, join employers' organisations because of their more traditional trade association activities. A number have arbitration schemes to resolve differences between supplier and customer, while others have the ability to remove an organisation from membership if they do not meet agreed standards (eg workmanship or quality). This can be a very effective sanction for a company who relies on the 'badge' of the trade association to help secure business (eg some of the building trades or electrical contractors).

Finally, we need to consider those businesses which, while they find industry bodies too parochial, do look for some external support. This may be from local organisations such as Chambers of Commerce or national bodies such as the Confederation of British Industry (CBI) or the Institute of Directors (IoD).

National and other representative bodies

The largest and perhaps the best-known national organisation is the Confederation of British Industry (CBI) whose roots go back to 1915 with the formation of the National Union of Manufacturers, later renamed the National Association of British Manufacturers (NABM). Within five years two further organisations, the Federation of British Industries (FBI) and the British Employers' Confederation (BEC), had been formed, and the CBI as an organisation was the result of a merger between them in 1965. Its membership includes individual companies (and nationalised industries), national and regional trades and employers' associations, and it sees as its overall task the promotion of policies for a more efficient mixed economy. It is estimated that around half of the total labour force work in organisations affiliated with the CBI. The CBI is basically a political lobbying organisation of which the major function is to provide for British industry the means of formulating, making known and influencing general policy in regard to industrial, economic, fiscal, commercial, labour, social, legal and technical questions.

However, while not specifically engaging in employee relations activities, the CBI does have a human resources programme to promote 'lifetime learning, employee ability and effective employee performance as a source of competitive edge for business' (*Annual Report*, 1995). And some of its lobbying activities can have an impact on issues that affect workplace employee relations. Recent issues on which the CBI has lobbied on behalf of employers include the Disability Discrimination Act and the new consultation requirements in respect of collective redundancies. Although as an organisation the CBI does not engage in negotiations with employee representatives, it does seek to maintain a working relationship with the Trades Union Congress (TUC) through joint membership of bodies such as ACAS.

Another organisation that has become increasingly influential with the UK Government in respect of employee relations policy is the Institute of Directors (IoD). The IoD is essentially a professional and influential business organisation which plays a key role in representing the views of business to the UK Government. Membership is on an individual rather than company basis, and to that extent its employee relations role is peripheral. However, there is no denying its influence. At the beginning of 1995, IoD members were on the boards of 750 of the *Times*' top 1,000 companies, which may explain why it tends to get listened to. This enables it to enter the debate on such employee relations issues as the minimum wage or statutory sick pay or legislation to restrict trade union activities.

One further organisation that needs to be considered, particularly in respect of the UK membership of the EU, is the Union of Industrial and Employers' Confederations of Europe (UNICE), which we briefly mentioned in Chapter 2 in the context of 'social partners'. UNICE is made up of employers' federations from over 20 European countries, including the CBI. In addition to its role as a social partner, its other purposes include the promotion of the interests of firms represented by its members and the provision of a coordinating function through which member organisations can develop their European policies. UNICE has contact with the European Commission, the European Parliament and the Council of Ministers, and its main employee relations priority is the development of social dialogue with the European Trades Union Confederation (ETUC).

TRADE UNIONS

Trade unions are organised groups of employees who, in the words of the relevant legislation, 'consist wholly or mainly of workers of one or more descriptions and whose principal purposes include the regulation of relations between workers ... and employers' (Section 1 of the Trade Unions and Labour Relations (Consolidation) Act [TULR(C)A]). In this book we are concerned mainly with independent trade unions – that is, unions who are not under the domination or control of an employer. The primary purpose of trade unions is to protect the jobs of their members and to seek improvement on pay and other conditions by the process of collective bargaining. Although overall membership of trade unions has declined in recent years, they still play an important part in the process of employee relations in many organisations. In some industries and sectors (eg printing, the health service), there is still a large union presence, and while the balance of bargaining power may have swung towards the employer, the role of the union within these workplaces cannot be ignored.

Union structure and growth

Union structure in this context refers to the external environment in which particular unions organise themselves, and their coverage of industries and occupations. The internal structure will be dealt with later in this chapter when we look at the relationship between a trade union and its members.

Britain's trade unions have a somewhat complex structure which in part owes something to our union movement's being the oldest in the world (Clegg, 1979). When unions began to come to prominence in the nineteenth century they developed, principally, as organisations of skilled workers whose main objective was to secure employment for themselves and other skilled craftsmen, but they did little or nothing for the labourers and other unskilled workers. Because of this, labourers' unions came into being by combining the labourers in craft industries with workers from previously unorganised industries and services. From these beginnings, union structure in the UK developed to the point where they (the unions) were grouped in three categories: craft unions, for those with a particular skill (such as electricians); industrial unions, for those in one industry (the construction workers' union UCATT is an example); and general unions, whose membership is open to all groups (the Transport and General Workers' Union, for example). However, because there have been so many union mergers and amalgamations over the past few years, definition, in this way is now difficult as the majority of current trade unions display the characteristics of more than one of these categories. The merger between the National Graphical Association (NGA) and the Society of Graphical and Allied Trades (SOGAT) provides us with a very clear example. The NGA, itself the result of other mergers, was considered to be a traditional craft union. Its members were traditionally drawn from apprentices and entry to the trade was strictly controlled by a quota system. SOGAT, although having some craft members, such as bookbinders, also embraced semi-skilled machine assistants and unskilled labourers. The new union, the Graphical, Paper and Media Union, now embraces all three categories. Is it a craft union, an industrial union or a general union? An examination of other merged unions will identify similar contradictions. In fact there have been so many union mergers and amalgamations over the past few years – in 1900 there were 1,332 unions; by 1976 this had fallen to 462; and today there are just over 300 – that typology of unions is becoming less and less important.

> If there is a union in your workplace or industry sector, has it been the subject of a merger or amalgamation? What category would you place it in?

Despite all this, and despite the mergers and amalgamations, the job that you do still effectively determines the union that you join. While legislative changes over the past two decades – which have seen the end of the closed shop and other restrictions – mean that individuals are free to join any union of their choice, the reality is somewhat different. Where unions exist in a workplace, and are recognised by the employer, most individuals who choose to join a union will want to join one that has a significant membership within their work group.

There is a downside to the job-centered tradition of Britain's unions. We referred above to the complex union structure which exists in the UK which is, in part, a consequence of the existence of job-based trade unions. This means that many unions can overlap and share jurisdiction in the same industry and even in the same company. There is a tendency to think that unions automatically support each other, but in fact this only happens when the job interests of different trade unions coincide. Only then do they show support and solidarity for each other. A more common feature is for unions to seek to protect their interests against other trade groups, and the overlapping to which we referred can very easily lead to demarcation disputes.

Inter-union disputes over who should do which jobs were very much a feature of the 1960s and 1970s industrial relations scene and often resulted in strike action, with the employer an unwilling victim of a problem largely outside his control. Such disputes have tended to decrease over the past two decades – partly as a result of legislative interventions and partly as a consequence of mergers and amalgamations. But such inter-union disputes do still happen, particularly where there is a suggestion that one union may be trying to poach another's members. The 1996 internal dispute at the Ford Motor Company, relating to alleged discrimination over driving jobs, is a case in point. Some drivers were threatening to leave their union (the T&GWU) and join the rival Union of Road Transport Workers (URT), because they felt that the T&GWU were not representing their interests. The T&GWU, in turn, accused the URT of encouraging its members to defect. How this particular dispute was resolved is not important – but what it does demonstrate is that inter-union rivalry can still be an issue and the employee relations specialist cannot afford to ignore its impact on employment relationships.

The unions would surely conclude that if they could start again they would probably not organise them around jobs. In Japan the union affiliation is company-based, while in Germany there are industry-based unions. The generally admired structure of German unions owes much to the fact that they were redesigned and reconstituted after World War II.

While some commentators may be critical of our own union structure and compare it unfavourably with Germany's, it does compare well with that of some of our other European partners. In most of the rest of Western Europe (ie France, Italy, Spain, Belgium and Holland) trade union affiliation is based on religion and politics, which can result in a fragmented and sectarian-based union structure. For example, a French schoolteacher must decide whether to join the Protestant teachers' union, the Communist teachers' union, the Christian Democrat teachers' union or the Catholic teachers' union. As a consequence, union membership levels are low, and the only way that an employer can get the employees to speak with a collective voice is for the state to impose the works councils system, which should elect individual employees without any regard to their religious or political affinity.

Trade union organisation
Most trade union members will have some kind of workplace organisation and will elect unpaid representatives of their union, who are usually called shop stewards. The term used may be different in certain industries – eg in printing and journalism the representative is called the Father or Mother of the Chapel (FOC, MOC); in some industries, they are called the works representatives. The role of the shop steward, in most instances, depends on the arrangements that exist between the particular trade union and the individual employer. In some workplaces the union is restricted to a representational role only; this means that the role of the shop steward is likely to be limited to issues surrounding discipline and individual grievances. If the union has full recognition, the role of the shop steward may be extended to issues such as pay and conditions, but the extent to which lay (unpaid) officials can get involved in pay bargaining is dictated by the particular bargaining arrangements in force for their organisation or industry.

If the organisation is party to a national agreement, shop stewards are unlikely to get heavily involved in pay bargaining. If, however, nationally determined increases are topped up with locally negotiated extras (eg for performance, productivity, etc), much more power will accrue to local representatives. In Chapter 2 we discussed some of the factors that had caused industrial relations to have such a poor reputation during the 1960s and 1970s, one of which was the devolvement of power from union national executives to local shop stewards who, in the opinion of many managers, exercised too much control and were too willing to use strikes as means of obtaining their objectives. The supposed anarchy that existed in industrial relations at this time was one of the major factors that led to the setting up of the Royal Commission on Trade Unions and Employers' Associations (the Donovan Commission) in 1965.

While it is easy to criticise the role that shop stewards have played in the past in respect of collective bargaining, they do have a wider role. They recruit new members to the union and also have a vital communication role between the union officials and the members inside the company. In companies where there are a number of trade unions recruiting members, and therefore shop stewards representing a number of trade unions, the stewards may form a joint shop stewards' committee to discuss strategy and to meet the employers in negotiation.

In most unions above the workplace organisation there is usually a branch structure which is geographically-based, and above this, depending on the union size, there may be a regional or area structure. The primary task of the branch structure is to act as a conduit between members and the union's decision-making body and to elect delegates to the union's decision-making conferences. At the apex of the union structure is its national executive, which is usually made up of elected delegates and full-time officials. It is the job of the executive to implement the policy of the annual (or, in many cases, biennial) delegate conference. In the Amalgamated Engineering and Electrical Union (AEEU) the process works as follows. Branches elect delegates to a regional conference, which in turn elects delegates to the biennial conference. There is one delegate per 1,000 members. Because of its size and various amalgamations over the years, the AEEU also has a number of conferences for specified industrial sectors. These are mainly geographical, but some are constituted on a national basis. The industrial conferences also elect delegates to the biennial conference – in fact, two thirds of the delegates come through this route.

Once its conference has decided a union policy, the implementation of that policy is carried out by the national executive. All unions have a number of full-time staff who conduct the affairs of the union on a day-to-day basis, but they would normally be responsible to the executive to whom they report on a regular basis (usually monthly). The principal full-time official in the majority of unions is the general secretary, who is supported by a number of national officers, regional officers (where appropriate) and branch secretaries. These are the individuals who would be involved in the operation of any of the dispute procedures that we referred to above.

It is normal for the general secretary and the national officers to be, *ex-officio*, members of the national executive committee, with or without voting rights, and because of the influence that they can sometimes have, the Trade Union Act (1984) and the Employment Act (1988), decreed that all members of union executive committees had to be elected by the membership every five years.

Unions and politics

In order to achieve their objectives, British trade unions prefer to use industrial rather than political methods. In most cases, despite some occasional rhetoric to the contrary, trade unions do not believe that it is in their interests to overthrow the elected UK Government in order to achieve their objectives. This position was confirmed at the Trades Union Congress in 1986, where it was stated that trade unions should be able to talk to, influence and persuade UK Governments, but should accept that if the UK Government does not take any notice, then they cannot change that. It is important to distinguish between the reason why trade unions are involved in politics, which is largely a pragmatic reason based on contemporary factors, and the reason why they are involved in party politics, specifically with the Labour Party, which is the result of a historical accident at the beginning of the twentieth century.

The association between the Labour Party and the unions, which goes back to this time, is of fundamental significance to any understanding of their political role, but it is important to be aware that this political connection was made from a pragmatic point of view, and did not have wider socialist aims. The formal relationship can be traced back to the formation of the Labour Representation Committee (LRC) in 1900.

The Trades Union Congress (TUC) had had its own Parliamentary committee since the late 1860s, and its principal aim was to lobby Parliament to support pro-union legislation. This lobbying had been very necessary, for up until the 1870s the criminal law had severely constrained the role of trade unions (Marsh, 1992). But the position changed when the then Conservative Government responded to the growth in unionisation by removing the criminal law sanction from trade disputes. Had the law totally disengaged from trade disputes it is entirely possible that the historic links between the trade unions and the Labour Party might never have been established. But it did not: employers sought to negate the impact of trade disputes on their businesses by taking civil action against the unions, and it was into this scenario that the LRC stepped. The results were not immediately positive. The judgement in the Taff Vale case in 1901, which held that unions could be sued by employers for losses sustained by strike action, was a major blow. But by 1906 the Liberals and the embryonic Labour Party had secured passage of the Trade Disputes Act (1906), which introduced the concept of 'in contemplation or furtherance of a trade dispute'. It is this 'golden formula' (Wedderburn, 1965) which created the immunities from legal action that unions – provided that they abide by the law on pre-strike ballots, etc – still enjoy today.

The fact that the LRC ultimately became the Labour Party is still a factor in the influence that the union movement has over the Party and the reason that it is granted certain powers within the Party constitution. However, as the Labour Party itself evolves, these constitutional rights have been, and continue to be, diluted. In recent years there is no doubt that the relationship between the two has changed, and 'New Labour' have made it clear that the unions will receive no preferential treatment when they are in UK Government. But even with these strictures about the limits of their influence, a constructive relationship between the unions and a Labour Government is much more likely than between the unions and a Conservative Government.

Trade unions are generally pragmatic rather than highly ideological organisations. The common interest between the buyers and sellers of labour can only be achieved by means of constructive compromise to reconcile the difference of interests, and compromise is a pragmatic solution to employee relations problems. The end result of most negotiations is a compromise between the interests of the employers and those of the unions. If one of the parties had strong ideological principles which did not allow it to compromise, then there would be no negotiation and no solution. The unions, who are keen to see policies like the minimum wage reach the statute book, are instinctively more inclined to seek compromise with Labour rather than Conservative Governments. The only significant factor that could set the unions on a collision course with a 'New Labour' Government is public spending. Although eschewing incomes policy, successive Conservative Governments have, since 1979, used limits on public-sector pay in their battles against inflation. The aspirations of public-sector unions in the health service, in teaching, etc, may create some serious problems for employee relations specialists in the years ahead. While a minimum wage might take some of the heat out of a potentially volatile situation, it is unlikely that any UK Government will be able to find sufficient resources during the next few years to restore public-sector pay levels to a point acceptable to the unions.

Future prospects for the unions
Some people would consider that the trade unions face a very uncertain future. Under a Conservative Government it is likely that there would be further attempts to reduce trade union influence either by indirect legislation or by indirect interference in trade disputes. The decision to remove the Post Office monopoly on the delivery of letters while Royal Mail was in dispute with the Communication Workers' Union in 1996 is one example of such interference. This dispute, together with those involving staff at London Underground, was the trigger for a 1996 consultative document issued by the UK Government proposing to limit the ability of public-sector unions to take industrial action. This proposal to further restrict union activities was not well received by either the CBI or the IoD. The latter, which hitherto had been an enthusiastic supporter of the UK Government's crack-down on union power, went so far as to describe the ideas as impractical, unworkable and liable to create a field-day for lawyers. The CBI felt that further legislation would simply lead to more uncertainty in the workplace. Under a Labour Government there is no reason to suppose that the trade unions would fare any better. They

may not have to operate in such an antagonistic climate, but there is little evidence that a Labour Government would introduce legislation significantly different from what we have at present. If the prospects for trade unions are to improve, therefore, they need to consider what steps they themselves can take to improve their position.

There is no doubt that the unions have suffered a significant decline in the past 18 years. There have been two major recessions, important legislative intervention, and radical changes in the labour market, all of which (Waddington and Whitson, 1995) have caused overall membership figures to decline every year since 1979. While this steady path of decline has caused unions considerable concern, it does not follow that there is a lessening of interest in union membership; it is simply that union activity in many unionised organisations has been very low-key. In Chapter 5 we look at initiatives in employee involvement and participation which have tended to become an important focus of employer/employee communication rather than the traditional union/management forums.

In organisations where unions do not currently have a presence, there is some anecdotal evidence that many workers would join if the unions put more effort into recruitment. Many of these workers are likely to be female and/or in part-time employment, working in service industries such as hotel and catering, who may have felt in the past – with some justification – that trade unions were not interested in them. If unions want to reverse the spiral of decline, then, in the same way that employers' organisations have had to reappraise their activities and widen their appeal to prospective members, so must the trade unions. The TUC has suggested that, collectively, unions need to recruit half a million new members per year just to remain at their 1996 membership levels. Against a background of perceived job insecurity, the unions could, with professional marketing, make some progress towards meeting this target. This means concentrating efforts on improving their communications to members and non-members so that individuals can more easily understand what relevance the union has to them. It also means putting time and resources into recruitment (UNISON the public sector union ran a very good TV campaign as a means of increasing membership) and then assessing the impact of such campaigns. If unions do start to increase membership levels, it is likely to have implications for employee relations, and employee relations practitioners in non-unionised companies should not be complacent about retaining this status.

> If there are individuals within your workplace who are not currently members of trade unions, what are the sort of issues, do you think, that would encourage them to join? What impact on employment relationships would an increase in union membership have?

Of course, it may be that despite all their efforts trade unions will continue to decline, but in many industries and workplaces they will continue to be an important element in the framework of employee relations – and as such they will retain a significant influence over the work of personnel professionals.

The Trades Union Congress

The TUC, which was established in 1868, has two major roles. Firstly, it acts as the collective voice of the trade union movement. Secondly, it attempts to maintain order between its individual affiliated unions. However, its actual ability to influence the actions of individual affiliated unions is limited. When the organisation was first set up it was very much the voice of craft unions, and these fiercely independent skills groupings were very wary of any sort of congressional structure. For this reason, when it came down to deciding on a constitution for the new body the trade unions were not prepared to devolve much power or resources to it or to allow it to interfere in their activities. This limitation still remains because the autonomy of the affiliated unions was, and still is, considered to be paramount.

The supreme authority within the TUC is its General Council, a governing structure that comprises four sections to which members are appointed in different ways. Section A consists of representatives of the largest unions in relation to their size – unions with between 200,000 and 399,999 members receive two seats on the General Council; unions with between 400,000 and 649,999 members receive three seats; unions with between 650,000 and 899,999 members receive four seats; unions with between 900,000 and 1,199,999 members receive five seats; and unions with over 1,200,000 members receive six seats. Within this framework, any union whose total number of women members exceeds 100,000, must reserve at least one of its designated seats to a woman delegate. Section B of the Council comprises one seat for each union with between 100,000 and 199,999 members. There are a further eight members in section C who are elected by, and from, unions with fewer than 100,000 members. The fourth section consists of four women members from unions with fewer than 200,000 members.

The TUC is still seen by many people as the voice of trade unionism in the UK although it is no more than the servant of its affiliates. It can take no actions that bind its individual members without their express approval, but it can intervene, and use its disciplinary powers, when it feels that a constituent trade union is acting contrary to the declared principles and policy of the Congress. This is a rarely used sanction, and between 1972, when unions that did not de-register under the Industrial Relations Act (1971) were expelled, and 1996, the sanction has been used only once. The TUC can also intervene when a trade union is considered to be behaving in a manner detrimental to the good standing of the union movement. The most recent example concerns the dispute between the print unions and News International when the latter re-located from Fleet Street to Wapping in London's Docklands. In this instance the print unions were arguing that another trade union (the electricians) had conspired with a hostile employer to put 5,000 members of other affiliated unions out of work, and should therefore be expelled. In such cases the matter is investigated, and if the complaint is upheld, the General Council lays out what an affiliated union must do to put the matter right. If the union does not comply, disciplinary and expulsion procedure can be invoked. In the Wapping dispute, the electricians' union was censured (see the TUC *Annual Report*, 1988), but not expelled. They were, however, expelled later in that year when they fell foul of the 'Bridlington Agreement'. This 1939 agreement was intended to stop the poaching by one union of another union's members, and complaints under its auspices are dealt with by the inter-union disputes committee. The complaint against the electricians related to single-union agreements that they had entered into with employers, to the supposed detriment of other unions. Under the terms of current legislation (the Trade Union Reform and Employment Rights Act (1993)), the TUC has had to revise its dispute procedures because an individual now has a legal right to join the union of his or her choice. Whereas the procedures under the Bridlington Agreement would have allowed for 'poached' members to have been handed back to their former union, this is no longer an option, and the only effective sanction the TUC can order is payment of compensation to the aggrieved union. The first case under the new procedures occurred in 1995 when the Amalgamated Electrical and Engineering Union (AEEU) was ordered to pay compensation to the Transport and General Workers' Union (T&GWU) and the Union of Construction and Technical Trades (UCATT). In real terms, however, the TUC has little authority and resources, and has to persuade its affiliates of the rightness of its decisions, sometimes without success.

Over the course of the last 18 years the influence of the TUC has declined not only among its own affiliates but with the UK Government, and, as Marchington and Wilkinson report (1996; p47), it was excluded 'from a number of principal advisory bodies'. More recently, it has begun to be more imaginative in its approach, introducing task groups to consider issues of importance, such as human resources management (Marchington and Wilkinson, 1996).

The TUC does not confine its role to Britain but plays a very active part in European and international affairs. It is a member of the European Trade Union Confederation and at world level is a member of the International Confederation of Free Trade Unions (ICFTU). ICFTU was established during the immediate post-war years and has its headquarters in Brussels. It has over 100 affiliated organisations from nearly 100 countries. The TUC also provides Britain's worker representative to attend the annual conference of the International Labour Organisation, a United Nations agency, and is represented on a number of its industrial committees. At the same time, the TUC has encouraged its affiliated members to play an active part in international affairs through their own industry-based international federations. For example, the Graphical, Paper and Media Union (GPMU) puts a lot of resources into developing and aiding other national unions. The European Trade Union Confederation (ETUC), in which the TUC now plays a leading role, comprises 36 affiliated national trade union organisations representing some 40 million workers. It plays a valuable role in building links with various committees and EU bodies based around Brussels, and has representatives on the Economic and Social Committee of the

European Parliament as well as on various specialist advisory bodies. It has an important role to play in the development of the Social Charter and European-wide labour law.

Recognising that the European dimension is important, trade unions are starting to examine the development of some form of EU-wide collective bargaining system. As a first step towards this objective the two biggest employees' organisations in Britain and Germany have signed an agreement that will give nearly 2 million workers in both countries dual membership. The agreement means that members of the two unions – the GMB general union in Britain and IG Chemie-Papier-Keramik in Germany, who are employed in the process industry – will have union protection when working in each other's countries. If such accords become commonplace, there could be a major role for the ETUC in the development of pan-European trade unionism.

Professional and staff associations
Staff associations are usually established within a single organisation and for a particular group of employees, and their funding and/or office accommodation is often dependent on a particular employer. The ability of such associations to represent truly the interests of employees must be questioned, but they may develop into trade unions by joining with other employee organisations, or by opening up their membership to others outside the one organisation which they originally represented. Many unions originated as staff associations, such as the National Union of Teachers (NUT) and the Banking, Insurance and Finance Union (BIFU).

Professional associations such as the British Medical Association or the British Dental Association often represent the interests of their members in negotiation with the relevant employers, but also function as organisations responsible for the education and certification of practitioners and the maintenance of professional standards among members. The dual roles of negotiators and professional standardbearers can sometimes conflict, as the medical and nursing profession has often found. It can be very difficult to take legitimate action in support of an industrial dispute without coming into conflict with a professional code of conduct.

THIRD-PARTY INTERVENTION

In this section we are concerned with those organisations that have a statutory role in employee relations, whether in respect of individual issues or collective issues. In the UK there are two such organisations: the Advisory, Conciliation, and Arbitration Service (ACAS), which is by far the more important, and the Central Arbitration Committee (CAC).

The Advisory, Conciliation, and Arbitration Service (ACAS)
In Chapter 2, we noted that the state plays a significant role in employee relations as both economic manager and legislator. In the context of employee relations institutions the state plays a further important role in providing third-party services in the field of conciliation and arbitration. The fact that it makes available an independent agency to help accommodate the interests of the other

two parties to employee relations is a very important consideration for personnel professionals.

The state's role in third-party intervention is not new. Before ACAS was established it used to provide the third-party services of conciliation and arbitration through the Employment Department. In its role as economic manager this interventionist activity was capable of causing the UK Government problems of impartiality, as was demonstrated when the UK Government introduced a series of incomes policies during the 1960s and 1970s. These attempts at pay restraint brought it into conflict with both public- and private-sector organisations and, as the provider of third-party services, there were clearly problems of compatibility. Indeed, during the period that the then Mrs Barbara Castle was Employment Minister, she refused to provide conciliation services in the case of pay disputes in companies which were already outside the incomes policy. This lack of impartiality removed the credibility of the service, and both the CBI and the TUC established their own private arbitration and conciliation arrangements. But despite this, both employers and unions were of the opinion that there was a clear need for an independent body to deliver a truly impartial service. In response to this lobby the Labour Government set up ACAS in 1974 as an independent organisation with its own independent Council, which could develop its own policy. Its chair is appointed by the Secretary of State for Education and Employment, and it has a council of nine members. One third of these are nominated by the TUC, one third by the CBI, and the remainder are independent.

When ACAS was created, it was intended that it should be the manifestation of a voluntary approach to employee relations. It was required to 'promote improvements in industrial relations and encourage the extension, development, and where necessary, the reform, of collective bargaining'. These requirements were changed by the Trade Union Reform and Employment Rights Act (1993), and ACAS is now required simply to promote and improve industrial relations.

One of the most widely misunderstood aspects of the work of ACAS is its involvement in industrial disputes. Such confusion often arises because of a lack of understanding about the difference between conciliation and arbitration. Conciliation operates at two levels: collective and individual. In collective disputes, one party can ask ACAS to intervene, but it will do so only if both parties agree, with the aim of achieving a settlement through the normal processes of collective bargaining. Generally, ACAS is reluctant to become involved in such collective disputes until all the agreed procedures have been exhausted – that is, all disputes procedures, where they exist, should have been exhausted. In its individual conciliation role ACAS does most of its work with individuals who have applied to an industrial tribunal for some form of remedy (eg unfair dismissal). The role of ACAS is to try and resolve the matter 'out of court', and its success rate in this area is very high. It has generally managed to reduce the numbers going to a full tribunal hearing by about two thirds, either by persuading the complainants to withdraw their claim or by successfully encouraging the parties to settle prior to any hearing.

The second of the ACAS roles is arbitration which, like conciliation, can involve both collective and individual issues. Arbitration, and whether to go down this route, is a mechanism that requires very careful thought. Once a management has decided to go to arbitration it must also recognise that it is relinquishing control over the settlement of differences with its employees. Arbitration can be triggered at the request of one party, but requires the consent of the other party or parties before an arbitrator can be appointed. In performing this function ACAS is obliged to consider whether the dispute could have been, or could be, resolved by the conciliation process. As with conciliation, arbitration cannot be offered until all agreed procedures for the negotiation and settlement of disputes have been exhausted. But assuming that arbitration is agreed, a decision needs to be made about the type of arbitration. Standard arbitration allows for the arbitrator to listen to the case presented by the parties and then to make an award based on the information given. In many cases this can mean 'splitting the difference'. 'Pendulum', or final offer, arbitration on the other hand does not allow for such compromises. The arbitrator must come down on one side or the other: acceptance of the union's or employees' claim or the final offer of the employer.

> Has your organisation ever used the services of a third party to help resolve a dispute? Under what circumstances do you think an employer might be prepared to consider agreeing jointly with its employees, and their representative body, to go to arbitration?

Although decisions about whether to use arbitration are important for management, it is important not to lose sight of the fact that two thirds of arbitration cases relate to individual concerns, such as job-grading, dismissal and discipline. There are three factors which make these important issues ideal choices for arbitration:

• They are not ones over which management would be prepared to face industrial action.

• The financial cost of implementing the arbitrator's decision if it went against the company would be low.

• The arbitrator's decision is unlikely to enter the public domain.

In short, employers appear to be willing to go to arbitration on small, but important issues where the cost of 'losing' is relatively low and the chances of adverse publicity virtually zero.

The arbitration role of ACAS is likely to be extended even further if new legislation in respect of unfair dismissal claims is enacted. Such legislation would allow claimants to take their case either to an industrial tribunal, as at present, or to opt for voluntary binding arbitration.

As one of the major institutions of employee relations there are four important points to note about ACAS. Firstly, it is independent and is held in high regard because of that independence. Secondly, ACAS does not have unlimited resources and it must therefore use its available resource wisely. Unfortunately, there are those who believe that ACAS is simply waiting by the phone to solve all manner of industrial problems. This is not true and employers, and employee relations specialists, would be better off ensuring from the beginning that they have effective policies and procedures in place to manage employee problems and disputes internally – arbitration or conciliation ought to be the process of last resort. Thirdly, with the passing of the Trade Union Reform and Employment Rights Act (1993), ACAS is now required to charge, where appropriate, for its services, whereas the services were formerly free. It is not yet possible to say how the words 'where appropriate' will be interpreted over time, but there is a real danger that if ACAS is placed under too much pressure to be 'cost-effective', its independence – on which its reputation has been built – will be compromised. Finally, as with referral to the Central Arbitration Committee (which is discussed below), referral to ACAS is voluntary. In Australia, for example, the compulsory use of arbitration is conversely a central plank of that country's industrial relations framework. There are those who would like to see some form of compulsory arbitration in the UK, and following the 1996 public-sector disputes involving London Underground and postal workers there were renewed calls for this to be imposed in certain types of public-sector dispute. To take such a course of action in isolation is, however, fraught with difficulties – not least because of the voluntary, non-legal status of collective agreements in the UK. To make changes simply to deal with one particular issue can be a very dangerous process and could lead to a worsening – not an improvement – in employee relations.

> Do you think there is a case for making third-party services compulsory in either individual or collective disputes? If it was introduced, what impact might it have on employee relations within your workplace?

In addition to its hands-on interventionist role, ACAS provides advisory services and issues publications and codes of practices. The best-known of their codes of practice is on discipline, but they have also issued other codes – on the provision of information to trade unions for collective bargaining and on time off for trade union duties and activities – plus a range of advisory booklets on matters as diverse as job evaluation and labour turnover.

The Central Arbitration Committee
This body was established in 1976 as an arbitration committee independent of the UK Government, but since the 1980s its powers have been drastically pruned. Its members are chosen in a similar way to those of the industrial tribunals, with an independent chairperson and representatives of employers and employees.

Apart from receiving requests to arbitrate directly from parties to a dispute, the CAC receives arbitration requests from ACAS. Additionally, it has powers to investigate complaints under the legislation which gives the right of information for collective bargaining purposes to independent recognised trade unions. However, there are now questions being raised about the rights of trade unions to such information, and if this right were to be repealed the continued existence of the CAC would be questionable.

The Certification Officer

Whether the Certification Officer truly qualifies as one of the institutions of employee relations may be questionable, but given the importance of this post to both trade unions and employers' associations, we felt it right to include an explanation of the role.

The Certification Officer is appointed by the Secretary of State for Education and Employment after consultation with ACAS, and is required to produce an annual report. He or she is responsible for maintaining a list of trade unions and employers' associations, and for making decisions on the independence, or otherwise, of trade unions.

Applicant unions who are deemed not to 'be under the domination' of an employer can be granted a certificate of independence. Where there is a dispute about independence, the union can appeal to the Employment Appeal Tribunal. The Certification Officer also has responsibilities in respect of union political funds, and can get involved in disputes about union mergers and amalgamations.

CONCLUSION

In this chapter we have tried to present a review of the institutions of employee relations rather than detailed study. Whether the subject is employers' associations, trade unions or state agencies such as ACAS, they all cover a wide field of activity and we have sought to provide an introduction to and an understanding of each one of them.

In respect of employers' associations, we have acknowledged that their influence in the field of national collective bargaining has diminished steadily since World War II and that for many employers they are an irrelevance. Nevertheless, we do believe that such institutions continue to have a major role to play in employee relations. Given that virtually all employers' organisations have expanded their role to provide a broad-based business support system, of which employee relations is a part, they do have the potential to add value to an individual business. Access to the functions provided by an employers' organisation might help a personnel professional in his or her everyday work – the provision of wage and salary information, satisfying employee relations training and development needs, advice on issues such as health and safety, updates on employment law and its implications for particular businesses are just some examples. However, we equally acknowledge that not every business will see the necessity for, or obtain value from, an employers' association. It is merely an option in the employee relations specialist armoury that needs to be considered from time to time.

In the section on trade unions and the TUC we tried to provide an understanding of their structure and internal organisation, but as for trade unions, each of them is subtly different and we could therefore only provide a general picture. Insofar as their future is concerned, it is very difficult to predict. Whatever political decisions the UK Government take over the next five years, it is reasonable to assume that the unions' role in employee relations will continue to change. Labour have made it clear that they do not intend any wholesale changes to the 1980s legislation and are unlikely to be as close to the unions as past Labour administrations. Any positive moves that they might make (eg statutory rights to recognition) are likely to come with a price-tag, such as public-sector pay restraint, attached to them. We also indicated that, like employers' associations, trade unions have to help themselves. If they wish to reverse the trend in membership decline, they have to make themselves more attractive to the large numbers of non-members. This may mean loosening their ties with the Labour Party and concentrating on effective service delivery.

Finally we looked at ACAS, an organisation that has added considerable value to the process of employee relations since 1974. Even so, in spite of its notable successes and enviable reputation for delivering results it is not immune from the process of change. Not only has its remit been narrowed by the 1993 legislation, it has had to take on the concept of charging – with all the potential effects on its impartiality that that implies – and now it is looking at a further expansion of its arbitration role. Clearly there is a need to improve the speed with which unfair dismissal cases are dealt with, and small firms in particular will probably welcome an arbitration process, but such a new process would need the consent of both parties and there may still be disgruntled ex-employees who will want their day in court.

FURTHER READING

ADVISORY, CONCILIATION AND ARBITRATION SERVICE. *Annual Reports*. London, ACAS.

CERTIFICATION OFFICER. *Annual Report*.

CONFEDERATION OF BRITISH INDUSTRY. *Annual Report 1995*. London, CBI, 1996.

4 Employee relations strategies and policies

INTRODUCTION

In the preceding three chapters we identified the main components of employee relations. In Chapter 1 we noted that the balance of bargaining power is affected by the economic, legal and technological environments, which in turn can be influenced by the prevailing management style. In Chapter 2 we developed these issues further as we examined the corporate environment and its importance to employee relations specialists. In this chapter we will be discussing the importance of employee relations strategies, and the type and style of employment policies that flow from such strategies.

First, we need to look at the whole concept of strategy and why, in recent years, it has become the subject of intense discussion and debate. It is because, although organisations have always had strategies, 'only since the 1960s has it been common to address explicitly the question of what their strategy should be' (Kay, 1993; p6). One of the reasons for the change in emphasis is, as we noted in Chapter 2, that economic fluctuations and intense competition have forced organisations to face a continuing process of change. This change has to be managed and requires that organisations develop clear business strategies which will then drive functional strategies, one of which is employee relations.

If the last two decades have taught us anything, it is that the pattern of employee relations has been constantly evolving and that this is likely to continue. The process of evolution has, quite clearly, been driven by the pace of change to which most businesses have been exposed, and has created a need for directors and senior managers to look more carefully at their approach to strategic employee relations management. They have come to accept that there are advantages to be gained in reshaping employee attitudes. This attitudinal change is of particular importance as organisations, in both the public and private sectors, have sought to maximise efficiency as a means of securing a competitive advantage. Competitive advantage is now as important an issue for the public sector as it is for the private sector. Three examples demonstrate this point: secondary schools which seek the more able pupils in a market-driven environment, health trusts that need to attract business from fund-holding general practitioners, and local authority departments faced with compulsory competitive tendering. Private-sector organisations have had their own challenges, very often linked to new technology or the growth of the global economy. Whatever the challenge, it will impact on and dictate the type of employment policies that the management of an organisation will seek to implement. When you have completed this chapter you should be able to

- explain what strategy is and the role that strategy plays overall in defining employee relations strategies and policies

- explain that strategic choices can be driven by the values, preferences and power of those who are the principal decision-makers

- explain that the choice of particular employment policies will often be a strategic decision

- explain the concept of management style and its importance to the process of employee relations

- explain why some organisations continue to embrace collective relationships and others prefer to remain non-union or anti-union.

WHAT IS STRATEGY?

The overall purpose of strategy is to influence and direct an organisation as it conducts its activities. It may be described as the attempt by those who control an organisation to find ways to position their business or organisational objectives so that they can exploit the planning environment and maximise the future use of the organisation's capital and human assets (Tyson, 1995). Clearly this is but one definition of strategy and many other writers have attempted to offer their own definitions, but out of them all a certain consensus does arise.

There are a number of issues with which strategy concerns itself, and these have been categorised by Johnson and Scholes (1993).

First of all, strategy concerns the full scope of an organisation's activities. It seeks to address fundamental questions such as What business are we in? Is the Benefits Agency, with its new focus on the customer, in the business of distributing public money or the business of preventing poverty? Is a local electricity board in the electricity supply business or something much wider? What of a newly privatised train-operating company – is it in the railway business or the transport business?

Secondly, strategy is concerned with the external environment in which an organisation has to operate, and this can be subdivided into three types. Type A is simple and static, an environment where nothing much changes year on year and where management decisions can be made on the basis of historical data. An example might be an organisation making or distributing fireworks. The timing of the main sales event of the year is known, and is unlikely to change; demand is unlikely to vary significantly; and the market is strictly controlled. In such an environment, an organisation could be forgiven if it considered itself immune from some of the pressures facing businesses in more fluid environments. But beware: such complacency can be very dangerous. Sudden changes in the external environment can cause immense problems. Given some very high-profile accidents in 1996, there is the very real possibility of further changes in the regulatory framework governing the sale of fireworks, which may have an impact on UK demand. Type B is an environment that is dynamic, that changes very quickly. Businesses operating in the field of computer technology, where software in particular seems to be out of date very quickly, could be described as operating in such an environment. Type C is a complex environment in which organisations providing a range of services for different markets operate.

Consider the environment in which your own organisation has to operate. How would you describe it?

A third aspect of strategy concerns the match between an organisation's activities and its resources. These resources can be physical (equipment, buildings) or they can be people. Strategies in respect of physical resources may require decisions about investment or even about the ability to invest. Strategies in respect of people might require decisions about the type of competencies needed for future development and where such resources are to be found. Having considered the relationship between activities and resources, a further strand of strategy concerns the resource implications that flow from such a matching process. If there is a need to improve the competencies of individual employees, does management invest in employee development or recruit externally to fill gaps in capability? Whatever the choice, it means that reward and relations strategies will need to be carefully thought out.

Two final, but important, aspects of strategy concern the beliefs and attitudes of those who formulate strategy and the long-term direction of the organisation. When we talk about the organisation in strategy terms, we very often mean the directors and senior managers for it is their values and beliefs that ultimately decide the type and style of employee relations policies that an organisation tries to follow. The senior management team may be very anti-union which, if there are trade unions within the workplace, can have a significant impact on the nature and style of collective relationships. Conversely, if the chief executive of an organisation is personally committed to the implementation of wider communication with the workforce, the organisation might seek to implement an initiative on employee involvement and participation. Similarly, the values and beliefs of those in power – such as Anita Roddick at Body Shop – will have a significant impact on the long-term direction of a business. In the case of the Body Shop, its strategic aim, formulated primarily by Anita Roddick, is to be an environmentally-friendly company and it is this vision that drives many of the things it does today.

To further understand the nature of strategy it may be helpful to investigate the process of strategy formulation: we can identify a number of different approaches. One of the oldest and most influential portrays strategy as a highly rational and scientific process. This approach is based on the importance of the fit between an organisation and its environment. Analyses are made of a firm's environment to assess likely opportunities and threats, and of its internal resources to identify strengths and weaknesses. This process is often referred to as a SWOT (strengths/weaknesses/opportunities/threats) analysis, and it is argued that through such rigorous planning senior managers can predict and shape the external environment and thus the organisation itself.

Other approaches to strategy formulation propose that the complexity and volatility of the environment may mean that a SWOT analysis is both difficult and inappropriate. This evolutionary approach believes that organisations are at the mercy of the unpredictable and hostile vagaries of the market. The environment in which they operate may be changing so frequently that any data that they use, either historical or current, may be worthless.

Some writers argue that it is not possible to apply either a rational or evolutionary label to the process of strategy formulation, but that it is behavioural – that strategic choice results from the various coalitions that are to be found within organisations. The most dominant of these coalitions will be at senior management level, comprising those who have to 'create a vision of the organisation's future' (Burnes, 1996; p168). Strategic choice will, therefore, as we said above, be driven by the values, ideologies and personalities of those in positions of power and influence. An example of how the personality of an individual or individuals can shape strategy can be seen in the example of British Petroleum (BP). When Robert Horton was appointed chairman and chief executive of BP in 1990, the company was, by most organisations' standards, doing reasonably well. It employed over 117,000 people worldwide and had an annual turnover of $50 billion. By 1995, having survived the recession, BP employed 64,000, of whom 22,000 worked in the UK. When Horton joined the business he realised that it was at a crossroads and lacked clear direction. An opinion survey just before his appointment showed that over half of the top 150 managers were unclear about where the company was going, and that the internal structure stood in the way of operational efficiency. Against this background Horton commissioned a review, 'Project 1990', to look at what the organisation needed for the 1990s and beyond. One of the main planks of Project 1990 was a massive culture-change programme aimed at changing attitudes and behaviour. Without this change programme driven by Horton's personal vision of where the company needed to be, there is some doubt as to whether BP could have survived the recession as well as it did (Blakstad and Cooper, 1995).

From this brief description it is clear that there is no one right way of formulating strategy. There are a number of approaches that can be adopted by an organisation, but it is important to understand that whichever one is adopted, it will be constrained by social, environmental, industry-specific and organisational factors, many of which will conflict with each other. If, for example, we take social factors: there can often be significant national differences in the way people approach work, and with the growth in multinational companies and internationalisation, this can have a major impact on workplace culture.

As we have said, the environment within which any organisation operates will, without doubt, constrain strategic choice. It may be a relatively stable and predictable environment where planning and predicting the future is not a particularly hazardous exercise. Alternatively, it may be a hostile, unpredictable and uncertain environment where planning is almost impossible. Whatever the environment, most organisations have to operate in a constantly changing world, and it is this change process that provides the link between business strategy and employee relations strategies. While environmental considerations may provide the stimulus for change, there is a clear consensus that the success or otherwise of individual change programmes is governed by the people in each organisation.

Types of strategy
It is important to consider not only the sort of strategic choices that organisations can make but also the levels of strategic decision-making. There are three levels with which we need to concern ourselves (Burnes, 1996):

- corporate-level strategy, which concerns the overall direction and focus of the organisation

- business-level strategy, which concerns day-to-day operational matters

- functional level strategy, which is concerned with individual areas such as personnel, marketing, etc.

Each of these levels is inter-related, but equally, each of them has its own distinctive strategic concerns. We now need to look at them in a little more detail.

Corporate-level strategy concerns itself with a number of questions and is usually formulated at board level. One of these questions will be about the mission of the organisation. What is the game plan? Is it, as Richard Branson is reputed to have said of Virgin, 'to be the greatest entertainment business in the world', or is it something a little less grandiose, such as improving shareholder value or offering clients complete business solutions? Whatever the mission, it needs to fulfil a number of criteria if it is going to be achieved. Firstly, it needs to be expressed in language that is understandable to the bulk of employees – this means paying attention to the communication process. Secondly, it needs to be attainable – that is, employees must recognise that the organisation has some chance of achieving the objectives that it has set itself. Thirdly, the mission needs to be challenging. For example, the Ford Motor Company once declared, as part of their corporate strategy, that by the year 2000 they would be the best car manufacturer in the world. One of the challenges within this mission is directed at their HR function. Their challenge is to provide the expert advice and counselling that will allow operational management to do its job. Operational management is seen as the means whereby the overall mission can be accomplished.

It the organisation in which you work has a declared mission, how does it compare with the criteria we describe? If it does not, how would you express it so that it met the need to be understandable, attainable and challenging? Alternatively, if no mission has been articulated, what do you think it should be? (Keep to our stated criteria.)

Another aspect of corporate-level strategy that we need to consider concerns those organisations that are large and diversified. Such organisations usually need to concentrate their corporate strategy on how their business portfolio should be managed, on whether to acquire or to dispose of particular businesses, and on what priority should be given to each of the individual businesses. An example of this is the Granada acquisition of Forte in 1996 when, as part of their declared strategy, Granada indicated which parts of the Forte business they would retain and which parts they would dispose of.

Business-level strategy is concerned with the way a firm or business operates in the short to medium term. Which markets should it attempt to compete in and how does it position itself to achieve its objectives? How does it achieve some form of 'distinctive capability' (Kay, 1993)? What should its product range or mix be? Which customers should it aim for? So far as products, markets and customers are concerned, Porter (1985) argued that there are only three basic strategies:

- cost leadership, which aims to achieve lower costs than your competitors without reducing quality

- product differentiation, which is based on achieving industry-wide recognition of different and superior products and services compared to those of other suppliers

- specialisation by focus – in effect seeking out a niche market.

All of these decisions have an effect on employee relations in that they impact on the way that the organisation structures itself internally and on the way that relationships are managed.

Functional level strategy is, in a sense, fairly straightforward. At this level strategy is concerned with how the different functions of the business, marketing, personnel, finance, manufacturing, etc, translate corporate- and business-level strategies into operational aims. But at this level it is important that the various functions pay attention to how they organise themselves not only in order to achieve their aims but to ensure synergy with the rest of the business.

Strategy and employment policies
Having identified how the process of strategy formulation works, we now need to look at how this links into employee relations in particular, but not forgetting that there must be a link with other aspects of the employment relationship – employee resourcing, employee reward, employee development.

Whatever means organisations choose for formulating their strategy, either at corporate or business level, maximising the organisations' competitive advantage has to be a major issue. This inevitably means that an organisation constantly needs to re-evaluate itself in order that it can sustain any necessary improvements. Employee relations strategies therefore need to be concerned with the design and management of employment policies and processes that will deliver and sustain business improvement. The process of change, and its impact on the development of strategy, present many challenges for the employee relations specialist. For example, as we discuss later in the chapter, there is the whole issue of trade unions. Where trade unions exist and are recognised within an organisation, the current trend towards individualism as opposed to collectivism means that strategic choices need to be made about whether unions are encouraged or marginalised. There is a clear link here with the management of reward. If the strategy leans towards rewarding individual performance it will not sit easily with a collectivist environment.

Overall, strategies and policies on employee relations need to have a direct relationship with the business strategy and need to be imaginative, innovative, clear and action-oriented. They need to be formulated by a continuing process of analysis to identify what is happening to the business and where it is going. In this context, the relevance of clear business objectives, as expressed through the medium of a mission statement, cannot be overstated. The key is to develop an employee relations strategy which is responsive to the needs of the organisation, which can provide an overall sense of purpose to the employee relations specialist, and which assists employees in understanding where they are going, how they are going to get there, why certain things are happening, and most importantly, the contribution they are expected to make towards achieving the organisational goals. Another key feature is to ensure that the employee relations policies and strategies do not stand alone but integrate with other employment policies and strategies.

If we examine some of the challenges facing the personnel specialist both now and in the future, we can identify some of the important links between the various personnel disciplines. In the area of employee resourcing, organisations face continuing challenges in developing policies on recruitment and selection, some of which inevitably spill over into the field of employee relations. New legislation on the recruitment of disabled people means that not only will recruitment procedures need to be reviewed but, in some cases, totally overhauled to ensure that no discrimination occurs in the selection process or in the terms under which an individual is offered a job. Once in employment, or in the case of those already in employment, the legislation sets out to ensure that no discrimination takes place in respect of opportunities for promotion, training or other benefits. While nobody would suggest that the legislation is unfair, it would be naive to pretend that it will not create problems, principally because it opens up the possibilities of employee relations tensions developing when able-bodied employees allege unfair positive discrimination. Similar tensions can arise with racial and sexual discrimination. Most organisations have reacted very well to the need for effective recruitment policies in these areas, but the fact that discrimination still takes place demonstrates a need for pre-employment policies and post-employment practices to complement each other. The embarrassment caused to the Ford Motor Company when the racial origins of some of its employees were changed in an advertisement demonstrates this very clearly. In this particular case, a product brochure aimed at the east European market, and which showed a group of Ford employees of both sexes and of different races, was changed to portray all the employees as white. Understandably, the Ford workforce and their union representatives were extremely upset, which demonstrates that policies and practices on discrimination are equally important post- as well as pre-employment. Further tensions might arise in respect of age discrimination, particularly if legislation is enacted to outlaw the practice.

In a similar way the relationship between employee relations and employee reward represents a continuing and continuous challenge to the personnel practitioner. Stimulating employee commitment, motivation and enhancing job performance are matters which will be discussed in Chapter 5, but among the issues that need to be considered is the balance between pay and non-pay rewards and individual versus collective bargaining.

So far as employee development is concerned, the personnel practitioner faces three challenges, all of which impact on employee relations. Firstly, is it in the company's interests to buy-in or to develop their own staff? Where do the long-term interests of the business lie? If you get the balance wrong and buy-in too much labour, there is a risk that existing employees will become disillusioned and assume that the organisation is not interested in investing in their future. Secondly, what sort of employees are required? Generalists or specialists? Personnel professionals have a significant role to play in helping to identify what value there is to the organisation in particular types of employee. Although it is popular to support the idea of multi-skilling, this concept does not always serve the organisation's best interests. Too many people may want to be trained in specific skills, some of which may never be fully utilised. This can then lead to resentment or to resistance to further training interventions. Finally, if investment is to be made in employee development, is it simply a question of training people to carry out the current tasks that they are required to fulfil, or is it strategically valuable to create a learning environment as many organisations have done?

All of these challenges are strategic issues that are inter-linked and have an impact on employee relations. In each case they will be conditioned in their scope and their impact by the type and size of the organisation.

> What external factors over the next five years are likely to affect corporate strategy, both in the wider business context and in the specific challenges that your own organisation is likely to face? How will these affect your employee relations strategy, if at all?

You should have looked at any trends in your organisation's business strategy that might have an effect, such as:

• plans for expansion

• proposals for new investment

• the need to improve profitability or productivity.

You need to consider the impact of changes to your employee relations strategies on the other policy areas – eg resourcing, reward, health and safety, development. Finally, you need to consider the impact of external influences – eg political (a change of UK Government), economic (interest rates, inflation, unemployment), social (demographic trends), new technology, and any possible changes in legislation, particularly European influences.

EMPLOYEE RELATIONS POLICY

Once it is clear what the overall philosophy of an organisation is, the employee relations specialist can use this knowledge to put together an employee relations policy for the business. This can then be used as the guiding principle against which individual policies are drawn up. The needs of an organisation in terms of its employee relations policy are potentially infinite, but could emanate from strategic business needs as diverse as:

• improving productivity

• greater employee empowerment

• introducing performance-related pay systems

• the attitude towards trade unions.

Let us look at the last of these for a moment. We have already discussed the impact that the values and preferences of an organisation's dominant management decision-makers have on strategy formulation. These values and perceptions will in part be determined by whether the organisation adopts a unitary or pluralist approach to its employee relations. The unitary approach emphasises organisations as harmonious and integrated, all employees sharing the organisational goals and working as members of one team. The pluralist approach recognises that different groups exist within an organisation and that conflict can, and does, exist between employer and employees. These are broad definitions and it must be noted that simply because an organisation is described as unitarist, it does not mean that management and employees share the same agenda. Unitarist organisations can be either authoritarian or paternalistic in their attitudes, and this – as we will examine later in the chapter – can have a major impact on management style. Pluralism, while generally used as a term to describe an organisation that embraces collective relationships, can emphasise co-operation between interest groups, not just conflict. It is this distinction in approach to the management of people that leads to variations in employee relations policies, ranging from the paternalistic no-union approach of Marks & Spencer through the single-union no-strike philosophy of Japanese firms like Nissan, to the multi-union sites of companies like Ford.

Two issues that need to be taken into account in drafting employee relations policies, and then implementing them, are the effects of external factors and of internal factors. We identified what some of the external factors were in Chapter 2 – in particular existing and future legislative constraints – but there are other influences. It is important to be aware of the type of policies other employers in your sector or industry are pursuing. These may have an impact in your own organisation if, for example, they have taken a particular stance on employee participation as a means of retaining key employees. This could impact on your own ability to retain staff. A third issue is what is considered to be prevailing 'good practice'. In this context 'good practice' means identifying those acts or omissions that distinguish the good employer from the perceived 'bad' employer. For example, if you fail to operate your disciplinary procedure in line with natural justice you may find that your ex-employees constantly file complaints with tribunals against you, and not only that but they win compensation as well. Many employers when drafting policies and procedures only scratch the surface. They either do not consider how the policy might operate in practice and whether it will meet the needs of their employees, or they are careless in its operation, with the result that it fails to meet the criteria of 'best practice', which is a standard that we pursue throughout this book. Whatever the policy, therefore, it is important to incorporate monitoring mechanisms within it so that checks can be made on its effectiveness.

MANAGEMENT STYLE

Although external constraints on employee relations policy formulation are an important factor, the internal constraints are probably of greater significance to the employee relations specialist. A key issue here is organisational size, ownership and location – factors which often determine managerial style. Style can be an important determinant in defining an employee relations policy, and is as much influenced by an organisation's leaders (like Bob Horton) as is business strategy. Since Fox first categorised management and employee relations as unitarist or pluralist, others have sought to define the topic in greater detail.

In particular, Purcell and Sissons identified five typical styles (Marchington, 1996). These were: authoritarian, paternalistic, consultative, constitutional and opportunist.

The authoritarian approach sees employee relations as relatively unimportant. There is no attempt to put policies and procedures in place, and as a consequence people issues are not given any priority until something goes wrong. Typically, firms with an authoritarian approach are small owner-managed businesses, and it is not unusual to find that the things that go wrong revolve around disciplinary issues. In many of the small firms that we have contact with, complaints against them of unfair dismissal is a common problem – an employer who has paid little attention to setting standards of performance dismisses an employee who makes a mistake, and then finds that the dismissed employee wins a tribunal claim for compensation. This is usually because no previous warnings were issued and no disciplinary procedure is followed. An analysis of the size and ownership of organisations that appear in tribunal cases would seem to support the view.

Paternalistic organisations share many of the size and ownership characteristics of the authoritarian type, but they tend to have a much more positive attitude towards their employees. A consultative or problem-solving organisation welcomes trade unions as partners in the enterprise and employee consultation is a high priority. Staff retention and reward are seen as key issues.

The type of constitutional organisation described by Purcell and Sissons also assumes a trade union presence. Although sharing some of the characteristics of the previous types of organisation, management style in employee relations is more adversarial than consultative.

In the opportunist organisation, management style is determined by local circumstances which indicate whether it is appropriate to recognise trade unions or not, or the extent to which employee involvement is encouraged. Purcell (1987, p535) moved his analysis of 'management style' forward to define it as 'the existence of a distinctive set of guiding principles, written or otherwise, which set parameters to and signposts for management action in the way employees are treated and particular events handled'.

So, a key issue in the drafting of your employee relations policy is to know and understand the prevailing management style. Purcell suggests that management style has two dimensions – individualism and collectivism – and each dimension has three stages.

Individualism is concerned with how much policies are directed at individual workers, whether the organisation takes into account the feelings of all its employees, and if it 'seeks to develop and encourage each employee's capacity and role at work'. The three stages in the individual dimension are: commodity status, paternalism and resource status. In the first the employee is not well regarded and has low job security; in the second, the employer accepts some responsibility for the employee; in the third, the employee is regarded as a valuable resource.

The collectivist dimension is, in a sense, self-explanatory. It is about whether management policy encourages or discourages employees to have a collective voice and collective representation. The three stages in this dimension are: unitary, adversarial and co-operative. At the unitary stage management opposes collective relationships either openly or by covert means. The adversarial stage represents a management focus that is on a stable workplace, where conflict is institutionalised and collective relationships limited. The final, co-operative, stage has its focus on constructive relationships and greater openness in the decision-making process.

> Can you identify the management style that operates within your organisation and contrast this with the style in other organisations with which you are familiar?

Remember: identifying a particular management style is not simply a question of labelling an organisation individualist or collectivist. Purcell points out that the interrelationship between the two is complex, and that simply because an organisation is seen to encourage the rights and capabilities of individuals it does not necessarily mean that it is seeking to marginalise any representative group.

Selecting employee relations policies
The ability to identify which policies are suitable and which are unsuitable for particular types of organisations is an important skill for the employee relations specialist to develop.

All organisations need to have policies on grievances, discipline, health and safety, pay and benefits and sickness absence, even if these may not all always be written down or consistently applied. It is also important to acknowledge that although each of the policies mentioned above might differ in scope and depth from one organisation to another, no one, irrespective of the type of organisation that he or she works in, would seriously question their selection in the range of employment policies adopted.

However, where we do need to examine seriously questions of selection is in respect of those policies which have a clear impact on corporate and business strategies and which can seriously affect relationships at work. As we enter the new millennium, an organisation's approach to strategy formulation, and thus its approach to employee relations, will continue to be influenced by UK Government actions and consumer preferences. This will impact on its decisions about the way it manages people and the policies that underpin these management processes.

In Chapter 2 we explained that for well over a decade the main thrust of industrial, economic and legislative policy has been to create a market-driven economy, and that 'from an industrial relations perspective, the most telling feature of this policy has been the successive pieces of legislation designed to limit the role and rights of trade unions' (Guest, 1995; p110). Because the question of why some firms recognise trade unions and others do not is so important to employee relations, it is dealt with separately within this chapter. For the moment we will concentrate on policy choices in other areas.

For many organisations who try to link policy choices in employee relations to their business strategies, the real question is not about trade unions but about how to ensure that the workforce is committed to the organisation. Obtaining employee commitment is one of the ways organisations can position themselves in order to achieve a competitive advantage, one of the necessary prerequisites of a successful business. However, employees will only give their commitment if they feel secure, valued and properly motivated – a sense of well-being that will, in part, be derived from the type of employment policies that are adopted. Such policies need to be capable of 'adding value' to the business – and for the employee relations specialist who may be trying to decide on the advice he or she gives in respect of a particular policy, this is of some importance. In respect of trade unionism, the question is not about pro- or anti-union stances, it is whether entering into a relationship with an appropriate trade union can add value to the business. It would be wrong to assume that the answer to this question will always be No. Two examples of this can be seen in the cases of News International and Nissan. When News International re-located their newspaper titles from Fleet Street to their new Docklands site at Wapping they made it quite clear to the printing trade unions that they were looking for a different style of employee relations from what had existed previously. When the printing unions (NGA and SOGAT) refused to accept the conditions on offer, the chairman of News International (Rupert Murdoch) sought to reach agreement with a different union altogether – a union he felt would be prepared to offer greater flexibility and thus add value to the business. The union in question was the electricians' union and their decision to enter into a collective agreement in respect of working areas outside their traditional spheres of influence caused major internal divisions within the union movement as a whole. Organisations like Nissan, who had the advantage of a new business starting up on a greenfield site, could certainly have established their north-east factory without a union presence. The fact that they chose not to do so, albeit with certain strings attached like pendulum arbitration, means that they must have seen a strong business case for recognition.

The search for competitive advantage and employee commitment are key issues, and if the concern is that policies should add value it may be necessary to look beyond the issue of trade unions. Do you move towards one of the new prescriptions such as the 'flexible organisation', the 'empowered organisation', the 'learning organisation' or some form of 'teamworking'? These questions will need to be answered whether trade unions are present or not. While these are clearly strategic choices which should be made at board level, the devising and implementation of policies to support them is usually devolved down to the appropriate level of management – in this case personnel.

The process of designing and implementing policies requires the employee relations specialist to develop certain skills. One of these is evaluation. It may be that you have been tasked by the board to establish whether a new fad or initiative will be suitable for your organisation. Evaluation is so important because there is a danger that organisations will invest in new ideas without thinking them through. Perhaps another business has publicised how well a particular initiative has helped it and the immediate reaction from your directors and senior managers is to 'introduce it here'. Quality-improvement initiatives, such as British Standard 5750 (BS5750), picked up a dreadful reputation for unnecessary bureaucracy among some organisations because they were introduced for the wrong reasons. Similarly, many organisations have questioned the value of Investors in People (IIP) because they did not evaluate it properly before seeking accreditation.

A further skill required by the employee relations specialist is that of gaining commitment. How do you convince your managerial colleagues that a particular policy or initiative is right for your company even though it may have board-level support? To demonstrate this we will look at one of the most recent initiatives which we identified earlier: empowerment. In Chapter 1 we stated that organisations need to make decisions about the way they manage people, and that this in turn requires a number of core skills, such as negotiating, listening, assertiveness, coaching and communication. We will use the possible introduction of an initiative on empowerment to show how these skills can help gain commitment.

The concept of empowerment 'is based on the belief that to be successful, organisations must harness the creativity and brain power of all their employees – not just a few managers' (Industrial Society, 1995; p3). The idea that everybody in the business has something to contribute represents a radical shift in thinking away from the old idea that managers managed and the workforce simply followed orders. The fact that empowerment does represent a radical shift in thinking explains why, in many organisations, the initiative has failed. It also points up some further valuable lessons for personnel specialists who might be tempted to try out every fad and fashion. Unless you are prepared to learn the techniques of evaluation in order to test the applicability of particular initiatives, spectacular failure might be the result.

Jenny Davenport, one of the Industrial Society consultants involved in the 1995 survey, says that where empowerment does not work it is because people do not think it through. To avoid such failures it is important to gain commitment from the chief executive and the senior management team, and then to cascade this down to other levels of management. Experience suggests that the hardest group to convince about empowerment and other similar initiatives are middle managers, because it is their jobs that are most likely to be affected. It is because these managers often have the most to lose that they have a tendency to undermine or delay implementation of a new policy. Such tactics are often born out of misunderstanding, and it is here that the skills we referred to above are so important. This, then, represents the first hurdle for the personnel specialist.

Secondly, it needs to be recognised that the introduction of most new initiatives – and empowerment is no different – will be an evolutionary process and that there is unlikely to be a 'big bang'. Any sort of organisational change can mean that responsibilities have to be altered, which means in turn that the boundaries of jobs need to be clarified and people given time to prepare.

Thirdly, it may be important to examine organisational structure. With something like empowerment instead of the traditional hierarchies, organisations need to be much flatter – a change that can give rise to considerable resentment and individual resistance.

Finally, it is important to ensure that other policies which would be required to underpin the initiative are themselves in place: eg equal opportunities, single-status workforce. For the personnel professional, applying the skills of evaluation and gaining commitment is not easy. Faced with any new policy there will always be those who oppose it, sometimes openly and sometimes covertly, and the professional employee relations specialist will recognise this. He or she will not assume that the process is complete just because an initiative has been properly evaluated and then properly communicated to all employees; he or she and will monitor implementation and seek ways to reinforce the initial communication about the policy change.

Even if the policy to be implemented is not a new fad or fashion, it still has to be applied; commitment still has to be gained. For example, a disciplinary policy, although a reasonably well-accepted part of working life, still needs to be applied properly and consistently. One way of gaining commitment to such policies is to identify the potential benefits that they can provide, and to explain the cost of not doing things properly. If you were trying to persuade colleagues about the value of disciplinary sanctions' being applied consistently, you might say that inconsistency would make it more difficult to justify a dismissal at an industrial tribunal.

Spelling out such downside effects to colleagues does not, however, always work. You may need to identify positive benefits for them personally. Many middle and first line managers seek to circumvent policies and procedures like those on discipline because they feel that they take too much time and are a constraint on their ability to manage. We have had many complaints from line managers to this effect. In Chapter 7 we explain in much greater detail the value of managing disciplinary issues properly, but before this can happen, commitment must be obtained. It is therefore important to demonstrate that using and applying procedures properly can help a manager to do the job more efficiently. The overall picture is very clear: good managers have little to fear from policies such as discipline. As far as complaints about the cost in time of following policy and procedures, it needs to be pointed out that more time is wasted by *not* doing things properly. Following 'best practice' when dealing with individual employees makes good business sense and can add value, not take it away. Putting this message across with clarity and conviction is one of the principal tasks of the modern personnel practitioner.

MANAGEMENT AND TRADE UNIONS

Although the influence of trade unions has been declining steadily since 1978, the question of trade unionism *per se* is very important to an employee relations specialist when trying to determine policies and procedures for his or her own organisation. Some companies seem to manage extremely well by being non-union; some organisations appear to be happy to embrace unions; some actively resist them; and, as we have already identified, one of the policy choices an organisation can make is the question of a company's relationship, or otherwise, with a trade union. If a trade union is already present in the workplace, do you continue with established relationships – for example by communicating only through elected representatives? Do you seek to involve people more as individuals without necessarily marginalising the union? Do you de-recognise the union altogether? As we have acknowledged elsewhere in this chapter, management style and philosophy will cause different managers to have different approaches to the role and involvement of unions. They will range from encouragement to active resistance and refusal, and it is important to understand why some businesses prefer to manage with unions and others do without.

Marchington and Wilkinson (1996) look in some detail at managing with or without unions. But before a decision can be made on whether it is in the interests of a business to recognise unions or not, it is important to be sure about the distinction between a unionised and non-unionised workplace. As Salamon points out (1992), the term 'non-unionism' can be used to describe two different types of organisation:

Type A – where an organisation has a policy not to recognise unions in relation to any employees or to particular groups of employees (such as managers) and, therefore, it is a distinct aim or element of the management's employee relations strategy to avoid any collective relationship (ie non-unionism results from management decision);

and

Type B – where union membership within the organisation or group of employees is low or non-existent and, therefore, unions are not recognised because of the absence of employee pressure for representation (ie non-unionism results from the employees' decision not to join unions).

But what of those organisations that have traditionally recognised unions – has there been some fundamental shift in attitude? Information on trade union membership shows that in the period following 1980 there was a significant decline in numbers, and this has been linked by some commentators with the ability of certain businesses to succeed in sectors with historically bad industrial relations – eg Rover (cars) and News International (printing). This decline in union membership has led to a belief that unions are a spent force and that managers therefore do not need to give them much consideration when it comes to formulating policy. This is a somewhat naive view. A major problem of looking at statistical data is that it can give a totally unrealistic view of activity within an individual workplace. One of the reasons for the decline in overall union membership figures relates to the scaling down or closure of hitherto heavily unionised industries, such as shipbuilding, mining, and steel-making. Our (admittedly unstructured) research shows that organisations which operated a closed shop when they were legal, or had almost 100 per cent union membership, have seen no significant decline in union membership. Even the legislation on check-off, which the unions initially feared would have an impact on membership, did not appear to do much to alter this picture. For employee relations specialists at Ford, or in the health service, unions have not gone away. The power balance may have changed, but this, as we have explained, can change. While data on union membership and density is an important factor in assessing union strength, of more importance is the extent to which managements recognise unions for the negotiation of pay and conditions. 'It is therefore important to identify the extent to which union recognition has declined and also to assess whether the decline can be explained mainly by changes in the structure of the economy affecting the composition of employment or by shifts in management attitudes and policies' (Clark and Winchester, 1994; p709).

De-recognition of trade unions

Assuming then that recognition is already in existence, and has been for some time, the policy question is: how appropriate would de-recognition be? The current fashion for individual contracts and a more unitarist approach to employee relations would suggest that de-recognition is a burning issue and has been much used by managers. There is no evidence to suggest that this is the case in any significant way. Research published by Claydon in 1989, the 1990 Workplace Industrial Relations Survey (WIRS) (Millward et al, 1992) and work by Gall and McKay (1994) suggest that when compared to other factors in the decline of union membership, de-recognition has not occurred in many workplaces (Marchington and Wilkinson, 1996). Claydon found 50 successful and four unsuccessful cases of de-recognition between 1980 and 1988, and interviewed managers and union representatives in 36 of the companies to establish reasons. The most common of them was not de-recognition of all unions in a company, but was grade-specific – often non-manual employees such as senior and middle managers or professional staff. In order to place his findings in some sort of context, Claydon looked for, and found, a number of common external pressures on the businesses that had de-recognised. These were increased competition, changes in technology, weak labour markets and UK Government legislation. However, for most unionised companies in Britain these were used not as the basis for de-recognition but to alter the balance of power, thus making it possible to negotiate or impose change through the existing bargaining machinery. Where there had been de-recognition, Claydon found two principal reasons for it: one, that the ownership of the business had changed; and two, that there had been specific changes in company industrial relations objectives and policies. Marchington and Wilkinson (1996) identify three: that union organisation and membership has 'withered away'; that de-recognition has been part of a tidying-up process in the possible move to single-union agreements; and because managements consider collectivism to be no longer appropriate.

Whatever the reasons for de-recognition, it is clear that issues relating to trade unions are more complex than is often apparent. A simple reference to the membership and density statistics, or to the apparent weakness of trade unions, may not be sufficient if you are to make the right choice for your organisation in respect of continued union recognition. Other factors will come into play. In trying to determine the correct path to follow, maintaining recognition or de-recognising is not really the issue. Where trade unions are present, the company may enjoy good industrial relations and therefore be reluctant to disturb existing relationships. Nevertheless, given the turbulent world in which all organisations have to operate, they may need to push through changes that will make them more adaptable, flexible or profitable. There is no reason that such changes cannot be achieved in a union environment. After all, being non-union is no guarantee that change can be implemented successfully either. But where industrial relations are not good and change is being hampered by the collectivist approach, employers need to ask very searching questions about maintaining the status quo.

Non-union organisations

One of the unsubstantiated myths of the last two decades has been the idea that non-unionism is the panacea for business success, with organisations such as Marks & Spencer and IBM put forward as prime examples of the concept. There will always be a debate between those who see trade unions as a negative influence and those, like most of our European partners, who see rights at work (including trade union membership and collective bargaining) as part of an important social dimension to working relationships. It is this polarisation which is behind much of the United Kingdom's animosity towards the social dimension of the European Union. Post-war industrial relations has given some commentators the opportunity to promote non-unionism as the ideal state to which we should aspire, and to suggest that to allow interventions such as the Social Chapter would be a massive step backward. While the debate about unionism versus non-unionism continues, the real question tends to be ignored – that is, is it easier to manage with unions or without unions? Personal prejudice ought not to come into the process of effective management, but many managers' attitudes towards trade unions have been conditioned by their negative experiences during the 1970s and 1980s, a period when the unions contributed to their negative image with some self-inflicted wounds. In too many organisations union representatives were allowed to take the initiative because managers were unsure of how to respond. There were two reasons for this: poor training in core skills like negotiation, communication and interviewing, and a lack of clear policy guidance. As personnel practitioners ourselves we have received many requests for help from organisations who are having difficulty in managing their employee relations. In almost all the cases blame is laid at the door of the union and there is no recognition that poor management might also bear some responsibility. When appropriate training interventions have been agreed and implemented we find that there is a complete turnaround. Not only do managers seize responsibility but they find that they are able to do so with little or no union resistance. In truth, union representatives were merely filling a vacuum that nobody else was interested in. These experiences have caused many managers to become very biased against unions, and many of those that we speak to genuinely believe that without the unions business success would be guaranteed.

This faith in managing without unions has meant that some of the larger non-union firms within the UK have become the focus of attention for developments in employee relations. Companies like Marks & Spencer and IBM, as we have said, have always been held up as exemplary non-union employers, but now others have joined the list. Companies such as Hewlett Packard, Texas Instruments, Gillette, and Mars. 'At the risk of over-generalisation, the generic characteristics of these non-union companies tend to be a sense of caring, carefully chosen plant locations and working environments, market leadership, high growth and healthy profits, employment security, single status, promotion from within, an influential personnel department, competitive pay and benefit packages, profit-sharing, open communications, and the careful selection and training of management, particularly at the supervisory level' (Blyton and Turnbull, 1994; p234). How many of the companies who yearn for non-union status would be prepared to make the investment in people management that the organisations which they envy have done? After all, as we have said, the real issue is how well a business is managed. That is what determines success.

One of the organisations most often quoted in support of non-unionism, is Marks & Spencer. So what is it that they do differently from the unionised firm? As Blyton and Turnbull report (1994), it starts from day one of employment. When employees are recruited to Marks & Spencer they receive a Welcome Pack which gives them information on the company and its principles. This is their introduction to the company's employee relations philosophy. A second booklet, *Facts for New Staff*, gives details of pay rates, the non-contributory pension, profit-sharing scheme, and details of extensive medical care, particularly preventative medicine. Marks & Spencer do not see themselves as anti-union but as non-union. Anybody who works for the company can join a union (it is their legal right anyway) and the company provides facilities for holding meetings in the stores. In common with other non-union organisations which we have mentioned, the question that trade union recruiters are likely to be asked by Marks & Spencer employees is, Why should I join a union? The opinion of their former chairman Lord Sieff is that so few Marks & Spencer employees join a union because the management provides them with everything that an active trade union could. Clearly not all large non-union organisations are as good employers as Marks & Spencer. There are many anecdotal tales relating to large companies in the hotel and catering industry who seem to have a poor record in employee relations but still seem to attract staff and resist the influence of trade unions.

Notwithstanding the influence of large organisations, data from WIRS (1990) indicates that non-union establishments are more likely to be small, single-plant establishments located in the private services sector. This result is not that surprising, given that over the past 15 years great encouragement has been lavished on the small firms sector. The number of business start-ups has risen and many of the new organisations have not been able to see the relevance of trade unions. Given that many of their employees may have been the victims of redundancy in older, traditionally unionised, industries, such a reluctance to embrace the supposed cause of industrial decline (trade unions) may be understandable. However, one must also question how active trade unions have been in trying to recruit from new industries and the new workforce. In Chapter 3, we suggested that trade unions needed to do more to market themselves if they wanted to attract members from previously untapped sources. Have the unions been so busy defending the interests of their existing members that they have not been able to devote sufficient resources to recruitment? Another question that needs to be asked is, How will people's feelings of insecurity about their long-term job prospects act as a feeding-ground for trade union recruiters?

These and other questions link back to the questions of policy choice. If a business wishes to be, or remain, non-union, it needs to be clear about the relationship it will have with its employees. To be a Marks & Spencer you need to be very people-oriented and to place great importance on respect for employees. This means highly developed and effective leadership skills, and that requires an investment in people. Gaining commitment and becoming a harmonious and integrated unitary workplace requires more than words: it can mean changing the established order, as Rover did.

Alternatively, a business can simply be anti-union. Such organisations very often employ people whose choice of job is limited – for example, ethnic minorities, single parents, students and the unskilled. Employees are expected to work hard and assist the organisation to meet sales and profit targets. Obtaining employee commitment is not really an issue for those who are unhappy, or leave, can usually be easily replaced. In the absence of any statutory regulation, those who find it unacceptable to work in such an environment and might be tempted to seek union representation have no means, other than persuasion, of achieving their objective. Even where there is a statutory right to recognition, employees may still be afraid to seek a legal remedy.

Irrespective of whether there is statutory support for the idea, organisations ought to be prepared to deal with a request from their employees for union recognition. The idea might be anathema to an anti-union organisation, but having an identifiable policy relating to trade unionism and trade union recognition can be very helpful. Organisations which are currently non-union should periodically consider whether they wish to discourage unions, retain a neutral stance, or openly encourage the development of trade union membership and recognition (Salamon, 1992) If a claim for recognition is received, the question of what has initiated it needs to be resolved. In such a situation it would be important to know how many employees had actually signed up to the union, as opposed to how many are thinking of signing up. Some form of investigation ought to be carried out to establish why people had joined the union. Perhaps some recent redundancies have created a climate of uncertainty. Perhaps there have been a number of grievances that have been either handled badly or simply not handled at all. There may be an issue over pay or general conditions. Whatever – unless the company has a history of treating its employees badly and those employees have now succumbed to the blandishments of a union recruiting drive, something will have changed for the worse in the employment relationship. If it is possible to identify some causal act, can something other than union recognition remedy it? A consultative committee perhaps. If granting some form of recognition is on the agenda, then it is important that management decides its own objectives and strategy. It would be important to decide on the level of recognition: would it be restricted to the union's right to represent people at grievance or disciplinary hearings, or would it be full-blown negotiating rights?

Employers and their use of the law
The laws that we now have on the statute book impact on employee relations in a number of ways, and, as we explained in Chapter 2, changes in the legislation have meant that trade unions are much more responsible for the actions of their members than they used to be. This in turn means that it is much easier for employers to seek a legal remedy when unlawful industrial action is taken against them. There is a much stricter definition of what constitutes strike action, which can be considered lawful only if it follows a properly conducted ballot, relates wholly or mainly to matters such as pay and conditions, and takes place directly between an employee and his or her employer. This is intended to rule out sympathetic or secondary action by those not involved in the main dispute.

Other provisions in the legislative package include restrictions on the numbers of people that can mount a picket outside a workplace, compulsory ballots to test union members' support for contributions to a political fund, and compulsory ballots to test whether union members within a particular workplace are still agreeable to their union dues' being collected through the check-off system. The law has also outlawed the closed shop – which is not to say that *de facto* closed shops do not still exist, because they do, most notably in the printing industry.

Against this background we need to consider the employers' use of such laws. Why do some employers seek legal assistance in the resolution of disputes and others do not? Much has been made of the rights that employers now have to take legal action against their employees, either to sue for damages caused by industrial action or to seek injunctions prohibiting action from taking place. Some of the cases involving employers and trade unions have had a very high profile – for example, Eddie Shah's action against the National Graphical Association in 1983 (which some say heralded the major changes in Fleet Street) and, more recently, London Underground's challenge to its employees over proposed industrial action.

Although such high-profile cases hit the headlines, there is no evidence to suggest that employers seek to exercise their legal rights every time they are faced with disruptive action. Indeed, there is probably more evidence to suggest that most employers resist the temptation to use the law, generally because they enjoy reasonably good industrial relations and are more interested in maintaining those relationships in the long term than they are in short-term victories. This is not to say that organisations like London Underground set out deliberately to alienate their workforce; it is simply that there are often other considerations. In the Underground's case it is the travelling public: if London Underground were seen not to challenge 'unnecessary' strikes it would run the risk of losing, perhaps permanently, many of its customers. For the same reason, any employer faced with the threat of industrial action would have to take seriously any concerns voiced by the customers and seek to balance these against his or her long-term relationship with the workforce. The customer dimension, particularly in the public sector, was a prime motive behind the Conservative consultative paper which we discussed back in Chapter 2. The circumstances in which an employer might have to consider using the law usually follow a breakdown in negotiations with a recognised union. Such a breakdown could lead the union to seek a formal mandate from its members supporting industrial action, or there could be some form of unofficial industrial action encouraged by lay officials. The response that an employer makes in such circumstances is extremely important and can have a critical effect on employee relations.

> Consider how you would respond to a ballot for industrial action in your organisation. What factors would you take into account?

If, for whatever reason, negotiations with a recognised union have broken down, there is every possibility that the union will seek to organise a ballot of its members. It may do this not just because its leaders have a desire to take industrial action but because a positive vote can be a very useful means of forcing the employer back to the bargaining table. The first thing to do when faced with a ballot for industrial action is to check that it complies with all the legal requirements. Firstly, was the ballot conducted by post? Before any form of industrial action can commence, all those employees who it is reasonable to believe will be called upon to take part in the action must have been given a chance to vote. Secondly, was the employer given seven days' notice before the ballot took place? Thirdly, has the union appointed independent scrutineers to oversee the ballot? Finally, did management receive notice of the result, and was this at least seven days before any proposed action?

Let us assume that all the legal requirements have been complied with. What are the legal options? Can any action be taken against the union? Not really, unless it can be demonstrated that the proposed action would not be a lawful trade dispute within the meaning of the legislation. There is, however, a right to take sanctions against individuals. It is possible to dismiss individuals who take industrial action – but this can be a high-risk strategy. If it is believed that the threat of dismissal will cause people to back down and not take industrial action, such a step can be justified. Unfortunately, such threats can merely cause attitudes to harden and what may have started as an overtime ban can become a full-blown strike.

Now let us examine a second scenario – one in which the ballot for industrial action was not conducted properly. In these circumstances, and before seeking a legal remedy, it is important to consider all the options. Decisions on using legal intervention should never be taken without a full and extensive evaluation. Firstly, it might be appropriate to sit down with those who organised the ballot to discuss concerns about its validity. It is possible that they are already aware of its flaws but are seeking merely to demonstrate the depth of feeling about a particular issue in order to secure a resumption of negotiations. Alternatively, it might be appropriate to talk to those who have been excluded from the ballot. They may be prepared to back the company in any dispute, and it is possible that their votes, in a re-run ballot, might overturn the original result. The third option is to seek an injunction against the union, restraining them from taking any action until a proper ballot is conducted. Again this can be a high-risk strategy because, in a re-run ballot, those who previously voted against the union might now vote with them on the basis of solidarity.

Conclusion

In this chapter we have looked at the link between corporate and business strategies and functional activities such as personnel. This has allowed us to see the relationship between the decisions of the board and the role of line managers in translating those decisions into actionable policies. We have looked at the process of strategy formulation and have seen that a number of different approaches are available. The methodology employed will, inevitably, differ, but as we saw in the discussion on types of environment, the markets that you operate in will have a clear impact on strategic choice. We have also tried to identify the link between business strategy and employee relations strategies and employment relations policies, but we also pointed out that employee relations, like every other function within a business, does not operate in a vacuum. This means that there has to be a relationship with employee development, reward and resourcing.

The chapter has also examined some of the issues that need to be taken into account when drawing up an employee relations policy. We have highlighted the need to incorporate monitoring mechanisms into policies so that checks can be made on effectiveness. We have also looked at management style and noted its role in the determination of an employee relations policy. Finally, in this part of the chapter, we looked at the skills required in selecting and applying particular policies to the organisation. Two key issues were identified. One was the need to evaluate new initiatives and ideas, and the second was the need to gain overall commitment to particular policies. In the context of gaining commitment we highlighted a number of core skills which we feel are an absolute necessity for the professional personnel practitioner.

In its final section the chapter examined the issue of trade unionism, union recognition, non-unionism and an employer's use of the law. We noted that different organisations have different approaches to the role and involvement of unions, but that in organisations where unions are already recognised there has been no mass attempt to de-recognise them. We examined the case for non-unionism and looked at some examples of non-union firms and whether their success was due to good management or the fact that they kept unions at arm's length. We concluded that good management was the most important factor. We identified the role that the law can play in management–union relationships and what factors employers should consider before they use the legal processes against trade unions or trade union members. We looked at some examples of where the law has been used to good effect by employers, but noted that decisions on whether, and when, to use the law can be quite complex and should not be taken lightly.

FURTHER READING

GALL G. *and* MCKAY S. 'Trade union derecognition in Britain, 1988–1994'. *British Journal of Industrial Relations.* Vol. 32, No. 3; pp433–48. 1995.

JOHNSON G. *and* SCHOLES K. *Exploring Corporate Strategy.* London, Prentice Hall, 1997.

PURCELL J. 'Mapping management styles in Employee Relations. *Journal of Management Studies.* Vol. 24, No. 5; p535. 1987.

TYSON S. *Human Resources Strategy: Towards a general theory of human resource management.* London, Pitman, 1995.

5 Employee involvement and participation

INTRODUCTION

Employee involvement and participation is a management technique designed to evoke greater commitment to, and identification with, the organisation's business objectives on the part of employees. Involvement refers to the degree to which employees accept the aims and needs of the organisation, and as such focuses on the individual employee. Participation, on the other hand, concerns the extent to which employees, often via representatives, are involved with management in the decision-making machinery of the organisation. By the use of employee involvement and participation, management seeks to gain consent from the employees for its proposed actions on the basis of discussion and consultation rather than by coercion.

After reading this chapter you should be able to

- explain the aims and objectives employers seek from introducing involvement and participation schemes

- assess the strengths and weaknesses of the various involvement and participation schemes available to management

- understand the essential conditions for the successful operation of involvement and participation schemes

- assess the situation in which involvement and participation schemes, in whatever form, are appropriate.

THE AIMS OF EMPLOYEE INVOLVEMENT AND PARTICIPATION

It is good business practice to involve employees in the activities of the organisation because a workforce more committed to the aims and needs of the organisation is more likely to be prepared to contribute to an improvement in the efficiency of its operations. The individual employees can use their greater knowledge to improve customer service and/or product quality. Employee involvement and participation schemes are said to enhance job responsibility by providing individuals with more influence over how they perform their tasks (employee empowerment). Each individual can make a personal decision on how to perform his or her tasks instead of being instructed on how to do so by management. When employees are involved, they have some influence over how they perform their job. This in turn is likely to increase their contentment with the job, the probability that they will remain in that job (reduced labour turnover), and their willingness to accept changes to the tasks that make up the job. Individuals who actually perform the job are the ones with the greatest stock of knowledge of its practical aspects. Individual employees are more likely to be effective members of the workforce if management taps into their knowledge of the job by seeking their opinion on how the job should be performed and how it can be organised better.

Financial participation schemes involve employees in the economic success or failure of the organisation. The theory predicts that if employees have a financial stake in the overall success of the workplace or unit, they are more likely to work harder for its ultimate success. This, it is argued, will particularly be the case if there is a direct and precise link between the financial success of the organisation and the financial reward received by individuals employed in that organisation. Supporters of financial participation schemes also argue that individual employees tend to work more effectively on behalf of the organisation if they have a sizeable control over the financial performance of the enterprise.

From a management perspective, the aim of introducing employment involvement and participation schemes is to gain a competitive edge in the marketplace. It is argued that this is achieved through individuals' gaining increased satisfaction from their work as they have more influence over how it is performed, and through the greater identification with the interests of the organisation which employees develop and which results in their understanding the importance of customer satisfaction to the growth and progress of the business. This, in turn, it is argued, enables the organisation to adjust more quickly to changing market requirements because employees are more willing to accept changes in working methods. Increased identification by employees with the overall interests of the organisation is also said to result in a competitive advantage because the employees understand better the necessity of an organisation to improve its performance and productivity, to adopt its methods of working to match new technology, and to draw on the resources of knowledge and practical skills of all its employees. It is further argued that if individual employees identify their own interests with those of the success of the business, they understand that the basis of their own job security lies in co-operation and partnership, not in conflict with the employer.

Table 5 **The aims of employee involvement and participation**

Involvement of and participation by employees in any organisation should aim to

- generate the commitment of all employees to the success of the organisation
- enable the organisation better to meet the needs of its customers and adopt to changing market requirements
- help the organisation to improve performance and productivity, and adopt new methods of working to match new technology
- improve the satisfaction employees experience in their work
- provide all employees with the opportunity to influence and be involved in decisions which are likely to affect their interests.

Source: IPD Code of Practice on *Employee Involvement and Participation in the UK*, 1995 (no longer available)

Employee involvement and participation thus aims to promote employee commitment to the enterprise. Commitment, however, is a two-way process. At the same time as promoting employee involvement, management needs to demonstrate a long-term commitment of its own to its employees in terms of their job security, pay and other employment conditions, access to training and re-training, and the provision of a safe working environment. It needs in addition to recognise that employees also have commitments outside the workplace (for example, families), and these have to be balanced against the employer's need for their services. Employers should seek to avoid giving the impression to their employees that unless they sacrifice everything for the good of the organisation they are not loyal and committed employees.

THE OBJECTIVES OF INVOLVEMENT AND PARTICIPATION

Ramsay (1996) points out that the means of achieving the aims of employee involvement and participation lie in action in five areas:

Table 6 **Possible management objectives for employee involvement**

Attitudes
  Improved morale
  Increased loyalty and commitment
  Enhanced sense of involvement
  Increased support for management

Business awareness
  Better, more accurately informed
  Greater interest
  Better understanding of reason for management action
  Support for/reduce resistance to management action

Incentive/motivation
Passive   Accept changes in working practices
        Accept mobility across jobs
        Accept new technology
        Accept management authority
Active   Improved quality/reliability
        Increased productivity/effort
        Reduced costs
        Enhanced co-operation and team spirit
Personal   Greater job interest
        Greater job satisfaction
        Employee development

Employee influence/ownership
  Increased job control
  Employee suggestions
  Increased employee ownership in the company
  Increased employee ties to company performance and profitability

Trade Unions
Anti-union   Keeps union out of company
        Representative needs outside union channels
        Win hearts and minds of employee from union
With union   Gain union co-operation
        Draw on union advice
        Restrain union demands

Source: Ramsay, in B. J. Towers (ed.) *The Handbook of Human Resource Management*, 2nd ed., Oxford, Blackwell, 1996

changing attitudes, increasing business awareness, improving employee motivation, enhancing employee influence/ownership, and the involvement of trade unions (see Table 6). This is not an exhaustive list but nevertheless demonstrates the need for the careful definition of objectives. Vague and general terms like 'changed attitudes' or 'greater incentive' are inadequate for evaluating whether employee involvement and participation schemes are operating as management intends. The list also illustrates the potential conflict between employee involvement schemes, or at least that there may be a certain strain between them. As Ramsay (1996) remarks:

> To exemplify this last point, a general sense of unity and belonging may sit poorly with the need to sharpen individual competition and incentive, and it may be advisable to use distinct kinds of scheme to achieve each if both require enhancement . . .

In organisations where trade unions are recognised and union membership is high, it is important that management involves trade union representatives and their officials in developing participation arrangements and procedures. Their co-operation, support and advice is likely to be an important factor in the success or failure of employee involvement and participation. Some employers, however, see employee involvement schemes as a means of restricting the scope of union influence, of winning the hearts and minds of employees from that influence, and of fulfilling the representative role need for employees from outside union channels. Evidence from WIRS (1990) published in the TUC report *Human Resource Management* (1994) showed that over the period 1987–90 inclusive, 54 per cent of establishments that de-recognised unions introduced forms of employee involvement. However, caution is required before drawing the conclusion that employee involvement is a route to union avoidance. The same study also showed that 43 per cent of establishments who de-recognised had made no attempt to develop wider employee involvement. Equally, 38 per cent of those employers without unions claimed to have implemented an employee involvement initiative during the same period.

For a management that already recognises unions to try to use employee involvement and participation to reduce their influence over its employees is a high-risk strategy. If a union has a high proportion of membership, controls its members, has bargaining power, and delivers on agreements, only an unprofessional manager would try to introduce employee involvement and participation schemes and de-recognise the trade union. If the union has a low proportion of membership, cannot control its members, has little bargaining power, and cannot keep to agreements, management will conversely have little difficulty in using employee involvement and participation schemes as a means of bypassing what is a weak trade union.

If the business awareness of employees can be improved, they are more likely to be better and more accurately informed, the rumour 'grapevine' will be reduced, and there is a higher probability that they will have greater job interest and greater support for (or resistance to) management action. Table 6 suggests that by using involvement and participation schemes to increase employee influence/ownership, management is more likely to provide its employees with greater job control and at the same time, via financial participation schemes, create increased employee ownership in the company and enhanced employee ties to company performance and profitability.

Ramsay (1996) claims that if management can change in a positive direction, employee incentive and motivation may have passive, active and personal effects. The employees may benefit from greater job interest, enhanced job satisfaction and increased opportunities to develop themselves. Active advantages may arise for the organisation stemming from improved quality/reliability of the product or service, increased labour productivity and effort, reduced costs and enhanced co-operation and team spirit. Among the passive advantages Ramsay notes as accruing to the organisation are a greater willingness on the part of employees to accept changes in working practices, flexibility across jobs, the implementation of new technology, and enhanced supervisory management authority.

If management can achieve a positive change in employee attitudes, it is likely to improve not only the morale of employees but also their loyalty and commitment to the organisation: their sense of belonging and involvement is also likely to be enhanced. In addition there is greater probability that employees will give greater support to management's position. Employee involvement and participation mechanisms are thus an important means whereby management can bring about organisational cultural change. However, such cultural change can only be achieved in any organisation on an incremental basis. The full benefits to the organisation from cultural change arising from the successful implementation of involvement and participation schemes will not accrue immediately. The attitudes of every employee, or manager, will not change in a positive direction at the same moment in time. Some will take longer than others to develop a positive change in attitude towards the actions of management. Positive changes in the morale of all employees will only come about over time. Management needs to be aware of the phenomenon of incremental cultural change when reviewing and monitoring the impact of the introduction of employee involvement and participation schemes.

INVOLVEMENT AND PARTICIPATION MECHANISMS

General principles
So far we have examined the aims of employee involvement and participation. We now turn to look at the various employee involvement and participation mechanisms available to management. In choosing an appropriate scheme, the guiding principle for management is the extent to which it will assist the organisation to achieve its corporate objectives. Management cannot select just any scheme – the one selected must be relevant to the purposes for which it is designed.

> Do you have employee involvement and participation schemes in your organisation? What do your managers expect to achieve from these schemes? If there are no involvement and participation schemes, why is that the case?

The IPD Code of Practice on *Employee Involvement and Participation in the UK* (though no longer available) provided guidance for organisations in implementing effective and efficient employee involvement and participation schemes. The listed directives related to their voluntary introduction, taking account of the organisation's needs, culture, costs and synergy. It set out eight principles for voluntary arrangements, though a ninth related to the general application of employer involvement and participation schemes to all types of employing organisations. The main eight principles were:

- The arrangements and procedures should be appropriate to the needs of the organisation.

- Agreement on arrangements should be arrived at jointly with the employees.

- The arrangements should involve trade unions where they are recognised by the organisation.

- The lead in establishing, operating and reviewing of the arrangements should be taken by the management.

- All employees in the organisation should be covered by the arrangements.

- Education and training should be provided to enable the participants in the arrangements to perform effectively.

- Employees' rights and trade unions' responsibilities should not be prejudiced.

Employee involvement and participation can be achieved through a wide range of schemes. However, those selected by management must be appropriate to the characteristics of the organisation, including the nature of its activities, its structure, its technology and its history. Processes and structures appropriate to older industries, for example, will not necessarily match the needs of newer organisations formed in a different social, industrial and commercial context. There is no one way of managing employee involvement and participation, and the guiding principle must be that the arrangements are compatible with the organisation's circumstances. It is not essential, for example, to establish employee involvement mechanisms to help improve product and service delivery quality if the organisation operates in a product market where competitive advantage rests with price and not the quality and reliability of the product.

Employee involvement and participation arrangements in organisations are best developed by joint agreement between management and the employees and/or their representatives. If arrangements are introduced on a jointly agreed basis, employees will have some 'ownership' of them and will have a greater commitment to ensuring the success of the scheme. If management imposes the arrangements, the employees have no ownership of them and therefore no stake in ensuring their success. Joint agreement by management and employees means joint commitment to operate the arrangements in good faith and as intended. Both parties have an interest in ensuring that they succeed. It is something they have jointly created. In addition, employees see advantages in their representatives' being involved in the management decision-making processes, if for no other reason than to act as the custodians of their interests and to ensure management accountability. Employees are desirous that all levels of management should take notice of their views and concerns.

It thus makes sense – on the basis of the joint agreement/joint commitment argument for best practice in introducing employee involvement and participation schemes into organisations where trade unions are recognised – that union representatives and their officials be involved in deciding the appropriate arrangement and in their operation. This helps reassure the trade unions that management's real agenda is not to undermine their influence. In initiating the necessary action to implement effective schemes the lead must come from management. Employee involvement and participation will not occur or develop of its own accord.

Two other key principles are: the opportunity for all employees, including managers, to participate in employee involvement participation schemes, and the provision of appropriate training and education for the participants in the schemes. The former principle enables all employees to have the confidence that the views being sought from them will be taken into account by management before it makes a final decision and not after it has made one. An important consideration in this regard is the quality of relationship between individual employees and their immediate superiors and managers. Best practice behaviour would require that if employees and employers are to play a constructive role in the operation of employee involvement participation schemes, both parties require training. It is reasonable for employees and managers to expect this. If the quality of decisions made by management is to be improved, the managers need to gain information by listening to what the employees have to say and by asking them appropriate questions. By the same token, employees require information from employers. Both employees and employers require training in communication skills, presentational skills and chairing meetings.

Employee involvement and participation arrangements do not relieve management of its responsibility for making business decisions that fall within the area of its own accountability, and for communicating such decisions, with relevant background information, to the employees. The quality of business decision, by management is likely to be improved if management takes into account the views of the workforce and/or their representatives before making a final decision. However, the employees do not have a veto on management decisions. The prerogative to make business decisions continues to lie solely with management.

Techniques

Employee involvement and participation arrangements fall into two broad types. First, there are direct participation techniques which involve face-to-face communication with individual employees and work groups. Such techniques include two-way communications systems, team-briefing, quality circles, total quality management (TQM) and financial participation in the form of profit-sharing and employee share ownership. Second, there are indirect participation techniques which involve the employees or their representatives in the organisation's decision-making machinery. These techniques include joint consultative committees, joint working parties, employee involvement councils, works councils and worker directors (employee representatives who sit on the board of directors of the company). These institutions all provide machinery by which employee representatives may seek to influence management policy- and decision-making machinery in the favour of employee interests.

Many considerations have to be taken into account by management in deciding which techniques to select (see Table 7). Consideration has to be given to the context in which the arrangements will be introduced and operated. If they are to be introduced as part of a coherent and consistent strategy to improve the performance of the enterprise, then the proposed arrangements to be introduced would be the result of a full evaluation of all the possible techniques. On the other hand, if they are being introduced to deal with a crisis situation it is likely that the arrangements selected will have been ill-thought-out and possibly rationalised on the flimsy basis that such employee involvement and participation arrangements have been successfully introduced in other organisations. Without any detailed assessment and evaluation, the management will be assuming that the arrangements can be transplanted successfully into its own organisation. Arrangements

Table 7 **Factors to be considered in the selection of appropriate employee involvement and participation schemes**

Context
• as part of a coherent and consistent strategy
• as part of 'crisis' management.

Single *v* Multiple arrangement
• the mix can vary
• the greater the mix does not necessarily mean a greater quality of arrangements.

Integration
• between the mix of arrangements (horizontal integration)
• with the strategic objectives of the organisation as a whole (vertical integration).

Success elsewhere
• why are the schemes successful elsewhere?
• could they be transplanted successfully elsewhere?

Legal
The Companies Act (1989)
• statement in directors' report describing action taken to introduce, maintain or develop information/communication consultation, financial participation and economic awareness.

European Works Council Directive (1994)
• European Union-wide information and consultation systems in pan-European companies.

introduced without proper analysis and evaluation are unlikely to be successful or to provide management with the expected advantages that might accrue from the implementation of employee involvement and participation schemes.

Research by Marchington (1993) into the operation of involvement and participation arrangements revealed that single measures designed to enhance employee commitment to the organisation are much less likely to succeed than a multiplicity of arrangements. Nevertheless, whatever the mix of employee involvement and participation techniques, those adopted must be appropriate to the organisation's needs as revealed by a thorough assessment and evaluation. Marchington (1993) found, for example, that in some small companies the mix of employee involvement arrangements was no more than one or two different practices, whereas in some larger manufacturing organisations there were as many as eight or nine different schemes for developing employee involvement and participation. However, he points out, it is dangerous to assume that the greater the number of employee involvement and participation arrangements an organisation introduces, the greater will be their overall quality. He warns that multiple techniques can lead to potentially conflicting pressures, and confusions or communication overload for the staff subject to these arrangements.

If a multiplicity of different employee involvement and participation schemes is held to be appropriate, then not only must they integrate with each other (horizontal integration) but they must be integrated with the strategic objectives of the organisation as a whole (vertical integration). This may require schemes to be 'customised' so they are relevant and appropriate to the organisation's needs and practices (see below). Since a wide range of employee involvement and participation schemes are available to organisations, giving careful consideration to all of them before attempting to implement one or more, is common sense. If employee involvement and participation arrangements are to make an impact, they must be integrated with the business objectives and be consistent with other management practices. Just because schemes have proved to be successful in one organisation, there is no guarantee they will work as successfully in another organisation which operates in a quite different context. Copying those arrangements that have been perceived to be successful elsewhere is a poor basis for selection. A full analysis and investigation of their appropriateness to another organisation is essential. Information is required on what factors made them successful in the original organisation. Do these factors exist in other organisations? Are there factors at other organisations that would prevent the practice from being successfully transplanted into another organisation?

There are also legal considerations that should influence management's choice of which involvement and participation arrangements to introduce. The Companies Act (1989) requires any organisation which employs more than 250 employees to include a statement in its directors' report describing the action taken in the previous financial year to introduce, maintain or develop arrangements in the following areas:

- *Information/communication* – providing employees systematically with information on matters of concern to them as employees.

- *Consultation* – consulting employees or their representatives on a regular basis so that the views of employees can be taken into account in making decisions which are likely to affect their interests.

- *Financial participation* – encouraging the employees in the company's performance through an employee share scheme or some other means.

- *Economic awareness* – achieving a common awareness on the part of all employees of the financial and economic factors that affect the performance of the company.

The European Works Council Directive (1994) provides for a European Union-wide information and consultation system to be set up in all organisations with more than 1,000 employees in any one European Union member state or employing more than 150 people in each of two or more member states. A pan-European Works Council (or alternative system) must be set up by the central management of a company and a Special Negotiating Body of employees elected from the various EU countries in which the company has productive capacity.

The Directive requires the establishment of a European Works Council of employee representatives with the right to meet central management at least once a year for information and consultation about the progress and prospects of the company on a pan-European basis. At this annual meeting, the employees' representative will receive information and be consulted about the enterprise's structure, its economic and financial situation, probable developments in its business and in production and sales, the employment situation, and likely trends, investments and any substantial change concerning the organisation – new working methods, production processes, transfers of production, mergers, cutbacks or closures of undertakings, establishments or important parts thereof, or collective redundancy. Employees also have the right in exceptional circumstances to trigger an additional meeting with management to be informed and consulted on 'measures significantly affecting employees' interests'.

UK and other foreign companies must comply with the Directive if their operations in the other European Union member states meet the thresholds. The UK operations of company headquarters located in other member states may be involved if central management wishes to include them. Companies with agreed pan-European information and consultation systems already in place before 22 September 1996 are exempt from the arrangements described above.

COMMUNICATIONS AND BRIEFING SYSTEMS

Communication systems

Employee communications means the provision and exchange of information and instructions which enable an organisation to function effectively and employees to be properly informed about developments. It covers the information to be provided, the channels along which it passes and the way it is relayed. Communication is concerned with the interchange of information and ideas within an organisation.

Whatever the size of an organisation, and regardless of whether it is unionised or non-unionised, employees only perform at their best if they know their duties, obligations and rights and have the opportunity to make their views known to the management on issues that affect them. With the trend towards flatter management structures and the devolution of responsibilities to individuals, it is increasingly important that individuals have an understanding not only of what they are required to do but why they should do it.

Good communication and consultation are central to the management process. All managers need to exchange information with other managers, which necessitates lateral or inter-departmental communications. Failure to recognise this need is likely to result in inconsistency of approach or application. The ACAS advisory booklet on employee communications and consultation lists the advantages of good employee communications:

- improved organisational performance, in that time spent communicating at the outset of a new project or development can minimise subsequent rumour and misunderstanding

- improved management performance and decision-making, in that allowing employees to express their views can help managers to arrive at sound decisions which are more likely to be accepted by the employees as a whole

- improved employees' performance and commitment, in that employees will perform better if they are given regular, accurate information about their jobs, such as updated technical instructions, targets, deadlines and other feedback; their commitment is also likely to be enhanced if they know what the organisation is trying to achieve and how they as individuals can influence decisions

- greater trust, in that discussing issues of common interest and allowing employees an opportunity to express their views can develop and improve management–employee relations

- increased job satisfaction, in that employees are more likely to be motivated if they have a good understanding of their job and how it fits into the organisation as a whole and are actively encouraged to express their views and ideas.

Communications policy

An organisation's communication policy needs to be well-defined and set out in a systematic way. The existence of such a policy is an effective way of establishing the attitude of the organisation, defining the responsibilities of the actors in the policy and dictating the means of communication to be used. ACAS holds that best practice in a communications policy covers:

* a clear statement of policy, including the purpose of communication, the fact that it is an integral part of every manager's job, and an acknowledgement of the importance of communication as a two-way process and not a one-off exercise

* a statement of who has responsibility for communication at each level

* the methods of communication

* the arrangements for consultation and participation

* the arrangements for training managers and employees in the skills and processes of communications

* how the policy will be reviewed and monitored.

A successful employee communications policy depends, above all else, on a positive lead from top management. Just approving a policy is insufficient: a *senior* manager should ensure the policy is put in practice, is properly maintained, is regularly reviewed, and that the chains of communications are clearly understood and followed by all concerned.

However, a crucial link in the success or failure of a communications policy is the line managers and supervisors. They have responsibility for passing on information in both directions as well as acting on appropriate signals and issuing instructions. Middle managers also have an important role to play. Direct communications between senior managers and employees is sometimes desirable, but best practice is to keep chains of communication as short as possible. It is advisable, however, that middle managers are not bypassed when information is given to employees. If senior managers do communicate directly with staff, middle managers must be kept informed. The personnel professional has a substantial interest in the provision of information for employees and in the way it is done. Personnel managers are well placed to identify needs, advise on policy and monitor arrangements. In particular, they are concerned with the provision of information about terms and conditions of employment.

> What are the principles that underpin the communications policy in your organisation? To what extent, and how, do you think your organisation's communication policy can be improved?

Communications is a two-way process which requires information to flow up from employees as well as down from managers. Good communications policies will provide information in three areas: contractual terms and conditions of employment, the job and its performance, and the organisation's performance, progress and prospects. Detailed information about what might be made available under these three areas is shown in Table 8. Employees have concerns

Table 8 **Information to be communicated**

Information about conditions of employment
- written statements specifying the main contractual details within two months of the commencement of employment
- written statement covering pay, hours of work, holidays, length of notice of termination and, where there are more than 20 employees, any disciplinary rules
- itemised pay statement.

Information about the job
- work objectives and performance requirements
- general information (administrative procedures, social and welfare facilities)
- arrangements for trade union representation
- operating and technical instructions (work to be carried out, use of equipment, standards to be met, reporting procedures)
- health and safety matters.

Information about the organisation
- the organisation's objectives and policy
- the organisation's past and present performance and progress
- future plans and prospects
- financial performance, state of the market, order book
- developments in technology and methods
- investment
- changes in products or services
- financial data – sales, turnover, income and expenditure, profit and loss, assets and liabilities, cash flow, return on investment, and added value.

Source: ACAS advisory booklet, *Employee Communications and Consultation*

and points they will wish to raise about their job and the organisation. A best practice communications policy will make provision for communicating information up as well as down the line. Job instructions and technical information are not sufficient. Employees also need to know how well they are doing in relation to what is expected of them, both on an individual and on a work group basis. This is important because of possible disciplinary proceedings (see Chapter 7). There is likely to be little gained if management begins proceedings against an employee who has never been told what standards of performance are required of him or her. How can an employee know that his or her performance is below acceptable standards if he or she has never been told what those standards are? An organisation that behaves in this way would have difficulty convincing an industrial tribunal that it had acted fairly and reasonably should it proceed to dismiss the employee.

The commercial sensitivity of some financial information and management fears of breaches of confidentiality are frequently cited as obstacles to good communication on the performance, progress and prospects of an organisation. However, the obvious need for confidentiality about such specific matters rarely justifies an overall restrictive approach to communication on all commercial matters.

A sensitive area for employees is job security. Changes in technology or in market conditions can give rise to fears among employees which become exaggerated if based on rumours or false information. Advance information and discussion of the organisation's future prospects is a way to alleviate or avoid such fears and assist employees to adapt to any necessary change.

The process of communication

To be effective, communication needs to be clear, easily understood and concise. Information is better received if it is presented objectively, in a manageable form, in a regular and systematic manner, and as relevant, local and timely as possible. In communicating with employees about how action proposed by the management will affect the organisation, it is best to start by explaining the likely impact on the employees themselves and then move on to explain to them the implications for the department, the operating unit, etc, and then the organisation as a whole. To go through process the other way round – organisation, department, employees – will result in the employees' failing to listen to the message being relayed to them. They are likely to feel that management's main priority of concern over the proposed change is for the organisation rather than for the employees, and that organisation consideration will prevail over employee interest regardless of what the employee says. To start with, a reference to the employees themselves demonstrates that management is concerned about the impact of the proposed change on the employees as a first priority. The failure of many an organisation's communication policy is the result of providing inappropriate information to the recipients of the message.

A variety of communication methods (spoken and written, direct and indirect) is available for use by management. The mix of methods selected will be determined by the size and structure of the organisation. Two main methods of communication can be distinguished. First, there are face-to-face methods, which are both direct and swift. They enable discussion, questioning and feedback to take place. It is often advantageous, however, to supplement these methods by written materials, especially if the information being conveyed is detailed or complex. The main formal face-to-face methods of communications are:

- group meetings – meetings between managers and the employees for whom they are responsible

- cascade networks – a well-defined procedure for passing information quickly, used mainly in large or widespread organisations

- large-scale meetings – meetings involving all the employees in an organisation or at an establishment, with presentations by a director or senior managers; these constitute a good channel for presenting the organisation's performance or long-term objectives

- inter-departmental briefings – meetings between managers in different departments which encourage a unified approach and reduce the scope for inconsistent decision-making, particularly in larger organisations.

Second, there are written methods. These are most effective where the need for the information is important or permanent, the topic requires detailed explanation, the audience is widespread or large, and there is a need for a permanent record. The chief methods of written communication include company handbooks, employee information notes, house journals and newsletters, departmental bulletins, notices, and individual letters to employees. Electronic mail (e-mail) is useful for communicating with employees in scattered or isolated locations, while audio-visual aids are particularly useful for explaining technical developments or financial performance.

WIRS (1990) showed that the use of multiple channels of communication was more common in unionised than in non-unionised workplaces, the implication of which is that unionised workers have greater opportunities to express their views to management than do non-unionised workers. Furthermore, in the unionised companies the communication methods were both 'top-down' and 'bottom-up' so that there was a two-way flow of information. The TUC *Report on Human Resource Management* (1994) noted that in the non-union sector the more anti-union the employer was, the less likely the employer was to use the full range of communication methods. The evidence revealed that most anti-union employers tend to use 'top-down' methods of communication with their employees through the use of meetings with senior managers or through the management chain. The problem with this approach, from a management perspective, is that most employees will be reluctant to express their views freely at such meetings. In general, the WIRS (1990) survey indicates that non-unionised employees have fewer opportunities to shape their working environment than unionised employees.

Monitoring
It cannot ever be taken for granted that communications systems are operating effectively, nor can it be assumed that because information is 'sent' it is also 'received'. The communications policy and its associated procedures need regular monitoring and review to ensure that practice matches policy, the desired benefits are accruing, the information is accepted, received and understood, and the management communicators know their roles. Monitoring is largely dependent on feedback from employees through both formal and informal channels, although other indicators include the quality of decision-making by management, the involvement of senior management, and the extent of employee co-operation. In monitoring and reviewing an organisation's communication policy, the criteria for assessing its effectiveness will therefore be related to outputs from the operation of the policy – for example, whether employee morale has improved, whether productivity has increased, whether there is a greater willingness to accept change on the part of employees and managers, and whether the employees have an improved understanding of the company and business generally. Review and monitoring should take place on a regular periodic basis – for example, quarterly or annually, depending on the size of the organisation.

Briefing groups
Dangers of the use of such groups, from a management perspective, is that as the information cascades down, it also becomes watered down, hedged around with rumour, out of date, and imprecise. As we noted above, many communications policies are less effective than they might be because a lot of information passed down from the top to the bottom of the organisation concentrates on the wider perspective, with the result that local receivers of the information do not take note of it simply because they do not directly appreciate the relevance of the

information. It relates to issues which to them are remote, marginal to their interests and concerns.

Of all the communication methods in use, team-briefing is perhaps the most systematic in the provision of top-down information to employees. Information is disseminated or cascades through various management tiers, conveyed by the immediate supervisor or team leader to a small group of employees, the optimum number being between four and 20. In this way, too, employees' queries are answered. This takes place throughout all levels in the organisation, the information eventually being conveyed by supervisors and/or team leaders to shopfloor employees. On each occasion the information received is supplemented by 'local' news of more immediate relevance to those being briefed. Meetings tend to be short but designed to help develop the togetherness of a workgroup, especially where different grades of employees are involved in the team.

Each manager will be a member of a briefing group and be responsible also for briefing a team. The system is designed to ensure that all employees from the managing director to those on the shopfloor are fully informed of matters that affect their work. Leaders of each briefing session prepare their own briefs, consisting of information relevant and task-related to the employees in the group. The brief is then supplemented with information which has been passed down from higher levels of management. Any employee's questions raised which cannot be answered at the time are answered in written form within a few days. Briefers from senior management levels are usually encouraged to sit in at briefings being given by more junior managers, while line managers are encouraged to be available to brief the shopfloor employees. Although team-briefing is not a consultative process and is basically one-way, questions-and-answer sessions do take place to clarify understanding. Feedback from employees is very important just as professional managers will explain management's view to the employees in a regular and open way, using examples appropriate to each work group.

There are, however, practical problems to be borne in mind in introducing team-briefing. First, if the organisation operates on a continuous-shift-working basis, how is it technically feasible for team-briefings to take place when the employees are working all the time except for their rest breaks? Second, management has to be confident that it can maintain a flow of relevant and detailed information. Third, if the organisation recognises a union, the management cannot act in such a manner that the union believes management is attempting to undermine its influence. Team-briefing cannot possibly succeed if the relationships between management and the representatives of its employees are distrustful.

TASK AND WORK GROUP INVOLVEMENT

The objective of these employee involvement and participation techniques is to tap into employees' knowledge of their jobs, either at the individual level or through the mechanism of small groups. These techniques are designed to increase the stock of ideas within the organisation, to encourage co-operative relations at work and to justify change. Task-based involvement encourages employees to extend the range and type of tasks they undertake at work. It is probably the most innovative method of employee involvement, given that it focuses on the whole job rather than centring on a relatively small part of an employee's time at work. Such techniques include job re-design, job enrichment, teamworking and job enlargement. Job enrichment involves the introduction of more elements of responsibility into the work tasks. Job enlargement centres on increasing the number and diversity of tasks carried out by an individual employee, thereby increasing his or her work experience and skill.

Teamworking is seen by its advocates as a vehicle for greater task flexibility and co-operation, as well as for extending the desire for quality improvement. Geary (1994) remarks:

> In its most advanced form, teamworking refers to the granting of autonomy to workers by management to design and prepare work schedules, to monitor and control their own work tasks and methods, to be more or less self-managing. There can be considerable flexibility between different skills categories, such that skilled employees do unskilled tasks when required and formerly unskilled employees would receive additional training to be able to undertake the more skilled tasks. At the other end of the spectrum, management may merely wish employees of comparable skill to rotate between different tasks on a production line or the integration of maintenance personnel to service a particular group of machines. It may not result in production workers undertaking tasks which were formerly the preserve of craft people or vice versa. Thus, flexibility may be confined within comparable skills groupings. In between, there is likely to be a diversity of practice.

Team size is usually seven to ten, though some are much larger. Task flexibility and job rotation can, however, be limited, partly by the sheer range of tasks and partly by the nature of the skills involved. Organisations operating teamworking programmes see major training programmes as a necessary accompaniment. Teamworking provides management with the opportunity to remove and/or amend the role of the supervisor and to appoint team leaders. However, research by Grapper (1990) indicates that management time saved in traditional supervision and control may be more than offset by the need to give support to individuals and groups.

Quality circles
In a specific section of the workplace, a quality circle aims to identify work-related problems that are causing a poor quality of service or productivity, and to recommend solutions to the problems. They provide opportunities for employees to meet on a regular basis (once a month, fortnightly) for an hour or so to suggest ways of improving productivity and quality and reducing costs. They typically involve a small group of employees (usually six to eight) in discussions seeking to resolve problems which are work-related, under the guidance of their supervisor. Its members select the issues or the problem they wish to address, collect the necessary information, and suggest to management ways of overcoming the problem.

In some cases the group itself is given authority to put its proposed solutions into effect – but more often it presents formal recommendations for action, which management considers whether or not to implement. Quality circles encourage employees to identify not only with the quality of their own work but also with the management objectives of better quality and increased efficiency throughout the organisation. Members of a quality circle are not usually employee representatives but are members of the circle by virtue of their knowledge of the tasks involved in their jobs. They are under no obligation to report back to their colleagues who are not members of the circle.

If quality circles are to be effective, a strong commitment from management is necessary. Management does not supply members to a quality circle but allows time and money for its members to meet, and provides them with basic training in problem-solving and presentational skills. A professional management treats all recommendations from a circle with an open mind, and if it rejects a proposal will give its reasons for the decision to the circle. If the organisation recognises trade unions, it is advisable to consult the unions on the establishment of quality circles and to encourage their support for a device which, if operated properly, could well contribute to constructive employee relations.

After a dramatic increase in their number, by the mid-1980s over 400 quality circles were known to be in existence. Their popularity then declined rapidly. Quality circles fail either at their introduction or after a short period of operation mainly because of a lack of top management commitment, a lack of an effective facilitator to promote and sustain the programme, a management unwillingness to bear the costs of operating circles in terms of time – including training time for participants, and time when employees are off the job – and because the suggestions from circles have not been followed up and acted upon by management.

Total quality management (TQM)
Total quality management programmes derive from a belief that competitive advantage comes not simply from low cost competitiveness but from high and reliable quality, achieved through the welding together of more stable and mutual relationships between suppliers and customers. Geary (1994) points out that TQM places considerable emphasis on enlarging employees' responsibilities, reorganising work and increasing employee involvement in problem-solving activities and that this search for continuous improvement is a central thrust. He further notes:

> The manufacture of quality products, the provision of a quality service and the quest for continuous improvement is the responsibility of all employees, managed and manager alike, and all functions. TQM requires quality to be built into the product and not inspected by a separate quality department. Where employees are not in direct contact with the organisation's customers, they are encouraged to see their colleagues at successive stages of the production process as internal customers. Thus a central feature of TQM is the internalisation of the rigours of the marketplace within the enterprise.

A second feature of TQM follows on from the first. Because each employee and department is an internal customer to the others, problem-solving necessitates the formation of organisational structures designed to facilitate inter-departmental and inter-functional co-operation. A consequence of this is that problems are best solved by those people to whom they are most immediate. Employees have therefore to be encouraged and given the resources to solve problems for themselves. Employees, it is contended, will embrace such job enlargement and undertake activities conducive to an improvement in the organisation's efficiency.

Ramsay (1996) argues that total quality management subsumes quality circles or teamwork arrangements into a more integrated approach and concentrates on stressing change throughout the entire organisational system. It is essentially a top-down management-driven process. If total quality management is to succeed, again top management commitment is essential. Departments have to be persuaded that resistance to integration is self-defeating while the employees need to have demonstrated to them that total quality management is not a cover for job rationalisation and redundancies. In short, the employees require evidence there is a stake for them in the total quality management 'world'.

FINANCIAL PARTICIPATION

Financial employee involvement and participation schemes link specific elements of pay and reward to the performance of the unit or the enterprise as a whole. They provide an opportunity for employees to share in the financial success of their organisation. There are two main forms of financial participation: profit-sharing and share ownership schemes. The former involves the payment of a cash bonus from the organisation's profits to the individual employee. The latter allocates a profit bonus to individual employees in the form of capital shares in their organisation.

Profit-sharing

These schemes aim to increase employee commitment by giving employees an interest in the overall performance of the enterprise. In this way management hopes to raise employees' awareness of the importance of profit to their organisation, with the underlying motive too that rewards which accrue from co-operative effort, rather than individual effort, encourage teamwork. Profit-sharing schemes ensure that employees benefit if the organisation makes a profit.

However, there are practical problems which must be addressed if profit-sharing schemes are to have the desired effect. Any scheme has to contain clearly identifiable links between effort and reward. Individuals must not feel that, no matter how hard they work in any year, that effort is not reflected in their share of the company's profits. There is also the issue of whether there is a clearly understood formula for the sharing of any profits so that employees can calculate their share often. Profits cannot be assessed quickly enough to secure early movements in pay in response to rapidly changing market conditions. Due account has to be taken of employee feelings of equity and fairness, or there is a risk of inter-group dissatisfaction in that some employees might believe that other groups have made less effort but received the same profit-share payment.

Share ownership

Share ownership takes financial involvement a step further by giving employees a stake in the ownership of the enterprise. It grants them shareholder rights to participate in decisions confined to shareholders who vote at the annual general meeting. Employee share ownership schemes seek to give individual employees a long-term commitment to the organisation and not just a short-term financial gain from a sharing of profit. Such schemes are usually linked to profit but the employee's portion is distributed in the form of shares, either directly to each individual or indirectly into a trust which holds the shares on behalf of all employees. Shares distributed to employees involve them in a tax liability, which formerly restricted the development of employee share ownership schemes. One way of avoiding this tax liability is employee share ownership plans (known as ESOP), which were given a boost when the UK Government provided important tax concessions for investment in such schemes in the late 1980s.

In employee share ownership plans the company shares are initially bought, using borrowed money, by a trust representing the employees. The employees may not be required to put down a cash stake. The transfer of a portion of the company profits to the trust over subsequent years, as laid down in the initial agreement, enables the trust to pay off the loan and to allocate shares to individual employees.

Employee share ownership plans are clearly a means of promoting employee involvement in ownership. They give individual employees democratic control over significant holdings of company shares. They also have limitations. Employees may view the shares as simply a source of income, which of course undermines the 'shared ownership' concept. Financial participation on its own is unlikely to give rise to a greater commitment on the part of the individual employee to the interests of the organisation.

Do you have any employee involvement schemes in your organisation? If you do, why have those particular schemes been chosen? To what extent and why are they effective?

REPRESENTATIVE PARTICIPATION

The main form of representative participation is joint consultation, which is a process in which management and employees or their representatives jointly examine and discuss issues of mutual concern. It involves seeking acceptable solutions to problems through a genuine exchange of views and information. Consultation does not remove the right of management to manage – it must still make the final decision – but it does impose an obligation that the views of employees will be sought and considered before final decisions are taken. We saw that employee communication is concerned with the interchange of information and ideas within an organisation. Consultation goes beyond this and involves managers who actively seek and then take account of the views of employees before making a decision. It affects the process through which decisions are made in so far as it commits management first to the disclosure of information at an early stage in the decision-making process, and second to take into account the collective views of the employees.

Consultation does not meant that employees' views always have to be acted on: there may be good practical or financial reasons for not doing so. However, whenever employees' views are rejected, the reasons for it should be carefully explained. Equally, where the views and ideas of employees help to improve a decision, due credit and recognition should be given. Making a practice of consulting on issues that management has already decided is unproductive and engenders suspicion and mistrust about the process amongst employees.

Consultation requires a free exchange of ideas and views affecting the interests of employees. Almost any subject is appropriate for discussion. However, both management and trade unions may wish to place some limits on the range of subjects open to consultation – for example, because of trade confidences, or because some topics are considered more appropriate for a negotiation forum. But, whatever issues are agreed upon as appropriate for discussion, it is important that they are relevant to the group of employees that will be discussing them. If consultation arrangements are to be effective it is important to avoid discussing trivialities. This is not to say that minor issues should be ignored. Although the subject matters of consultation are a matter for agreement between employer and employees, there are a number of issues upon which employers are legally required to consult with recognised trade unions. These are:

- the Health and Safety at Work Act (1974), which places a duty on employers to consult with safety representatives appointed by an independent, recognised trade union

- the Transfer of Undertakings (Protection of Employment) Regulations (1981), which provide for trade unions to be consulted where there is a transfer of a business to which the regulations apply; this consultation must take place with a view to reaching agreement on the measures taken

- the Trade Union and Labour Relations (Consolidation) Act (1992), which requires employers to consult with trade unions when redundancies are proposed; such consultation must be undertaken by the employer with a view to reaching agreement and must be about possible ways of avoiding the dismissals, minimising the numbers to be dismissed, and mitigating the consequences of any redundancies

- the Social Security Pensions Act (1975), which requires employers to consult with trade unions on certain matters in relation to contracting-out of the state scheme for an occupational pension.

Joint Consultative Committees (JCCs) or works councils as they are sometimes known, have long been used as a method of employee consultation. They are composed of managers and employee representatives who come together on a regular basis to discuss issues of mutual concern. They usually have a formal constitution which governs their operations. The number of members in a JCC will vary depending on the size of the organisation. However, as a general rule the size of the committee should be as small as possible, consistent with ensuring that all significant employee groups are represented. In order to demonstrate management's commitment to consultation, it is necessary that the management representatives on the committee include senior managers with authority and standing in the organisation and who regularly attend its meetings.

Every meeting of the JCC should have as its focus a well-prepared agenda, and all members should be given an opportunity to contribute to the agenda before it is circulated. The agenda should be sent out in advance of the meeting so that representatives have an opportunity to consult with their constituents prior to the committee meeting. A JCC needs to be well chaired if it is to be run effectively. It is important that employee representatives know exactly how much time they will be allowed away from their normal work to undertake their duties as committee members, and what facilities they are entitled to use. Employee representatives need to be reassured that they will not lose pay as a result of attending committee meetings. If joint consultation is to be effective, the deliberations of the committee should be reported back to employees as soon as possible. This can be done via briefing groups, news-sheets, noticeboards and the circulation of committee minutes.

> Do JCCs exist in your organisation? If so, what forms do they take, and are they successful? How could they be improved? If there are no JCCs, what mechanisms are in place to consult with the workforce? Would a JCC be useful? Why/why not?

THE INTRODUCTION OF EMPLOYEE INVOLVEMENT AND PARTICIPATION SCHEMES

In implementing employee involvement and participation schemes, employee relations managers will be mindful that different organisations operate under very different environmental circumstances, and that what is good for one may not necessarily be appropriate for another. There are a number of necessary conditions to be met if employee involvement and participation arrangements are to be successfully implemented and operated. First, a good employee relations climate is essential. Second, if a strong commitment to the introduction and operation of the schemes is not forthcoming from top management, there is little likelihood that the schemes will have much chance of survival beyond their initial establishment. If such commitment is forthcoming, there is a greater likelihood that there will be a free flow of information up, down and across the organisation, that employee involvement mechanisms appropriate to the organisation's needs will be selected, and that the impact of the operation of the schemes on the value and credibility of other employee

Figure 4 **Conditions for the successful implementation of employee involvement and participation schemes**

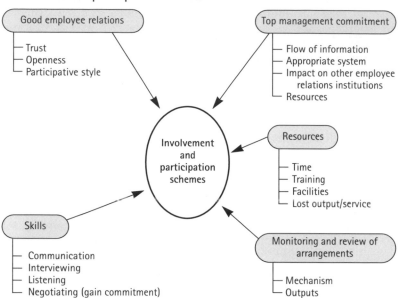

relations institutions and procedures will be protected. A management prepared to commit resources in terms of time, lost wages, training, facilities and lost output/service to support the operation of employee involvement schemes is increasing the probability that they will be successful. Appropriate mechanisms to review and monitor the operation of employee involvement and participation arrangements, to ensure they are achieving their objectives, is also a necessary condition. However, it is not a condition sufficient on its own to improve their chances of success. Management requires the skills of oral and written communication, interviewing, listening and team-building. It also needs negotiating skills to gain the commitment of managerial colleagues and the workforce to the implementation of the employee involvement and participation schemes selected. Without management and employee commitment, employee involvement and participation schemes will not survive very long.

Let us now look at these conditions in more detail.

Good employee relations
Employee involvement and participation schemes are more likely to be effective if there is a willingness on the part of both management and employees/union to be open in their attitude and behaviour. Employee involvement and commitment will not be gained in an atmosphere of lack of trust or motivation. Effective schemes require 'openness' and trust of each other on the part of employees and employers. They cannot operate effectively in a background of disputes and confrontation. If there is insufficient motivation on the part of management and employees to make involvement and participation techniques work, or there is insufficient mutual trust to allow them to,

it is this lack that is more likely to be the cause of their failure than the substance of the arrangements. If management introduces employee involvement and participation schemes but shortly afterwards changes its management style to one that is less open and participative, the employees are likely to regard this behaviour as an attempt by management deliberately to sabotage the schemes. Employee scepticism towards employee involvement and participation schemes will emerge and the schemes will be less effective.

Good employee relations is thus a necessary precondition for effective employee involvement and participation schemes. An open style of management in which employee support for the proposed action is gained by consent, and not coercion, is essential. However, by itself a good employee relations environment is not a sufficient condition for the successful implementation and operation of involvement and participation schemes. Implementation and operation also require unquestioning commitment from top management.

Commitment by top management
This is a key condition but again is not sufficient on its own to deliver effective involvement and participation schemes. Such schemes are likely never really to be effective unless top management, by its own behaviour, visibly demonstrates a belief in them; top management's commitment requires not only to be felt positively but to be seen to be so by employees. All managers should accept the value of employee involvement and participation schemes and not give the impression they are supporting a fad in management practice or are spouting rhetoric behind which there is no substance. While a good committee structure may be important for some participation schemes, it is totally irrelevant if individual managers are not committed to their success. Support for introducing employee involvement and participation needs to be secured throughout the whole management structure. If management is not committed to their success, employees will view the arrangements as a 'tokenism' and not as genuine attempts to gain their commitment, loyalty and support.

If managers wish employee involvement schemes to succeed, they must ensure that there is no loss of momentum following the initial enthusiasm of their introduction. Management commitment has to last longer than just the introduction of schemes – many are costly in management time if they are not run properly. Nothing destroys employee participation schemes more quickly than management action that is inconsistent with the philosophy of worker involvement. This is particularly so when management's behaviour conveys to the employees that it really considers employment involvement and participation of little significance, something that is hastily set aside when short-term production/service provision pressure to meet customers' needs arises. Care must be exercised by management in deciding the timing of meetings. If they are scheduled late on a Friday afternoon and there is little opportunity to explore issues in sufficient depth, employees will question management's commitment to employee involvement as a means of improving management decision-making. The same applies if employees feel that their views do not really count when they find their contributions are dismissed without serious examination.

Two important causes of failure of employee involvement and participation schemes are the attitudes of middle and lower managers to such schemes and what Marchington (1993) calls the 'lack of continuity caused by the dynamic career patterns of managers who are the driving force behind the schemes'. Middle and supervisory management often lack commitment to, and support for, the development of employee involvement and participation schemes. Some regard them as mechanisms by which senior/top managers 'pander' to the employees and their representatives, and which at the same time undermine supervisory authority over employees. They perceive top management in supporting employee involvement and participation, as being 'soft' on employees whom they perceive as only too pleased to be paid while not working, and who, as a result, will always have issues they want to discuss with employers.

In large multi-divisional firms, managers frequently expect to stay at an establishment for only a short period of time; their time there is regarded as part of the development package en route to senior management positions. Marchington (1993) refers to this phenomenon as the 'mobile champion', reflecting a picture of the manager who introduces a scheme then moves on to other duties, frequently at another site, or to employment elsewhere. The successor often has different priorities and any employee involvement scheme that was the 'baby' of the predecessor lapses because of operational difficulties or because the successor sees no kudos forthcoming from his or her senior managers in administering another individual's creation.

The introduction of employee involvement and participation arrangements on the basis of fashion and fad will quickly create feelings of disillusionment amongst employees, and feelings too that management has no real focus to its current and future activities. A management committed to employee involvement, however is highly unlikely to select arrangements on the basis of fad rather than on what is appropriate to the organisation's commercial and business needs. Proper analysis of the objectives desired from any participation arrangements before their introduction should prevent any possible confusion or conflict between the arrangements introduced. This is particularly important when the organisation is introducing a multiplicity of schemes. Rather than just select any scheme, it can be helpful to management to give extremely careful consideration on how it will apply and modify any schemes introduced to the needs of the workplace. Schemes which are 'customised' (see above) offer better prospects for success than those that are lifted down from the shelf and which may clash with production or service provision considerations.

An all too common mistake made by management when introducing involvement and participation schemes is that management becomes seduced by the prevalence of public relations accounts into believing that any scheme introduced is a panacea that will solve product market problems. The impact of employee involvement and participation in securing a positive change in employee attitudes and behaviour is less profound and permanent than is often claimed if the schemes selected turn out to be inappropriate to that organisation's needs. The inappropriate choice of systems is most noticeable, Marchington (1993) claims, amongst companies which bring in consultants to advise them on how to implement a new scheme without establishing its relevance or purpose. A company might decide to introduce a system of monthly team-briefings. However, it is a waste of time to do so without having assessed whether there will be sufficient information to sustain meetings on that basis or whether the supervisor has the necessary skills or motivation to make them work. This difficult problem becomes further complicated if different management functions or levels in the management structure have a responsibility for introducing employee involvement, often at the same time and with conflicting objectives. Such a situation arises especially in service-sector companies, where the issue of customer care often falls within the province of both the personnel and the marketing departments.

A management fully committed to employee involvement and participation will ensure that those participating in such schemes have access to a free flow of information to enable them to operate effectively. This flow of information is most effective if it is up, down and across the organisation. A willingness to listen, evaluate and act on views expressed by employees at all levels is a sensible approach. There are many traps into which management can fall with respect to the information it makes available in the workplace to participants in the employee involvement schemes. Management needs to strike a balance between providing too little information and providing too much information. Otherwise, employees can become confused. Managers have to avoid too much 'tell and sell' because that triggers employee mistrust of involvement and participation schemes, especially if most information is bad news and is accompanied by rallying calls for belt-tightening and restraint.

Effective employment involvement and participation involves two-way communication. To focus on downwards communication carries the risk that employees and/or their representatives might feel they are being informed of changes or decisions only after the event, rather than before. This may seem an obvious statement, but unfortunately commonsense is not common practice for many managers. A further problem that management faces is the tendency for employee involvement and participation schemes to regress, rather than grow and develop, from their original position with respect to their expected objectives. Several involvement and participation schemes that are successful in one organisation have come apart in another because in the latter their scope collapsed to the level of 'canteen tea discussions syndrome'. When the subjects discussed become non-controversial or less interesting, employee indifference – if not scepticism – develops. Given that employees are the principal objects and recipients of many employee involvement and participation schemes, this is potentially perhaps the most common cause of failure. A management fully committed to involvement and participation, introducing it for the right reasons, and having selected the schemes appropriate for its business objectives, will provide no opportunities for employee sceptism to occur.

A professional management will also ensure that participation schemes do not become ineffective because their operation produces adverse impacts on the workings of other employee relations institutions in the organisation. Some of the most successful involvement and participation programmes have been established in unionised companies with the joint involvement of management and unions. In contrast, arrangements set up independently of trade unions, where they are recognised and are fully representative of their members' views, have often led to difficulties. This can happen because unions – especially those which are weakly organised – regard the introduction of an independent system of employee involvement as an attempt to bypass them and undermine its relationship with its members. In strongly unionised organisations, involvement and participation schemes are unlikely to be used to undermine the normal bargaining process with the trade unions. Attempts to bypass or undermine established trade union channels are likely to backfire and founder on union opposition taken to the point of withdrawal – for example, a refusal to sit at the same table as non-unionists. In non-union companies, the danger that employee involvement schemes may adversely effect other employee relations institutions is less likely to be a potential hazard for management.

A management committed to employee involvement and participation will adopt an open and participative style of management, will select appropriate schemes tailored to the organisation's needs, will ensure there is a full flow of information up, down and across the organisation, and will commit the necessary resources in terms of time, finances, paid time off for employees, and people and physical assets to support the operation of participation schemes.

Resources

If employee involvement and participation schemes are to be effective, resources are required to meet the direct and indirect costs (time lost, production/service foregone, meetings, training, paid leave, etc) associated with introducing, operating and maintaining them. An uncommitted management is likely to regard them as a cost without any benefit and seek to ensure that there is insufficient business to be discussed by those participating in the schemes. The employee relations manager has an obligation to persuade his or her colleagues to view employee involvement and participation schemes in a positive light, and to educate them as to the value they can add to the business if they are embraced by all levels of management.

The impact of employee involvement schemes is often diminished by a lack of skills or knowledge on the part of the participants. It is important, therefore, to provide both managers and employees with training in the skills required to operate involvement and participation schemes in an effective way. This involves acquiring and developing skills of chairing meetings so that people keep to the agenda, bringing out suggestions and ensuring that employees' contributions are appropriate to the subject matter under discussion. Managers also need training in presentational skills to present information by word of mouth or in writing and through the use of visual aids. In addition, they require interviewing skills to be able to question employees to gain information and seek clarification of employee views. Listening skills are essential, for consultation involves management's listening to what the employees have to say. In participating in involvement schemes managers therefore need to limit their contributions and let the employees do most of the talking. By listening, employers acquire additional information. Managers also require the skills of negotiation to gain the commitment of their managerial colleagues, at all levels, and in all functions, and of the workforce for the effective operation of employee involvement and participation mechanisms. If an organisation's management provides training for its managers and employees to prepare them to participate in employee involvement schemes, it is best practice periodically to evaluate the effectiveness of any training undertaken.

Spending resources on training for all involved in the operation of employee involvement and participation schemes is an investment by management. It demonstrates openly to all concerned its commitment to the schemes. To do otherwise invites employee disillusionment with the schemes. A serious and continuing commitment to employee involvement is not easy to achieve and requires significant support from the highest levels of management. The gaining of employee commitment, via employee participation and involvement, is a time-consuming process. It is much easier to undermine the operation of the schemes than to continue them. Financial resources are necessary to ensure that training is executed effectively and efficiently, and that sufficient time, balanced against production and customer service needs, is set aside for joint consultation meetings, briefing groups and regular management walkabouts, etc.

Management needs to be alert to the potential problems that face employees and/or their representatives operating in participation arrangements. For example, employees may lack knowledge of the subjects under discussion and may have problems in coping with the social situation of rubbing shoulders with top management. They may also experience undue pressure from their constituents who have an unreal expectation of what employee involvement and participation schemes can achieve in protecting and advancing the interests of the employees. A professional management will assist employee representatives and individual employees to overcome these problems by providing them with the necessary facilities to keep communication channels open between themselves and their constituents. It is of little value to an organisation committed to employee involvement schemes to have employee representatives who are unable to represent their members or to report back to them, or to have union representatives that suspect management is really opposed to their activities.

Monitoring and review arrangements
The establishment of mechanisms for the regular monitoring and reviewing of the operation of employee involvement and participation schemes is essential. Monitoring takes place to assess whether the schemes are producing the desired outputs of improved efficiency,

productivity, quality of service, a greater willingness on the part of employees to accept change, etc. The effectiveness of employee involvement and participation mechanisms is measured against the outputs of their operation in terms of contributing to the achievement of the overall objectives of the organisation. The outcomes of the operation of the schemes are, thus, the important criteria against which their effectiveness must be judged.

Assessing effectiveness in this way precludes the deception of management and employees into accepting a public relations image of what is no more than an alleged success of the operation of employee involvement. Nevertheless, it is not easy to quantify the contribution of employee involvement and participation schemes to the achievement of corporate objectives. There are problems of identifying appropriate benchmarks and isolating the influence of other factors.

The results of any monitoring exercise are best discussed with employee representatives and, where appropriate, recognised trade unions. If the monitoring process exposes weaknesses, remedial action should be taken as soon as possible. Regular monitoring and review also enables an organisation to assess the cost-effectiveness of its employee involvement and participation schemes.

FURTHER READING

GEARY J. F. 'Task participation: employees' participation enabled or constrained', in K. Sisson (ed.) *Personnel Management*, 2nd edn, Oxford, Blackwell, 1994.

MARCHINGTON M. 'The dynamics of joint consultation' in K. Sisson (ed.) *Personnel Management*, 2nd edn, Oxford, Blackwell, 1994.

TOWNLEY B. 'Communicating with employees' in K. Sisson (ed.), *Personnel Management*, 2nd edn, Blackwell, 1994.

Part 4

MANAGING EMPLOYEE RELATIONS

6 Negotiating skills

THE PURPOSE OF NEGOTIATION

Negotiation involves the coming together of two parties (such as individuals, companies, employers, trade unions, employee representatives) to confer with a view to making a jointly acceptable agreement. It is a process whereby management, as the purchaser of labour services, resolves its conflict of interests with its employees, as the sellers of labour services, over the 'price' at which labour services are to be exchanged. Both parties must understand what they have jointly agreed, or they run the risk of frequently differing with each other over whether they are correctly applying and/or interpreting what has been agreed. Making an agreement means that the parties have a commitment to operate under its terms until they agree jointly to change it. The agreement must be capable of standing the test of time.

Negotiation involves two main elements: purposeful persuasion, and constructive compromise. Each party attempts to persuade the other by using arguments backed by factual information and analysis as to why they should accept their case (request). However, the probability that one party can persuade the other to accept its case (request) completely is extremely low. If an agreement is to be reached, both parties must move closer towards each other's position. To achieve this, they must identify common ground within and between their positions. Constructive compromises can then be made within these limits. Compromise is only possible if sufficient common ground exists between the two parties. The overriding objective of any negotiation is for the parties to reach an agreement and not to score debating points or save the face of one or both parties.

After you have read this chapter, you should be able to

• understand the different negotiating situations in which a management may find itself

Figure 5 **The purpose of negotiation**

```
┌─────────────────────────────────┐
│   Negotiation:                  │
└─────────────────────────────────┘
  │
  │ is the coming together of two parties (social inter-action)
  │ to confer with a view to making a jointly acceptable
  │ agreement.
  │
  │   Negotiation involves
  │
  │   • purposeful persuasion
  │   • constructive compromise
  │
```

- explain how employee relations negotiations differ from commercial negotiations

- identify the different stages in the negotiating process

- understand the steps involved in preparing for negotiations

- explain the activities involved in conducting and concluding negotiations

- understand the skills required by an employee relations manager involved in the negotiation process.

This chapter provides an overview to the negotiation process. Chapter 8 deals in more detail with managing employee grievances, and Chapter 9 does the same with bargaining.

There are methods other than negotiation by which an agreement between employers and employees can be reached. We saw in Chapter 5 that consultation involves a willingness by the employer to exchange information and views with trade unions or other bodies who represent the interests of employees. Management gives full consideration to their views whilst reserving the right to implement a decision without their formal agreement. Where negotiations fail to produce an agreement it is, in certain circumstances, possible for an employer, with the consent of the other party, to achieve this objective via an arbitrator's award which then becomes the 'agreement' between the parties. An agreement between employers and employees can be made by the former's imposing one on the latter. If one party, for whatever reason, accepts the right of the other to make unilateral decisions, then negotiation has no place in their relationship. Whether they accept this situation voluntarily or through a fear of the consequences of not doing so makes no difference because one party has been given, or has taken, unilateral rights over the other.

The purpose of negotiation is to solve a problem – but there are circumstances in which the parties might not find it possible to reach an agreement. The interests of the parties will be irreconcilable if one sees its difference with the other as being a matter of principle upon which it cannot compromise. This would be the case where one party views the other's behaviour as in breach of an existing agreement to which they have both given their word. For example, in the 1996 London Underground dispute, the Rail, Maritime and Transport Union members undertook industrial action because they claimed London Underground had broken an agreement to reduce the working week. A fundamental principle of any agreement is that in accepting the agreement both sides trust each other to keep to its terms. If one side does not keep its word on one aspect of the agreement, how can it be trusted to keep its word on other aspects of that agreement? Parties to an agreement have to accept all the terms of that agreement. They cannot pick and choose which parts they will accept and implement and which part they will reject and refuse to implement. To act in breach of an agreement is probably the worst employee relations sin that can be committed.

An agreement between employer and employee may also not be possible if the employer thinks that granting the union's claim (for example, for a 35-hour working week or six weeks paid holidays) will increase the company's labour costs so significantly that its product market competitiveness will be undermined. A further set of circumstances in which an agreement may not be possible is where one party does not have the authority to settle and has to seek consent from a higher level of management or trade union. A failure to reach agreement can also arise where one party is over-confident and regards making concessions to the other party as unnecessary because it believes its own superior position/arguments will eventually prevail. Other situations management needs to avoid if it is to negotiate an acceptable settlement with its employees include: becoming unjustifiably committed to an extreme position; a clash of personalities with a member, or members, of the other party; having to deal with a party that is unreasonable, dishonest or not negotiating in good faith; and becoming involved with a party whose ability to deliver its part of the agreement is questionable. Many of these potential non-agreement situations are avoidable if management develops an understanding of its employees (ie knows how they are likely to react to situations) and their representatives, and if it prepares properly for negotiations.

DIFFERENT TYPES OF NEGOTIATING SITUATIONS

Figure 6 identifies four main types of negotiating situations. Two – grievance-handling and intra-/inter-management – involve negotiation to resolve an issue that is normally confined to an individual. However, if an individual worker's concerns are not handled with care they can develop into an issue of concern to a group as a whole. The other two situations – bargaining and group problem-solving – involve negotiation to resolve issues which are normally of concern to a collective group of employees. However, bargaining can, and does, take place between management and individual employees, resulting in employment on the basis of a personal contract.

Between individual members of management
The most common negotiating situation in which employee relations managers are likely to find themselves in is the one shown in the top right-hand quadrant of Figure 5 – negotiation with and between

Figure 6 **Different types of negotiating situations**

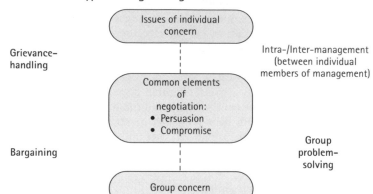

management colleagues. Every day managers find themselves negotiating with their colleagues, either in the same management function or in another management function (eg marketing, finance, sales, operations management). These managers will be of the same, higher or lower status than themselves. The negotiations will be over issues such as suggested courses of action (eg how to deal with an employee complaint against management behaviour), the introduction of new employment practices and procedures (eg the introduction of a new incentive scheme), and the allocation of additional financial, staffing and equipment resources to support the people function.

Two or more employee relations managers may have differing views on how a problem should or might be resolved. One employee relations manager will seek purposefully to persuade the others of the merits of his or her proposed solution to the problem. If other managers disagree with their colleague's approach, they will seek to persuade their managerial colleague to accept or adopt a different way of proceeding to resolve the problem. If managers with different views and approaches cannot persuade each other to accept their own favourite solution to the problem, they will have to make constructive compromises (move closer to each other's preferred course of action) if an agreed management position on how the problem might be resolved is to be achieved.

If two or more employee relations managers cannot agree how a problem may best be resolved, then a senior manager will intervene and decide how management wants it solved. Employee relations managers will also be frequently participating in negotiations with senior managers to gain their support to make resources available to implement new policies, procedures and practices that they have devised on their own initiative or at the request of a more senior manager. Negotiation between managers involves parties who are protecting the same economic and political interest, and the style of negotiations will be friendly and constructive.

Managers in any management function and at any level of seniority cannot assume that their intended actions, policies and arrangements will be accepted without question by their management colleagues. There is likely to be some opposition from management colleagues who have different interests and priorities. If unanimous management commitment to and support for a proposed course of action (eg a major change of policy, such as to recognise or de-recognise a trade union) is to be gained, it has therefore to be achieved by intra- and inter-management negotiation. So we see that negotiation is not, as is popularly thought, an activity confined to relationships between managers and employees and their trade unions or other representative bodies. It is an activity in which all managers are involved daily. Negotiations take place day in and day out between managers of different and similar levels of executive authority and between different managers from different management functions. Nevertheless, some managers have difficulty in treating these intra- and inter-management relationships as negotiating situations and prefer to think of the process as 'influencing others'.

> When were you last involved in a negotiating situation in which the other party was a management colleague? What arguments did you use to persuade him or her that your view of handling the problem might be the right one? What counter-arguments did he or she put forward? How were your differences of approach to solving the problem overcome?

Grievance-handling

A grievance is a complaint, real or ill-founded, laid by an employee against the behaviour of the management. A complaint by the management against the behaviour of an employee is referred to as a disciplinary issue. Complaints about management behaviour tend to come from individual employees and can range over a wide range of issues. Examples include a bonus payment that has been calculated incorrectly, a disciplinary penalty imposed that is too harsh, promotion that has been unreasonably denied, access to a training opportunity that has been denied, a job that is currently under-graded, the sexual harassment of one employee by a senior employee, and insufficient car-parking spaces in the company car park. Although complaints about management behaviour usually come from individual employees, if they are not handled sensitively they can develop into collective employee complaints.

In handling grievances, management treats each on its merits, appreciating that an individual's grievance is an important and serious issue for that person even though it may seem trivial to management. In resolving an employee's grievances, management has to proceed on a one-by-one basis. It settles one person's grievance before moving on to resolve that of the next person. Management cannot offer to settle one person's grievance in exchange for getting other employees to agree to drop their grievances. In grievance-handling neither management nor employee representative takes part in 'trading' (ie you drop that grievance and we shall accept another employee's grievance). A professional manager will not fall into the trap and be dragged into a situation of dealing simultaneously with a list of grievances from a number of employees. He or she will deal with them sequentially, one at a time.

Chapter 1 showed that according to WIRS (1990) most organisations have grievance procedures. Employee relations managers need to be knowledgeable about those procedures. When an employee raises a grievance against management behaviour, it does not automatically start up the procedures. Indeed, the vast majority of grievances are resolved outside the procedure in an informal manner. Employee grievances usually revolve around the interpretation and/or application of particular 'rules', procedures and practice.

Some employees who have a grievance against management may not initiate the grievance procedure because they fear (rightly or wrongly) that to do so may result in the management's initiating some adverse action against them (eg overlook them for promotion or a merit payment). Grievances can thus fester and remain hidden. This is not a situation which management can allow to continue. Employees need to feel confident that management will see their grievances as important and will be dealt with quickly, fairly and consistently. A professional management prefers employees to bring their individual complaints about management behaviour into the open. To this end they will create an environment in which employees feel they can bring up grievances confident that they will be dealt with in a fair and consistent manner.

Bargaining

Bargaining is a situation where the parties involved have a 'shopping list' of demands to make of each other. One party (usually the employees collectively) proposes a list of improvements to employment conditions – a pay rise, a shorter working week, longer holidays, etc – while the other responds with counter-proposals such as changes in working practices, changes in the pattern of working hours, etc. In a bargaining situation, unlike a grievance-handling one, 'trading' takes place over the items that have been flagged up for negotiation. Identifying which items in their shopping lists the parties are prepared to trade is a key activity in bargaining. The aim of the parties is to use trading to advance or protect their own interests and thus to create new 'prices' (new rules) at which labour services will be bought and sold.

Bargaining is about trading with the other party and not about conceding to the other party. Something is gained in return for trading something. However, there are bargaining situations – especially in the public sector – where an employer gives pay increases to the employees who trade nothing in return. For example, the pay increase is given to the workforce to compensate for an increase in the Index of Retail Prices. In a bargaining situation, the parties are seeking to defend and enhance their economic interests. The tenor and style of negotiations is likely to be relatively more adversarial than in other negotiating situations.

In most academic literature the words 'negotiation' and 'bargaining' are taken to mean one and the same thing. This is incorrect.

Bargaining is only one of a number of different types of negotiating situations in which a management might find itself. Bargaining is usually a process for changing employment conditions. It is a means of creating new employment rules. Negotiation is any situation in which two parties come together to make a mutually acceptable agreement by purposeful persuasion and constructive compromise.

Explain the difference between grievance-handling and bargaining.

Group/joint problem-solving

This is a situation in which two or more parties negotiate the details whereon they will co-operate with each other to resolve a problem which is of common interest to them. For example, an organisation may be performing reasonably well in terms of sales, profitability, etc, but recognise that in the near future product market competition will become more intense. The top management decides it needs now to consider possible policy initiatives that might now be implemented to offset any adverse consequences in terms of sales, etc, when the greater product market competition becomes a reality. As a first step, the organisation may decide to invite a team of consultants to examine its work organisation and systems to produce a feasibility study on what action or policies it might introduce to improve its future product market competitiveness. The management of the organisation will have decided to take no action on the outside advisers' report without consultation and discussion with the workforce. If the consultants are to gain full information to produce their report they will need to speak to the workforce. Management requires the full co-operation of the workforce with the work of the outside consultants. The workforce has an interest in the organisation's efficiency improving because that enhances their job security. It therefore has an interest in co-operating with the consultants. However, it may have objections to the firm of consultants to be used and of some of the methods whereby the consultants are to go about their work. The workforce is not against the use of consultants as a matter of principle.

The negotiations between the employer and the unions will centre on the details of the conditions upon which the workforce will co-operate fully with the work of the consultants to enable them to produce a report which will be helpful to both the employer and the employees in their common interest to improve the organisation's future competitiveness. Management will be seeking the co-operation of its workforce to some proposed action to gain information which can then be used to solve a problem as a result of which there will be mutual gain. In group problem-solving negotiating situations, management is normally seeking the support and co-operation of its workforce to gain information upon which proposed action can be based and from which both will gain mutual advantage. The management negotiating style will not be adversarial. Management will offer 'carrots' to its employees' representatives to gain their co-operation with its own proposed action. To bang the table and to be insulting to the employee representatives would be inappropriate to the situation and unlikely to secure the management's objective of gaining employee co-operation with its proposed action.

Attempts to change the negotiating situation

The four main negotiating situations set out in Figure 5 are all different: each is conducted by the parties involved in a different style with different attitudes. It is important that management is clear about which negotiating situation it is in, adopts the appropriate style, and resists attempts by the other party to drag it into a different negotiating situation where that party feels more comfortable. For if either party feels uncomfortable (or on the defensive) in a particular negotiating situation, it will try to change the attitudes and approach of the other party. Efforts will be made to switch the negotiations from their present situation to a different one in which that party feels more confident and in which the attitudes of the parties towards each other is changed. For example, if management is handling an employee grievance and the employee and his or her representative see their case is not as strong as they had thought, then in an effort to strengthen their position they may introduce a whole list of other grievances which other employees have against the employer.

By behaving in this way, the employee is attempting to shift the negotiations from a grievance handling situation to a bargaining situation. He or she hopes to lull the employer into falling into the trap of trading grievances ('I'll let you win this grievance if you will drop that grievance') instead of dealing with each one on its merits independent of the others. Management needs to concentrate carefully when involved in grievance-handling to watch for such behaviour by the employee and/or the representative. If the employee and/or the representative try to change the focus of the negotiations, management should politely inform them that they are in a grievance-handling, and not a bargaining, situation. Management would then tell the union that it was prepared to discuss the additional grievances raised, but on another occasion, and that for the moment management was prepared to deal with only the specific grievance under negotiation.

The tactic whereby one of the negotiating parties attempts to influence the expectations of the other is also commonly used prior to the start of bargaining. Before negotiations begin in companies over the annual pay increase, for example, it is not uncommon for management to make a statement designed to lower the expectations of its employees over what improvements in conditions might be achieved. The statement will stress intensifying product market competition, the squeeze on its profits and increased labour costs. Such statements are likely to imply that any improvements in employment conditions will be small and will have to be self-financed by increased labour productivity. Trade unions also engage in such behaviour prior to bargaining. It is not uncommon for them to issue a statement that their members are so outraged by their declining relative pay that they must be given a significant pay increase and a share in the increased prosperity of the enterprise (or industry) or it will be difficult for the unions to control them. These statements prior to negotiations are usually rhetoric rather than substance, and are part of the ritual that accompanies bargaining (see below).

INDUSTRIAL NEGOTIATIONS v COMMERCIAL NEGOTIATIONS

Industrial negotiating situations are very different from commercial contract negotiations. Many managers outside of the employee relations function find it difficult to understand why industrial negotiators go through the ritual they do, and why they take so long to conclude their deal. It is important that employee relations managers understand *how* employee relations negotiations are different from commercial contract ones.

The main differences between industrial and commercial negotiations are:

• Industrial negotiations involve an on-going relationship.

• Industrial negotiations are carried out by representatives.

• Industrial negotiations are always conducted on a face-to-face basis.

• Industrial negotiations do not result in legally enforceable contracts.

• Industrial negotiations make more frequent use of adjournments.

Commercial negotiations tend to be conducted on a more polite basis than in grievance-handling or bargaining situations. In commercial negotiations, purchasers tend to buy from individuals or organisations they prefer while sellers can give preferential deals to those they like. In industrial negotiations, the parties cannot deal only with those they prefer. Each party selects its own representatives. Both parties have to develop a professional relationship towards each other regardless of their feelings towards each other. Industrial negotiations are always conducted by representatives of the parties who must report back to their constituents. Commercial contract negotiators are accountable not to constituents but usually to a line manager.

Management may dislike the employee representatives. This should not prevent it from developing a professional respect for them and dealing with them, in negotiating situations, on the basis of equal status. Management represents the employer's interests. The employee representatives represent those of their members. Both sides in industrial negotiations are of equal status. Dealing with employees on the basis of equality is difficult for some managers to accept because they are used to instructing members of the employees' side in the work situation. They cannot distinguish between dealing with employees as representatives of the workforce and dealing with employees as employees under their supervision. This equality of status of negotiators is discussed further in Chapter 8.

Many negotiations in the commercial field do not take place on a face-to-face basis. They may be held by telephone (eg tele-ad sales for newspapers) or even by letter. Industrial negotiators always meet on a face-to-face basis. The use of adjournments is less common in commercial negotiations than in industrial ones. In this latter case management (or union) negotiators may adjourn several times during bargaining, but usually on fewer occasions than in grievance-handling, to consider a union (or management) proposal. Adjournments enable the parties to obtain more information, to reassess their objectives, aims, strategy and tactics, to regroup as a team where negotiations are being conducted via working parties, to gather and analyse new information, and, on occasions, to allow emotions to calm down.

A very important difference between industrial and commercial negotiation is the legal status of the agreement that emerges. In the commercial world the contract agreeing the conditions of the sale is legally binding and its conditions can be enforced via the courts. The agreement that emerges from industrial negotiations, as we saw in Chapter 1 is not legally binding but binding in honour only. Neither party can enforce its rights as contained in the agreement via the courts.

Industrial negotiations take place against an assumption that the parties have to have an on-going relationship. When the negotiations are over, the parties who have met on a basis of equality have to meet again the next day and continue their employer-employee relationship in which the latter is in a subordinate position relative to the former. Industrial negotiators, unlike commercial contract negotiators, cannot simply walk away from the party with whom they are currently dealing and make a more favourable agreement with another party. The continuous relationship between industrial negotiators at the workplace acts as a restraining influence on their behaviour during and after the negotiations. Each party must retain its dignity and self-respect relative to the other. Management needs to avoid any implication that the negotiated outcome indicates that the employee or the trade union has 'lost' while management has 'won'. Once the negotiations have been concluded, regardless of the outcome, the parties have to return to a constructive working relationship as soon as possible. For management to use its 'victory' over its employees to humiliate them is not constructive behaviour. The result will be decreased employee morale, increased absenteeism and a reduced quality of product or service. In industrial negotiations, unlike commercial contract ones, the negotiators have always to bear in mind the importance of preserving the quality of their future relationships.

> List at least four ways in which industrial negotiations are different from commercial contract negotiations.

THE BARGAINING RITUAL

Bargaining is surrounded by a ritual, a behaviour which the parties feel obliged to carry out even though they both are fully aware that such behaviour is for the benefit of their constituents and the other party is not taken in by it. The ritual is best seen from a management perspective when it publicly expresses 'surprise and disappointment' at the union's claim. It is seen from a trade union perspective with statements through its membership communication channels (ie its monthly journal) that it is 'pushing hard against an intransigent and unreasonable management' to gain its bargaining objectives.

The ritual also operates in that the constituents of the management and the trade union negotiators expect the bargaining processes to last a minimum length of time or they feel that their economic interests have not been properly protected. If an agreement is made relatively quickly, the management negotiators are likely to be accused by their colleagues of having made unnecessary trading concessions or of trading before it was necessary to do so. Union negotiators would face the same accusations from their members with the added danger that where wage agreements have to be accepted by the members in a ballot, the members may reject the proposed agreement perhaps despite its being highly beneficial. When this happens, the two sides have to return to the bargaining table for a period of time which reassures their constituents that their economic interests have been properly protected. The reopening of negotiations often brings only marginal amendments to the original deal rejected by the party's constituents. However, the deal is then accepted and praise is showered on their respective negotiators by the employer and the employees.

Both management and union negotiators nation-wide have tried on a number of occasions to short-circuit this aspect of the bargaining ritual and convince their constituents that a 'relatively quick settlement' does not mean compromising the protection of their economic interests. However, they have had little success and have quickly seen the wisest course to be to return to play the ritual game. The constituents of bargainers and grievance-handlers still continue to believe that negotiations must last some minimum period of time before their economic interests have been properly defended by their 'skilful and able' negotiators.

The distrust of the constituents of negotiators of the relatively quick settlement is perhaps best illustrated by a story told to the authors by a general secretary of a trade union about when he first became general secretary. This position also made him the lead negotiator for the union in its annual negotiations to review the national agreement it held with the nation-wide employers' organisation. They too had a new lead negotiator. We were told by the general secretary that he and his new employer association counterpart were determined to conclude the next set of national negotiations more quickly than had been the case in the past and to avoid achieving an agreement only after an all-night and all-day bargaining session.

The two lead negotiators quickly convinced their respective negotiating teams of the value of their proposed new style of bargaining. The negotiations were completed relatively quickly compared with what had happened in the past. The union had negotiated the best-ever deal for its members in terms of new money. However, when the general secretary and his negotiating team took the proposed agreement back to their national executive council, the council refused to accept it. It complained that the agreement had been made too quickly, and that the negotiators by sticking to the negotiations for a longer time period could have gained an improved offer from the employers. When the employer's negotiating team presented the proposed settlement to its own council for approval, it too refused to endorse the intended settlement. It said that the negotiations had concluded too quickly and their negotiators must have offered improvements in terms and conditions at too high a level for the union to accept the offer so quickly. The employer's negotiators were accused of trading items before it was necessary and gaining too little from the union in return.

The general secretary was now concerned. He had given the employer's lead negotiator his word that the new style of negotiation would deliver an acceptable deal. He wondered how he could inform the employers. Unbeknown to the general secretary, the employer's leader was experiencing the same feeling. Eventually the general secretary plucked up the courage to telephone the employer's leader, who was relieved to hear that they both had the same problem, and who had himself wondered how he could tell the general secretary that the employers would not accept the deal.

The two negotiating teams were recalled, and decided that the deal could only be improved in a minor way. The two sides then spent four weeks discussing matters of mutual interest to both sides. The amended agreement was then taken back to the union's executive, which accepted the deal and congratulated the general secretary and his team on the excellent deal they had achieved. The same happened to the employer's negotiators. However, during the recalled negotiations, the union's journal contained headlines declaring that their negotiators were pushing the intransigent employer for a substantial increase. The employer's communication channel was reporting in banner headlines that their negotiators were fiercely resisting unreasonable and unrealistic claims from the union's negotiators.

STAGES IN THE NEGOTIATION PROCESS

The stages in the negotiation process are:

• preparation

• presentation

• searching for and identifying common ground

• concluding the agreement

• writing the agreement.

All negotiating situations involve the stages shown above although the length of time each stage lasts and the degree of formality in the stages will vary. For example, in an intra- and inter-management negotiating situation, the 'agreement' on how to handle a problem will not normally be written down except perhaps in the form of a letter and/or an internal memorandum to management colleagues.

The preparation stage
There are three stages in preparing for negotiation. These are shown in Table 9 and are: analysis, establishment of the aims to be achieved

Table 9 **Preparing for negotiations**

There are three stages in preparing for negotiations:

1 analysis
2 establishment of aims
3 strategy and tactics.

Analysis
• the facts/sources of information of the incident, claim, etc
• any relevant rules (company) agreements or 'custom and practice'
• any relevant precedents or comparisons
• attitude of management on the issue(s)
• what issues are tradable? which issues will the other party trade?
• significance of the issues for the employees, their representatives and their trade union.

Aims
• ideal (like to achieve)
• realistic (hoped-for)
• fall back (must have)
• consider feasibility of aims against relative bargaining power.

Strategy and tactics
• size of team
• who is to speak? in what order? on what subject?
• anticipation of most likely of the other side's arguments and counter to them
• be familiar with the meaning and intent of the agreements, procedures and rules of your organisation.

Preparation is vital

wrong analysis = incorrect aims = failure to achieve objectives

Golden Rule

failure to prepare

is

preparing to fail

in the forthcoming negotiations, and planning the strategy and tactics to be used in those negotiations. The analysis component involves management's collecting and analysing the relevant information (facts) to substantiate its view. In grievance-handling, for example, the information will be collected by word of mouth from those who witnessed the alleged incident/behaviour, etc, complained of by the employee. These witnesses are likely to include other employees and managers as well as those directly involved. So in managing employee grievance, the management requires to be competent in interviewing skills if it is to gather and then analyse all the facts surrounding the employee's complaint (see Chapter 8). On the other hand, in bargaining situations, the information is likely to come from internal company records, local pay and salary surveys, and external sources of data, such as the Index of Retail Prices or the New Earnings Survey.

The analysis stage also involves management's checking whether any company rules, any collective or individual agreements, other arrangements or 'custom and practice' are relevant to the forthcoming negotiations. However, the most important activity in the analysis stage is the identification of the key issues involved in the negotiations and of which issues management is prepared to trade and which, if any, are for management non-tradable. In a grievance-handling situation, management needs to identify clearly what the employee's complaint is and why he or she believes it is a problem. In a bargaining situation the employer's representatives will consider each of the items in the employee's claim and decide which of these they are prepared to trade in return for some move from the employees on the employer's counter-claim. In making this decision, management must weigh up the significance of the issues at stake for itself, for its employees and for the trade union.

Having decided which issues it is prepared to trade, management anticipates which issues the employees will be prepared to trade. In the process of identifying potential tradable issues (and therefore in common ground with the employees) management is helped if it understands what motivates the employee representatives with which it has to deal. Having analysed the issues involved in the forthcoming negotiations and identified which items are likely to be traded, management goes on to establish the potential areas of common ground between itself and its employees and which are expected to form the basis of an agreement between them. This can be done by constructing an aspiration grid. This is discussed in Chapters 8 and 9.

The second phase of the preparation stage is the establishing by the management of the objectives it wishes to achieve in the forthcoming negotiations. It also requires management to consider the negotiating aims and objectives of its employees and/or their representatives. Again, this task can be more competently done if the management knows and understands the representatives of the workforce with whom it has to deal. Getting to know them does not necessarily mean agreeing with their position. However, it is only by knowing what makes them tick (eg their attitudes, the pressures upon them, their personalities) that management can predict with any reasonable degree of certainty how the employees' representatives might react to management proposals, the issues they might be prepared to trade and what negotiating style and strategy and tactics they might adopt.

Management determines three negotiating objectives. First, what would management ideally like to achieve? In actuality, the ideal is unlikely to be realised so management establishes an objective which represents what it believes can realistically be reached. However, management also establishes a third objective often referred to as the fall-back (or sticking-point/bottom-line) position. This represents the least package at which management will settle. If this minimum fall-back position cannot be achieved, management will prefer to enter into a dispute situation with its employees. It implies that management in the ultimate is prepared to see the employees impose industrial sanctions against them. This being the case, management needs to devise a plan of action to minimise the impact of such action on the organisation's position.

A management that enters negotiations without having firmly fixed objectives is increasing the probability of reaching an unsatisfactory outcome or entering into a dispute. However, before establishing feasible negotiating objectives, management should undertake a detailed analysis and then make an assessment of the relative balance of bargaining power between itself and the groups of workers with whom it is to negotiate. As we saw in Chapter 1, this involves considering such questions as whether the group has the power to inflict costs on the employer, and if if does, whether it appears willing to use that power. Consideration has also to be given to whether the work group has the leadership necessary to impose any industrial sanctions. Management's answer to these questions will be significant factors in determining its negotiating objectives.

The third phase of the preparation stage is the planning of strategy and tactics. Management works out a plan by which it hopes to achieve its negotiating objectives. This involves deciding the size of the negotiating team, the selection of the team leader, the note-taker, the observer (who will listen and watch but not speak) and the strategist, who will discern whether the expected common ground and anticipated tradings have been identified correctly. If they have not, the strategist will suggest how the management's negotiating objectives should be changed. The strategist will also assess and monitor proposals from the other party as they are made. The management's negotiating team, if more than one person, before meeting with the other side will decide who will speak, in what order and, if appropriate, on what issues or items.

An important part of planning the strategy and the tactics is the anticipation of the arguments mostly likely to be used by the other side and how they might be countered. In this regard, it is helpful if someone on the management side can play the 'devil's advocate' by probing management's case for its weak points and so exploring how the employees' and/or their representatives' arguments against management's case might be countered, whether in a grievance-handling, bargaining and/or joint problem-solving negotiation situation. When management has completed its preparations for negotiation, all members of the negotiating team should understand, and have agreed on, the negotiating analysis, aims, and strategy and tactics.

Of all the four negotiating situations we have identified, the preparation stage is the most important. If management's analysis of the information it has gathered – whether by interview techniques or from statistical data – is incorrect, it will establish inappropriate negotiating objectives, plan the wrong strategy and tactics, and the chances of achieving its negotiating objectives will be reduced. If it does achieve its objectives, despite inadequate preparation, it will be because management holds the upper hand in the relative balance of bargaining power stakes or by good fortune.

The golden rule to remember is:

Failure to prepare
is
preparing to fail.

If management fails to prepare adequately, it need not be a disaster. The situation can be resolved by a reassessment of its analysis, objectives and strategy and tactics in the light of the information it has now gained and which was not available at the preparation stage. Indeed, it is important for management to reassess its objectives every time it gains information it did not have or did not take into account when preparing for the negotiations. During grievance-handling, bargaining and joint problem-solving, negotiating-situations management must frequently monitor and review its objectives in the light of how the negotiations develop and progress.

Justify the actions that a manager needs to take in preparing to resolve a grievance raised by an employee against the behaviour of the organisation.

The presentation stage

At the first meeting with the other side, it may be necessary to break the ice. If the negotiators are unknown to each other, the formal introduction of the respective members of the negotiating teams takes place. (If the negotiators are well known to each other this is unnecessary.) It can be appropriate at this initial meeting in grievance-handling situations for management to suggest a procedure whereby the negotiations may proceed and to suggest a schedule for their completion.

If management is making the initial presentation, then it gives a summary of its case. It tells the employees or their representatives the issues (demands) it is going to raise and then substantiates its case using facts and recorded information. Management emphasises its proposals and the rationale behind them. In dealing with employee grievances, when meeting with an individual and his or her representatives management should propose remedies for the employee's complaint and not just state a rejection of the grievance. It is good practice to inform the employee of any overall solution that management sees to the complaint, but management should not at this initial stage go into details of its arguments. The first part of the presentation stage of negotiations involves both parties' telling each other what they want from each other.

Although it is perhaps not the normal expectation, it is good practice for both parties to put all their proposals on the table. Each party should state its position on all issues to be considered in the negotiations and not just present its views on selected issues. Some negotiators see advantages in 'keeping something up your sleeve to hit them with later'. This is a dangerous tactic. What is being kept up the sleeve might be a non-negotiable issue for the other side or one on which they are prepared to trade only if the alternative is no agreement at all. If this turns out to be the case, the the probability that the negotiations may break down, despite agreement on some issues, is increased significantly. The purpose of negotiations is to solve a problem, not to score points.

Another danger of the 'keep something up one's sleeve' tactic is that it can destroy the mutual trust between the two leaders of the respective negotiation teams. Negotiators do not like to have negotiated in good faith, and have openly and honestly raised all their issues to help achieve an agreement, only to find that the other party has behaved differently. A further problem is that if one party behaves like this all the time, the other will consider it part of that party's negotiating ritual and will discount it in future negotiations. The intended surprise, and with it the possible further improvements in offers from the other side, is nullified. At most, a management will get away with the 'up one's sleeve' tactic once. Best practice requires an employee relations manager to be a completely open negotiator who puts all issues to be considered in the negotiation on the table from the outset.

If management is receiving a proposal from its employees' representative, it listens to what he or she is saying and does not interrupt the presentation. When the employees' side has completed its presentation of its proposals, management should avoid an unconsidered (ie knee-jerk) reaction to proposals. By the same token, management should not immediately respond with counter-proposals unless they have been agreed after thoughtful consideration by the management team or its representatives. If management is receiving proposals or listening to an employee's complaint for the first time, it should confine its response to asking questions to seek clarification of the employee's proposals. For example, typical questions might be: what does the proposal really mean? What is the source of the statistics quoted? Can you just remind us of the individuals you have interviewed in connection with the alleged management behaviour of which you are complaining? It is also good practice on receiving the employee's case for the first time to summarise back in a neutral manner what management understands has been proposed to it. Management should then arrange to meet with the employees at a future date so that a considered response can be given after a detailed analysis and assessment of any proposal(s).

By the end of the presentation stage, both parties will have put to each other their ideal positions. There is unlikely to be much common ground between them. However, the issues to be resolved during the negotiation will be known to both parties. The parties now begin the task of seeking confirmation of their predicted common ground and anticipated tradable issues.

Identifying common ground
The emphasis of the negotiation now switches from concentrating on differences to identifying points of common interest and possible agreement. Management recognises the point has been reached at which both it and the employees must now seek to confirm the common ground identified between themselves during the preparation stage of the negotiations. Management will have anticipated possible areas of common ground and made an assessment of which issues or details it expects the other party will be prepared to trade on. Management now needs to obtain information from representatives of the workforce which will enable it to confirm whether these expectations (aspirations) are correct. Each negotiating session can now be used constructively to gain the desired information from the

other party. At the same time, management needs to supply information to the other party so that the employees can have their expectations confirmed as to management's position on the issues. Negotiation sessions which do not provide information by which the two parties involved can confirm their expectations of their anticipated areas of common ground are not a constructive use of time. However, negotiation sessions can arise in which neither party gains relevant information because one merely wishes to score points, to lay blame, to threaten the other side, to shout it down, or adopt a sarcastic attitude. Such behaviour is unprofessional and does nothing to help the negotiation process solve problems.

Management can seek to confirm expectations of where any common ground with the other side lies by a number of techniques. The most important of these are:

- 'if and then' technique (if you move closer to our position on issue y then we shall move closer to your position on x), which deliberately emphasise a requirement for the other side to move: it is a conditional offer

- discussion

- questioning (interviewing)

- watching the other party's reaction to management's proposal

- listening carefully to what is being said, including any conditions placed on any offers or proposals: if the other party says 'We are not prepared to discuss that at this stage', what it is telling management is that it is prepared to trade on that issue but does not feel it necessary to do so at this stage.

These techniques are discussed in greater detail in Chapters 8 and 9.

Another technique for testing whether management's understanding of the common ground is correct is the use of periodic summarising of the other party's position on an issue. Confirmation of the employees' position can be achieved by management's summarising the points they have made during the negotiations. This is particularly helpful if the issue involved is complex. Each separate negotiating meeting begins with one party's summarising the stage the negotiations have reached. Such a summary indicates areas of agreement and the outstanding issues still to be settled. In any negotiating situation, the linking of issues is crucial if the exact issues and details the parties are prepared to trade are to be identified. By linking issues, management can ensure that the negotiations have a momentum (see below). By separating issues, negotiators narrow their negotiating scope. If the use of the techniques listed above leads to the emergence of new information, an adjournment can be called, if thought necessary, to consider the implications of the new information, including whether management needs to reassess its negotiating aims, analysis and strategy and tactics.

Confirmation of the common ground enables the negotiations to take on a momentum. If the negotiations get bogged down on one particular issue, the momentum can be sustained by switching to a new issue. This reinforces the importance of the negotiators' putting all issues on the table from the outset. Any difficult issue can be returned to later – and if it is then the only issue outstanding towards an agreement being secured the parties are likely to readjust their attitudes towards the issue. They are, after all, faced with a stark choice. Either an accommodation is effected on the issue or no agreement is reached and all the issues upon which consensus has been achieved fall by the wayside. The party that feels the strongest on the difficult issue is faced with a 'do-we-throw-the-baby-out-of-the-bath-with-the-bathwater?' type of choice. It may regard the issue as so central to the survival of the business that it prefers to go into a dispute situation rather than make an accommodation with the other party. If this course of action is chosen, management would be well advised to plan how it might neutralise the impact on the business of any industrial sanctions the other party might impose upon it.

Outline the various techniques by which a management negotiating team can search for the common ground and thereby the basis of an agreement with representatives of the workforce. Which of these techniques do you consider to be the most important, and why?

Concluding the agreement

After completing the identification of the common ground, the negotiations move to their concluding stage. Entering this stage is a matter of timing and judgement. To be able to recognise that the best deal in the circumstances has been reached, and that it is one that will be acceptable to the constituents represented in the negotiations, is an important skill for employee relations managers to acquire. This is particularly the case in a bargaining situation.

There are a number of considerations for management to bear in mind when closing negotiations. It needs to be satisfied that all the issues have been discussed and agreed, and that both parties fully understand what they have accepted. If there is any uncertainty about the meaning of the agreed proposals, management should go over what has been agreed perhaps by explaining how it sees the proposal working in practice (the 'play-back' technique). However, if it turns out that there has been a misunderstanding over what has been agreed, negotiations must recommence. It is crucial that both sides have the same understanding of what they have agreed. If there is any lassitude, then when the agreement is put into operation both parties will find themselves squabbling again and again over whether the agreement is being applied or interpreted properly.

In concluding the agreement, the management has to convince the other party that its final offer is final. Management must at all costs avoid claiming, *as a bluff*, that its position is the final one. A series of 'final offers' from management will destroy its credibility and undermine its ability to convince the other party that it has really reached its bottom line. It is of little value for management to tell the employees that there can be no further improvement because management has reached its bottom line (ie its fall-back position) if the threat of industrial pressure from the employees – for example, by undertaking a successful industrial ballot result – brings a further concession. Management has demonstrated to the other side that it has *not* reached its fall-back position, and the employees will begin to suspect that even further improvements can be made. If management tells the employees that its offer is final, management must mean that, and not give in to any threat of industrial pressure.

The authors once heard a personnel director referring to the fact that he always had four sets of final offers, each one hidden away in a different pocket. This may sound amusing – but if he was to pull out all four of these offers he would forever destroy his negotiating credibility with the trade unions. To tell them that management had reached its final offer would never again be believed, because what the director was saying was that he was prepared to change his 'final' offer at most four times over. What could he do if the fourth offer was not believed? In future negotiations the employees will never know when the final offer has been made by the company. A management negotiator *must* retain the respect and credibility of the other party. Final-final-final offers will not achieve this.

Writing the agreement

After the deal is done, the agreement is written up. In the case of an employee grievance this may be no more than an internal memorandum. The agreement will state who are the parties involved, the date it was made, the date upon which it will be implemented, its contents, how disputes over its interpretation and application will be dealt with, and its duration, and will be signed by the parties to the agreement. It is usually drafted by management and then sent to the other party, who usually initials the clauses the wording of which it accepts. Only when both sides are happy with the wording of the agreement is it printed and signed.

Both management and trade unions or other employee representative bodies have responsibility for implementing the agreement. As we have already pointed out, unless the agreement is understood fully by both parties, its operation will cause endless disputes over its interpretation and application. Agreement means commitment. It is important that the wording is right. There is a big difference between a clause which states that 'employees may be dismissed if they report for work with the smell of alcohol on their breath' and a clause which states that 'employees *will* be dismissed if they report for work with the smell of alcohol on their breath'. The first clause implies that there may be circumstances in which dismissal may not take place. The second leaves no room for doubt. If management really means that turning up to work smelling of alcohol is a dismissal offence, it must be stated in any agreement in a way that can leave no room for doubt so that every employee knows that if he or she behaves in this way exactly what will happen. The importance of making sure that the agreement is drafted correctly is probably best illustrated in that UK employee relations managers can point to many examples of disputes about the meaning of poorly worded agreements.

THE OUTCOME OF NEGOTIATIONS

The best outcome of the negotiating process occurs when both parties make some gains – the so-called win/win situation. This is normally achieved by professional negotiation which concentrates on achieving well-prepared objectives, on maintaining long-term relationships between the parties, on emphasising a pragmatic approach, and on making an agreement that is not unacceptable to anyone and meets the needs of both parties. However, the relative balance of bargaining power between the two parties still heavily influences the outcome of the negotiations regardless of the professionalism that management may display.

The opposite outcome of the win/win situation is the lose/lose situation. Here, because of a lack of professionalism on the part of the negotiators, the objectives of neither are achieved. No agreement is secured, long-term relationships are soured, the constituents of the negotiating parties no longer respect or trust their negotiators, and both parties become disillusioned with the negotiating process.

A third possible outcome is the win/lose situation in which one party dominates the other and secures a something-for-nothing deal. This outcome is often the result of unprofessional negotiations on the part of one or both parties. In such negotiating situations, there exists an 'us and them' distinction between the parties: individuals' energies are directed only towards victory ('I win, you lose'), a strong emphasis on immediate solutions regardless of whether the long-term objectives are met, too many personalised conflicts rather than challenging facts, information, arguments, etc, an emphasis is on short-term concerns, and the implications of the continuing relationship are forgotten.

SKILLS REQUIRED IN NEGOTIATING PROCESS

So far we have examined what a negotiator does. These tasks have included the establishment of aims to be achieved from negotiation, the planning of strategy and tactics, the anticipation of the other side's reactions and arguments, the reassessment of objectives in the light of previously unknown information becoming available, and the continuing personal relationship with the other party to the negotiations. However, describing these tasks does not identify the skills required of a negotiator. The key skills are interviewing, note-taking, presentation, listening, watching, analysis and judgement.

Interviewing skills
Much of an employee relations manager's job is dealing with employee problems and/or complaints. This requires the collection of information, upon which a manager can analyse the complaint, can establish aims and can plan strategy and tactics as to how the complaint may be dealt with in the best interests of management. Most of the information required to undertake these tasks will be collected from individuals (both employees and managers) by word of mouth. Competence in interviewing skills is therefore crucial to employee relations managers. It is on the basis of information obtained from interviewing the individuals concerned that employee relations managers prepare to resolve employee grievances. Interviewing skills

are also necessary in presentation, in identifying the common ground and in concluding the agreement stages of different negotiation situations. In the last-named stage, they are important in helping to clarify what the other party is proposing and to test its understanding of what it understands it has agreed.

The purpose of an interview is to gain information which must be complete and consistent. All the facts, including those that weaken the case, as well as strengthen the case, must be obtained. Incomplete information will mean incomplete preparation for negotiation. It is important that the interviewer relaxes the interviewee so that he or she will be more willing to talk. An implication of this is that during the interview, the interviewer should limit his or her contribution. The interviewer should be listening. If he or she talks too much, is preoccupied with formulating the next question or is looking at (reading) papers, he or she may miss useful information or limit the opportunity to evoke relevant information. It is useful to find a quiet place to conduct the interview, preferably where it is possible for the interviewer and interviewee to sit down and talk without fear of interruption. The interviewer needs to be sympathetic to the interviewee and avoid creating the impression that a cross-examination is taking place. Interviewers need to be relaxed and informal in their approach, but at the same time be business-like. An environment must be established which supports the exchange of information. This sometimes is not a problem, especially in grievance-handling situations where the individual tends to be angry and only too willing to talk. The trouble for the interviewer in such a situation is that the individual employee is likely to be telling only one side of the story and not the complete story. It may be that the other half of the story is the vital one for management.

In an interview, therefore, it is not only a case of obtaining all the facts but also of being sure that they make a complete and consistent story. A useful guideline for collecting the basic facts is the '5Ws' technique:

What – What is the employee complaint or proposal about?

When – When did the cause of the complaint, etc, take place – note the dates, times, etc.

Where – Where did what is being complained about happen? From where did the information come?

Who – Who was involved?

Why – Why does what happened create a problem for the employee? Why is a particular remedy being sought? It is important to understand what it is that the employee is asking the organisation to do on his or her behalf.

The 'why' question is the most difficult. Individuals always like to give a favourable view of their behaviour but employee relations managers need also to know the downside of each interviewee's behaviour. In addition, they require to know the background information of the interviewee – for example, length of service, domestic situation – to help gain a full picture. Interviewers are likely to have to probe behind the answers they receive from interviewees by asking for more information and evidence to support for what has been said. The taking of notes during an interview is essential.

The information received from each interviewee must be complete and consistent – put crudely, the story must add up. An interviewer can check for completeness and consistency by recalling to the interviewee the information he or she has given. If the facts are inconsistent, the interviewer explains to the interviewee that this is the case, and why it is necessary now to have the missing information. The interviewer might, for example, say to the interviewee, 'What you have told me is interesting but does not add up. The manager, who I know well, has no record of behaving in that way. Why should his behaviour have changed? There is something you have not told me. What is it?' And then the interviewer follows this with a pause. Invariably such pauses result in the interviewee's saying things he or she has previously found hard to say or has wished to hold back because it makes their case look less open and shut.

Another technique an interviewer might use to obtain missing but vital information is the 'play-back' by which what the interviewee has said is gently recounted back to him or her. This technique has a number of advantages. It demonstrates that the interviewer has been listening, thereby increasing the interviewee's confidence in the interviewer and increasing the probability of the interviewee's volunteering information on the case which he or she would prefer not to reveal. It also enables any misunderstanding by the interviewer to be corrected.

Whether the facts given by the interviewee are consistent and complete can also be checked by corroborating his or her account by interviewing another individual who has an interest in the outcome of the same issue that was the subject of the original interview. A clue that an interviewee might be withholding important information is his or her facial and body movements in response to open-ended questions like 'What else would you like to tell me?' If eye-contact changes (the head goes down or sideways) or the posture changes significantly, these are outward signs that the interviewee may well be withholding important information which would put the problem in a different perspective.

At the conclusion of an interview, it is good practice to summarise what has been agreed. This helps avoid misunderstandings. It is also good practice to write up the notes of the interview while it is fresh in your mind. There is no general rule for taking notes during an interview except that if notes are taken they should be brief and not break the flow of the interview. In some situations, the making of brief notes indicates to the interviewees that what they are saying is regarded as sufficiently important for notes to be taken. However, in some other situations, note-taking can create an inhibiting environment. In this case, notes should be written up as soon as possible after the interview.

Interviewing skills are crucial to the employee relations manager. Defective interviewing skills mean gaining imperfect information and undertaking an inaccurate analysis of the situation. They are a crucial source of information for the manager.

Explain why competent interviewing skills are crucial to a manager.

Note-taking skills

This is another vital skill for employee relations managers: to be able to take accurate and clear notes. If the manager does not make notes, he or she may promise to do something but forget – may agree something with a managerial colleague, an employee or a representative of the employees, and forget what was agreed. Accurate and clear notes are helpful for producing a report to management. They reduce the probability of missing something out. Without notes it may be difficult to prove that colleagues and/or employees have been informed of something or that they had agreed something. A way to avoid these problems is to carry a notebook and take regular notes when you promise management you will do something, when you agree something with employees or their representatives, when you make a telephone call, or when you go to a meeting. As an employee relations manager it is likely you will need to take clear and accurate notes from documents and articles that are read. Note-taking skills will be needed at every stage in the negotiating process.

A problem with note-taking is how much detail to record. However, it is good practice always to note background details such as subject, date and time, place, and the people involved (the 5Ws), and to record only the key points. It is bad practice to try and produce a word-for-word account of a meeting or interview. Your concentration must be on recording essential information. This may seem obvious advice but it is surprising how many people do attempt to make a word-for-word record of a meeting, speech, etc. It is also good practice always to keep a careful note of conclusions made at meetings and any follow-up action that is proposed to be taken.

However, on some occasions, employee relations managers might need to take word-for-word notes. This would be the case if they were taking a statement from a management colleague or employee who, say, witnessed an accident in the workplace. It would also be the case when agreeing the wording of an agreement concluded with the workforce. Accurate notes are particularly important at this writing-up stage of an agreement. There is for instance a big difference between an increase in basic pay and an increase in earnings (basic pay, overtime, shift premiums, etc). A clause in an agreement which states management may grant employees an additional day's paid holiday after five years' continuous service is different from one that says management *will* grant employees an additional day's paid holiday after five years' continuous service. The first clause gives management discretion; the second imposes an obligation on the employer.

There are three main styles of setting-out notes. These are the 'Brain-pattern' or 'Bubble' style, the 'Chronological' style, and the 'Presentation' style.

The 'Brain-pattern' or 'Bubble' technique can be used to structure rambling speeches, long and complex statements, arguments or discussions. It operates on the premise that an individual's brain thinks in pictures of associated ideas and themes and not in lines of typewritten script. The basis of the technique is that the mind is chaotic but within this chaos a pattern can be identified. It moves away from the traditional note-taking style of a layout in a vertical pattern to produce a record in a pattern that replicates the working of the mind. Because the note is directly related to the individual producing it, the patterns (bubbles) can take a variety of forms and to another individual can be unintelligible. The most important aspect in the construction of the note, however, is the identification and summary of the key elements of the subject that is being discussed, using words that are meaningful to the note-taker. The 'bubbles' are key words which along with associated words trigger the individual's memory.

An example of the 'Brain-pattern' or 'Bubble' technique is shown in Figure 7, which represents notes taken at a management meeting to discuss the possible introduction of a new shift system. The meeting was chaotic in that those present kept continually switching from one aspect of the proposed new system to another and to topics unrelated to the subject. The meeting started by discussing when the new system would be introduced and then began to talk about the size of shift premium. It then turned back to the proposed implementation – only for a discussion to start up about the party some of those present had attended the previous night. The meeting then returned to discussing the period of notice that would be given to introduce the new shift, going straight on to implementation dates again, and then the meeting started to talk about the performance of the company's sports team,

Figure 7 'Brain–pattern' or 'Bubble' technique

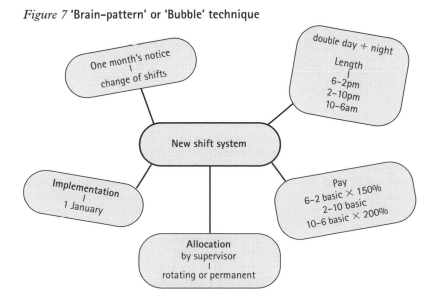

before returning once more to shift premium. The meeting carried on on this way until it ended after three hours.

Figure 7 demonstrates that the meeting discussed five key elements (period of notice, implementation date, allocation of shifts to employees, shift premium rates and the times of the shifts) although they were not discussed in any logical sequence. Each of the key elements is shown as a 'bubble' around the topic of the subject under discussion – the new shift system. Within each 'bubble' are words that trigger the memory of what was agreed in each key element involved of the introduction of the shift system. For example, the shift premium key elements shows that the meeting decided that the 6.00am to 2.00pm shift would carry a 150 per cent premium, the 2.00pm to 10.00pm shift no premium, and the 10.00pm to 6.00am shift a 200 per cent premium. A highly structured and logically sequenced report of what was a very chaotic meeting can now be given. From the notes, the report would be something like this :

> Yesterday, I attended a meeting of senior management which discussed the introduction of a new shift system. It discussed, and made decisions in, five aspects of its introduction, namely: the length of notice to be given to the workforce for its introduction, the date of implementation, the allocation of the shifts to employees, shift premium, and the timing of the three shifts to be introduced. Turning to the date of implementation of the new system, it was decided this would be the first of January. Turning to the timing of the shifts, it was decided that there would be three and the hours involved would be 6.00am–2.00pm, 2.00pm–10.00pm and 10.00pm–6.00am. On the question of the allocation of shifts to employees, it was decided this would be done by the supervisor. Turning to shift premium, it was decided as follows: 6.00am–2.00pm a 150 per cent premium, 2.00pm–10.00pm no premium, 10.00pm–6.00am a 200 per cent premium. Finally, it was decided that the employees would be given one month's notice as to the implementation of the new system.

The 'Bubble' style can be used in negotiations to take notes of longwinded and disjointed oral presentations of the other parties' proposals and/or arguments. It can also be used to take notes during formal and informal interview situations in, say, grievance-handling. In addition, it is a useful technique to use when taking notes during committee meetings or meetings at which management is preparing for grievance-handling, bargaining and group problem-solving negotiation situations.

The 'Chronological' style of note-taking is a technique which can be used when it is important to record how an interview, discussion or negotiating session evolves in terms of who 'responded' to whom, what with, and when. The notepaper is divided in two, with management's words recorded on one half and those of the employees or their representatives on the other. Table 10 records the verbatim exchange between the manging director (MD) and a shop steward (SS) over the disciplining of an employee. The whole negotiating session is not recorded but hopefully Table 10 contains sufficient information for you to understand the general principle of the chronological style of note-taking. It is particularly useful to use in a negotiating situation, particularly in bargaining. It enables the note-taker, in adjournments,

Table 10 'Chronological' style of note-taking

	Management		Union
		2.30pm	
MD	To discuss the grievance of Ms Jones. Thank you for coming to this meeting. Management believes it is correct in the action it has taken to discipline Ms Jones for swearing at her supervisor.	SS	We understand what your position is. However, the union believes the disciplinary penalty is too harsh given that the alleged swearing was only in the presence of, and not at, the supervisor.
PM	Management cannot accept that a disciplinary penalty should not be imposed. The loss of pay for such an offence is a matter of fundamental principle to us.	SS	That may be the case but we believe the length of her suspension and the loss of pay for that period are too harsh. We believe they should be reduced to one day.
MD	The need for a disciplinary penalty remains. We might give consideration to the reduction of the length of suspension, but the issue of pay lost is not for negotiation.	3.00pm	
		3.05pm	

MD = Managing director
SS = Shop steward
PM = Personnel manager

to spot immediately if the negotiations have a positive momentum or are making little progress because the two parties keep interrupting each other or will not let each other say what they are seeking – in short, that neither is listening to the other. It also enables the note-taker to keep an eye on what issues have been agreed and what issues remain outstanding. The note-taker can summarise the state of progress of the negotiations and ensure that no issues are left unresolved or inadvertently forgotten. By using the 'Chronological' style, the note-taker to the negotiation team will record when, by whom, and what was actually agreed. When it comes to writing up the bargained agreement, the exact record of the note-taker becomes invaluable. It is from that record that the clauses of the agreement are drafted and finalised. For the reasons outlined above, the note-taker on the negotiating team is a key player. His or her role far exceeds that of merely being the 'secretary' to one side of the negotiations.

The 'Presentation' style is a technique for converting detailed notes that may have been taken into a summarised form which can then be circulated to management colleagues and, if appropriate, employees and/or their representatives for information. It is particularly useful for recording decisions taken and actions required for entry into an official record, and for informing management of decisions taken at particular meetings, etc. An example of the 'Presentation' style is shown in Table 11.

When taking notes, employee relations managers should choose the style best suited to the situation in which they find themselves. They may need to use just one of the three styles outlined above.

Table 11 'Presentation' style of note-taking

MANAGEMENT COMMITTEE MEETING
22/3/97: 4.00pm

Present: J Wade, A N Other, B Jones, L Dixon, J Jones, T White

1. Sick pay

   — Complaints from employees about sick pay not being paid on time have increased. It was decided the matter should be investigated and a report, containing recommendations should be given at next meeting.

   Action: B Jones and T White to undertake investigation and production of report for next meeting.

2. Overtime working

   — It was discussed that overtime working should be reduced by half.

   Action: J Wade to brief all supervisors of this and report on progress to next meeting.

3. Fumes in press area

   — Complaints have been made about fumes from solvent and new inks in machine room.

   Action: safety representative to investigate immediately.

Alternatively, they may like to develop a note-taking style which is a combination of all three styles.

Presentation skills

Employee relations managers rely heavily upon the spoken word, and although some have natural gifts as presenters, most need to acquire and develop such skills. The best advice is that they should develop a style which suits their own personality and situation.

An oral presentation should have a well defined structure. It should contain:

- an introduction which captures the audience's attention and which outlines what it will be told: a broad-brush-pen-picture of management's position and/or proposals. For example, management might say: 'We want to talk to you about redundancies, and our proposals will cover the need for redundancy, the measures we intend to introduce to reduce the need for redundancy, and the basis on which individuals will be selected for redundancy.'

- a main section which spells out in detail management's position backed by facts, arguments and illustrative examples. Management explains, for example, the causes of the need for redundancy, explains (together with reasons) the personnel and production/ provision of service measures it will introduce to minimise the number of redundancies, etc. In the main section of an oral presentation, the management tells the audience the details of its case.

- a conclusion in which management summarises the proposals it has put to its employees or their representatives. Management will use language such as, 'So what we have been explaining to you is why we need redundancies, how we intend to minimise the number required, what compensation we propose to give to redundant employees, and the ways in which we intend to select employees for redundancy.' The concluding section should sum up to the audience what it has been told, with the use of such terms as, 'In a nutshell, what management has been saying is . . .'

Before making a presentation of management's case in, say, grievance-handling and bargaining, an employee relations manager should examine his or her intended presentation in relation to:

Content – Have you said all you want to say?

Sequence – Is the presentation logical, and has each part been linked?

Balance – Does it have the right weight and emphasis?

Objective – Will it work to achieve this?

In making an oral presentation, preparation is just as vital as it is for negotiations: there are a number of key tools an employee relations manager can use to make it a success. First, there is the voice. Its volume and pitch should alter during the presentation, and its speed should vary. There is value to be gained in emphasising and repeating particular words and phrases, introducing effective pauses, employing gestures and conveying meanings by expression. However, if these would complicate an already nerve-wracking experience, managers would better forget about them and concentrate on delivering their presentation in as interesting a way as possible.

Second, there is body language – but an audience can be distracted by mannerisms to the point where they turn off from the presentation and concentrate instead on the presenter's performance. Mannerisms are to be avoided (eg theatrical postures): effective presenters behave naturally and do not attempt to put on an act. Third, there is eye-contact, which involves the oral presenter looking directly at the audience. In practice, many people find this difficult, but if eye-contact can be developed it brings advantages: individuals (or groups of individuals) are more likely to listen if spoken to directly. The eyes of the listeners reveal the effect that the manner of the presentation and what is being said is having upon them. Fourth, there is the attitude of the presenter. An effective communicator is enthusiastic about what he or she is saying. If a speaker wants to convince somebody of something, he or she must believe in it personally. It is this belief that helps to get the message across.

Listening skills

Employee relations managers cannot operate merely by issuing instructions. They need information and intelligence, one source of which is interviewing management colleagues and employees. Another major source of information is listening to what is being said by individuals. A good listener makes a more competent employee relations manager. The ability to listen is too often taken for granted.

Too frequently it is not regarded as a skill. However, effective listening is a management skill which needs to be acquired and developed.

There are three main problems associated with listening skills. First, there is normally no chance to hear what has been said again. The spoken word must be absorbed immediately. Second, there is the problem of interpretation. What one person means by a particular word or phrase may not necessarily be what another person means by that same word or phrase, so confusion can arise. Third, individuals can think more quickly than a person can talk, so once someone outlines the issue to be considered, the listener might have started to think ahead about how the supervisor will deal with this particular question. If this happens before the person has finished telling the listener all the facts, the listener may miss vital information through lack of concentration.

There are barriers to effective listening other than mind-wandering. There are the physical barriers of fatigue, discomfort (or excess comfort) and a stuffy room. For example, a tired listener will seldom devote full attention to a speaker, nor will a listener who is wriggling around in an uncomfortable chair. There are also mental barriers of indifference and/or prejudice. If people are not interested in a subject they 'switch off' mentally. Similarly, there is a tendency for listeners to make up their minds about a subject (or speaker) early in a talk – to stop thinking about what is being said and again to switch off.

From this examination of the characteristics of, and the barriers to, the listening process it is possible for an employee relations manager to develop effective listening techniques. These fall under three main headings: attention, comprehension and absorption. Effective listening requires concentration. Among the physical measures a listener can take to increase his or her attention is to sit where the speaker is clearly visible, so as to watch the speaker at all times. The speaker's facial expressions and other gestures will help to emphasise different parts of the presentation. Individuals can accommodate at least 500 words per minute in thinking and 150 in listening, so they only use something like one third of their mental capacity. The remaining two thirds of the mind will wander if not otherwise used. So employee relations managers need to use it. The best uses for the spare capacity are in thinking ahead and in making notes of what is said. Note-taking while listening also helps comprehension and absorption.

Comprehension will be easier if the listener has done some homework and thinks ahead of the speaker. By means of such preparation, the listener increases his or her capacity to understand. It also makes the listening process easier, in that the talk will be more readily understood and more retentive of the listener's attention. Similarly, if the listener mentally summarises the speaker's argument as the speaker is talking, and thinks ahead about its consequences, he or she may well further enhance his/her understanding. An effective listener must set aside any preconceived personal bias and listen to the message of the speaker. If the listener disagrees with the speaker, her or she should think of reasons to think differently. Along with mental summaries of what the speaker is saying, it is sensible to write down some kind of note. The writing itself helps to formulate thought and aid comprehension. An employee relations manager who disciplines himself or herself in this way ensures that he or she does not switch off.

Individuals all have different sections to their memories. Immediately after they have read a sentence they can probably recall it word for word. A few minutes later they can probably recall the concept but not the actual words. By the next day they will probably barely recall reading the sentence. The process of understanding a talk is fundamental to, but not the whole of, the process of transferring relevant information to the long-term memory. Few people retain more than half of what they hear after a few hours. The best way of improving this absorption rate is again for the listener to make notes of what he or she hears. The act of making a note helps to fix information in the memory. A review of the note, perhaps a day later, will fix a little more information for a little longer. A further review in a week or so will fix the information even more permanently. A written note preserves the gist of the transitory spoken word.

Other skills
Information is exchanged not only by word of mouth but also by people's expressions, eyes, gestures and postures, physical distances and orientations. Individuals' bodies give indications of how they feel. Employee relations managers therefore need to acquire and develop the skills of obtaining information by watching people (or as it is more commonly referred to, 'non-verbal communication'). However, this is not a simple skill for the employee relations manager to acquire and develop. It is easy for the wrong information to be picked up from non-verbal communication, and particularly so if individuals are good at hiding their inner feelings. Watching skills are generally acquired through familiarity with other people's behaviour, through trial and error, and through observing responses to verbal instructions from other people.

In negotiation situations, employee relations managers require the skills to anticipate the likely positions and reactions of the other party to the management's behaviour. This can be acquired by getting to know and understand the workforce and/or its representatives. If a manager understands those with whom he or she has to deal, it becomes easier to anticipate their objectives, strategy and tactics in any negotiation. A most difficult skill for the employee relations manager to acquire is judgement. By this we mean the ability to be able to decide, for example, whether the best possible negotiated agreement has been reached and will be acceptable to the groups who have an interest in the outcome of the negotiations. This skill is acquired by knowing the other parties and by experience.

7 Handling disciplinary matters

INTRODUCTION

This chapter and the one that follows cover two related topics, discipline and grievance. And although they are to be dealt with separately it is important to recognise that both are two-way processes and concern complaints, real or imagined, by one party against another. A second factor is the way in which the two subjects are treated by the law. Disciplinary procedures and practices are covered by a specific code of practice, which we shall examine in detail later in the chapter, and this tends to give the disciplinary process a much higher profile within organisations than grievance procedures.

Discipline is an emotive word in the context of employment. The dictionary offers us several definitions of the word *discipline*, ranging from 'punishment or chastisement' to 'systematic training in obedience', and there is no doubt that discipline at work can be one of the most difficult issues with which a manager has to deal. It is an issue that brings to the forefront of our attention matters relating to an individual's performance, capability and conduct. In the context of employment, the definition I think we should adopt is 'to improve or attempt to improve the behaviour, orderliness, etc, of by training, conditions or rules' (*Collins Concise Dictionary*). In this chapter we will be examining the principles of discipline-handling, the characteristics of a fair and effective disciplinary procedure, the legal aspects of discipline and dismissal, and the monitoring and evaluation of disciplinary procedures. As we will identify, a fair and effective disciplinary procedure is one that concentrates in improving or changing behaviour, not one that relies on the principle of punishment.

Many managers have a real problem with the disciplinary process because they believe that the process used is cumbersome and ineffective, or that the law on employment rights is heavily biased against them. This can often result in problems being ignored because it is felt that effective action against individual employees either takes too long or is liable to mean an appearance before an industrial tribunal. Because many managers share this basic misconception, it is the responsibility of the employee relations specialist to advise and guide his or her managerial colleagues through what, to many, is a minefield.

It is important that managers, at all levels, appreciate that the effectiveness of the business can be undermined if issues relating to conduct, capability and performance are not handled professionally and consistently, or if such matters are ignored altogether. This chapter will look at the concept of 'best practice' in relation to discipline at work, at the steps that need to be taken when managers are trying to alter behaviour, and at how to ensure that all employees are treated fairly. Best practice is an important principle because not only does it help to ensure fairness and consistency, it makes good business sense and can add value. When you have completed this chapter you should be able to

- explain the development of disciplinary procedures

- explain how the law supports the use of disciplinary procedures and protects individuals from unfair treatment

- explain the importance of clear rules about conduct

- explain the importance of counselling to the disciplinary process

- explain how to use the disciplinary process to manage different disciplinary problems.

THE ORIGINS OF DISCIPLINARY PROCEDURES

Up to the beginning of the 1970s employers had almost unlimited power to discipline and dismiss individual employees and in many instances they were not slow to exercise this power. While it was possible for a dismissed employee to sue for 'wrongful dismissal' under the common law, this was rarely a practical option because of the time and heavy costs involved. The only time that employer power was likely to be restricted was where trade unions were present in the workplace and dismissal procedures were established through the collective bargaining process.

This was all to change with the passing, in 1971, of the Industrial Relations Act. This Act gave individual employees the right, for the first time, to complain to an industrial tribunal that they had been unfairly dismissed. Industrial tribunals themselves had only been established in 1964, and in 1971 were a relatively new feature of business life. As well as introducing the right not to be unfairly dismissed, the 1971 Act also instituted, in 1972, the Industrial Relations Code of Practice. This introduced us to the idea that there was a right way and a wrong way to deal with issues of discipline, but it has since been superseded by the ACAS Code of Practice *Disciplinary Practice and Procedures in Employment* which we will deal with in more detail later in the chapter.

The 1971 Act was a turning-point in the relationship between employer and employee. The relative informality of industrial tribunals and the fact that access to them did not depend on lawyers or money meant that for many employees the threat of dismissal without good reason disappeared or diminished. This does not mean that employees cannot be unfairly dismissed – they can, because the law has never removed from management the right to dismiss who it likes, when it likes, and for whatever reason it likes. All that has happened since 1971 is that where employees are deemed to have acted unreasonably and unfairly they can be forced to compensate an individual for the consequences of those actions. Most employers have accepted this legal intervention without serious complaint and seek to manage disciplinary issues in as fair a way as possible. Some clearly do not, and take a cavalier attitude to individual employment rights; others, as was mentioned in the introduction, suffer from a misconception as to what they can do and how the law impacts upon their actions.

THE CURRENT LEGAL POSITION

Up until 1996, the law relating to discipline and dismissal was contained in the Employment Protection (Consolidation) Act 1978 (as amended), but in August of 1996 the Employment Rights Act (1996) came into force, consolidating provisions contained in the 1978 Act together with provisions of the Wages Act (1986), the Sunday Trading Act (1994) and the Trade Union Reform and Employment Rights Act (1993: TURER).

The starting-point for the disciplinary process is to be found in Section 1 of the 1996 Act, which deals with an employee's right to a statement of employment particulars. Section 3 states that any statement of particulars shall include a note:

(a) specifying any disciplinary rules applicable to the employee or referring the employee to the provisions of a document specifying such rules which is reasonably accessible to the employee.

The section goes on to state that the statement of particulars must also specify who an employee can appeal to if he or she is dissatisfied with any disciplinary decision that is made. Given that this has been the law in one form or another since 1971, it is surprising that many employers still have no effective disciplinary code or appeals procedure.

Sections 94 to 134 of the Act deal specifically with unfair dismissal, and these set out the legal definition of dismissal, the specific reasons for which it is deemed fair to dismiss an employee (with the overriding proviso that the employer acted reasonably), the position of shop workers who refuse to work on a Sunday, the position of trade union officials, the position of pension trustees, and the position of health and safety representatives.

There are three ways in which individuals can be legally dismissed: their employment is terminated with or without notice; they are employed under a fixed-term contract and that contract comes to an end without being renewed; or they resign (with or without notice) because of the employer's conduct. This book is not intended as a legal text: more detail on the meaning and applicability of these three definitions can be found in *Essentials of Employment Law* by David Lewis.

The Act defines a number of reasons for which it can be fair to dismiss an employee. These are: conduct, capability, qualifications, redundancy, breach of statutory provision, or some other substantial reason. Dismissals relating to capability, conduct or some other substantial reason are probably the most common and have the most links with the disciplinary process. They are examined in greater detail below.

Although the Act sets out minimum qualifying periods of employment for the acquisition of some employment rights, these limits can be, and have been, changed. It is always disturbing when we hear, as we do, managers talk of having a free hand to take whatever actions they like during an individual's first months of employment. Not only can the qualifying periods change, but making distinctions about how to deal with discipline based on an individual's length of service is to invite the possibility of inconsistency creeping into the process and so to lay the organisation open to legal challenge. To avoid this possibility it is prudent for all managers and employee relations specialists to treat disciplinary issues in exactly the same way.

DISCIPLINARY PROCEDURE

We have already stated that the ACAS Code of Practice *Disciplinary Practices and Procedures in Employment* is of significant importance in the management and resolution of disciplinary issues. While breach of the code of practice is, in itself, not unlawful its provisions and impact are central to an understanding of the disciplinary process. The legislation makes it very clear just how central this is:

> A failure on the part of any person to observe any provision of a Code of Practice shall not of itself render him liable to any proceedings; but in any proceedings before an industrial tribunal or the Central Arbitration Committee any Code of Practice ... shall be admissible in evidence, and if any provision of such a Code appears to the tribunal or Committee to be relevant to any question arising in the proceedings it shall be taken into account in determining that question.
>
> Employment Protection Act 1975, Section 6(11)

Given such a very clear statement of the Code's status, it is a very foolish organisation that does not take it seriously or is not prepared to invest time in devising its own disciplinary procedures based on its provisions. Since the 1960s, when very few establishments had formal procedures, the intervening years have seen significant growth in their use. Now only a small proportion of establishments do not have some form of mechanism for dealing with discipline and dismissal (Edwards, 1994). Our own research indicates that it is usually establishments with fewer than 25 employees who do not have formal procedures. Because of the importance that ACAS places on drawing up disciplinary procedures and company rules, ACAS has produced an example procedure which is set out in the advisory booklet *Discipline at Work*. This shows what the scope and purpose of a disciplinary procedure ought to be, the principles of the procedure, the procedure itself, and finally the appeals process. If you examine your own organisation's disciplinary code against the ACAS template, you are likely to identify if not a mirror image, remarkable similarities. The starting-point for the actual procedure should be an oral warning, followed by a written warning if the required improvement is not forthcoming, and then a final written warning if conduct or performance is still unsatisfactory. The ultimate stage would be dismissal.

There are a number of important points to note about this staged procedure. Firstly, it is important that a record be kept of every disciplinary warning issued, even an oral or verbal warning. Secondly, it is important to advise individuals how long a warning will be 'live'. 'Live' in this context indicates the length of time that a particular disciplinary sanction will 'stay on the record'. 'Live' warnings can be taken into account if further disciplinary issues arise; warnings that have expired cannot. Many organisations will have different time-scales for different levels of warning: an oral warning might only be live for six months, whereas a written warning might be live for 12 months. Finally, it is important that employees are advised of what will happen next if no improvements are made.

The purpose and scope of a disciplinary procedure should be very clear, and however it is written it should allow all employees to understand what is expected of them in respect of conduct, attendance and job performance, and set out the rules by which such matters will be governed. The aim should be to ensure consistent and fair treatment for all.

> To what extent does your organisation's disciplinary procedure meet the criteria of clarity? Does it set out the time that individual warnings will be 'live', and is it capable of ensuring consistent and fair treatment for all employees? You may consider it worth reviewing your procedure against these benchmarks.

When we look at handling discipline later in the chapter, you will note that the only way to ensure consistency is by recognising that a disciplinary procedure is more than just a series of stages – that there are a number of principles that underlie the procedure which are extremely important and help to ensure good personnel management practice. As with the mechanics of the procedure itself, ACAS offers guidance on these principles which are set out below:

- No disciplinary action will be taken against an employee until the case has been fully investigated.

- At every stage in the procedure the employee will be advised of the nature of the complaint against him or her and will be given the opportunity to state his or her case before any decision is made.

- At all stages the employee will have the right to be accompanied by a shop steward, employee representative or work colleague during the disciplinary interview.

- No employee will be dismissed for a first breach of discipline, except in the case of gross misconduct when the penalty will be dismissal without notice or payment in lieu of notice.

- An employee will have the right to appeal against any disciplinary penalty imposed.

- The procedure may be implemented at any stage if the employee's alleged misconduct warrants such action.

Although it is to be hoped that any disciplinary problems within an organisation can be resolved at the earliest opportunity, and without recourse to all levels of the procedure, the world of work is not so simple. Many managers complain that having given an individual an oral warning or, in some cases, having got all the way through to final written warning stage, the problem to which the disciplinary action related resurfaces once the warning ceases to be 'live'. It is then assumed, mistakenly, that the whole process must begin again. Not so: two points need to be considered. Firstly, for what length of time do warnings stay 'live'? If it is for too short a time, you run the risk of only achieving short-term changes in behaviour – but on the other hand you do not want it to be too long. A sanction that remains on an employee's record for an excessive period of time relative to the original breach of discipline can act as a de-motivating influence. Secondly – and this is a very common mistake – has the warning been too narrow? Very often it makes more sense to issue a warning in such a way that an employee is left in no doubt that 'any further breaches of the company rules will result in further disciplinary action'. As the ACAS principles which we set out above identify, the procedure may be implemented at any stage. If you have an employee against whom you constantly have to invoke the disciplinary procedure, or if the offence is serious but does not amount to gross misconduct, then it may be appropriate to begin with a written rather than an oral warning – and in extreme cases, a final written warning.

Before leaving procedural requirements it is necessary to examine what 'gross misconduct' means. You will have noted above that according to the ACAS principles it is permissible to dismiss an individual without notice if he or she has committed an act of gross misconduct. Gross misconduct can be notoriously difficult to define and often difficult to prove, and ACAS very helpfully provides a list of actions which would normally fall into this category. These are: theft, fraud, deliberate falsification of records, fighting, assault on another person, deliberate damage to company property, serious incapability through alcohol or being under the influence of illegal drugs, serious negligence, and serious acts of insubordination. While that is quite an extensive list, it is also notable for its lack of precision. For example, what is an act of serious insubordination? Would it cover a refusal to carry out instructions received from a supervisor? What is serious negligence, or serious incapability through alcohol?

The potential difficulties caused by this lack of precision mean that whatever procedure you establish, it reflects the organisation's structure and culture – the norms and beliefs within which an organisation functions. This is where the writing of clear company rules is so important. Not only do they help to distinguish between ordinary and gross misconduct, but they provide employees with clear guidelines on what is acceptable in the workplace, both in terms of behaviour and performance.

> How sure are you, that your organisation's procedure is working as it should? What criteria would you use to assess whether it is or is not?

RULES IN EMPLOYMENT

Rules should be written for the benefit of both employer and employee. Their purpose should be to define and make clear exactly what standards of behaviour are expected in the workplace. Typically, rules will cover the following areas:

• time-keeping

• absence

• health and safety

• misconduct

• use of company facilities

• confidentiality

• discrimination.

There are some (including ACAS) who would argue that rules about poor performance should also be included, but we believe there are some practical difficulties about writing rules in respect of poor performance. Clearly, if rules relating to behaviour are broken and, as a consequence, performance is impaired (eg by drunkenness), then it is easy to see a link between poor performance and rule-breaking, and the disciplinary procedure's being used to correct the problem. But if someone is simply not competent to carry out the tasks for which he or she has been employed, then it is hard to identify what sort of rule has been broken, notwithstanding the fact that the disciplinary procedure may be used as a means of correcting the problem. This however, is a minor point, the important maxim is to ensure that the following principles are followed whatever rules are established: one, that they are clear; two, that they cannot be misinterpreted; and three, that they are capable of distinguishing between ordinary misconduct and gross misconduct. Failure to be clear and failing to make a proper distinction between types of misconduct have caused many organisations to suffer losses at industrial tribunals. It is no good having a very clear procedure, laying down the type and number of warnings that an individual should receive, if the rules which are being applied are imprecise or do not reflect the attitudes and requirements of the particular business. 'How people expect to behave depends as much on day-to-day understanding as on formal rules. Workplaces may have identical rule-books, but in one it may be accepted practice to leave early near holidays; in another, on Fridays; in a third, when a relatively lenient supervisor is in charge; and so on' (Edwards, 1994; p563).

There is also a need to ensure that rules reflect current industrial practice, as is illustrated by the following case. The applicant, who was a union representative, had been dismissed for gross misconduct after gaining unauthorised access to his employer's computer system. He had gained access to a part of the system that would normally be inaccessible to him by using another employee's password. In his defence it was argued that 'he had only been playing around' with the system, and that there had been no intent to obtain information to which he was not entitled. Furthermore, that while he might have been doing something wrong, it was not 'gross misconduct' and could have been covered by a disciplinary warning. In upholding the dismissal for gross misconduct, the Employment Appeal Tribunal (EAT) stated:

> The industrial members are clear in their view that in this modern industrial world if an employee deliberately uses an unauthorised password in order to enter or to attempt to enter a computer known to contain information to which he is not entitled, then that of itself is gross misconduct which *prima facie* will attract summary dismissal, although there may be some exceptional circumstances in which such a response might be held unreasonable.
>
> <div align="right">Denco <i>v</i> Joinson (1991) IRLR 63</div>

In essence the EAT was making the same point that had been made some years earlier in C. A. Parsons & Co. Ltd *v* McLaughlin (1978) IRLR 65 – that some things should be so obvious that it ought not to be necessary to have a rule forbidding it. However, to avoid any doubt, the EAT went on to say in the Denco case that

> It is desirable, however, that management should make it abundantly clear to the workforce that interfering with computers will carry severe penalties. Rules concerning access to and use of computers should be reduced to writing and left near the computers for reference.

While the comments of the employment appeal tribunal to the effect that certain things ought to be obvious may seem perfectly reasonable, it should be remembered that employers have an absolute duty to demonstrate that they have acted reasonably when they dismiss somebody. And, in Denco, even the EAT acknowledged that there might be circumstances in which an employer's particular response might be 'unreasonable', even over something which is supposedly obvious. The message is very clear: if something is not allowed, then say so, and spell out the consequences of breaching the rule. Because technology, or the ownership of businesses, can change – what may have been acceptable once may now be frowned on. The prudent employee relations specialist will ensure, therefore, that the organisation rules are the subject of regular monitoring to reflect properly the organisation's current values and requirements.

The need to be clear about the behavioural standards that are expected in any workplace, and about the sanctions that will be applied for non-compliance, is particularly important in distinguishing between gross and ordinary misconduct. Very often organisations will commit the error of making vague statements in their company rules to the effect that certain actions *may* be treated as gross misconduct or that failure to do something *could* leave an individual liable to disciplinary action. We have already highlighted the importance of discipline's being applied fairly and consistently; how can this happen if different managers are given the opportunity to apply different standards to the same actions? One way to avoid this problem is to make positive statements – for example, that theft will be treated as gross misconduct.

But even here there is room for doubt and confusion. If an employee stole a large sum of money from the company, there is little doubt that he or she would be charged with gross misconduct and, if the allegation was proved, dismissed without notice. What, though, would happen if the alleged theft were of items of company stationery or spare parts for machinery? Would every manager treat the matter as one of gross misconduct and dismiss, or would the value of the items taken be a consideration? Employee relations specialists need to be aware of these potential contradictions when helping to frame rules that govern the employment relationship. If it is normal practice to turn a blind eye to the misappropriation of items like stationery, it can cause problems when someone is accused of a more serious theft. Allowing different managers to take a different view about the seriousness of certain acts of theft brings inconsistency into the process; this could prove very costly at an industrial tribunal. A better rule on theft than the one shown above might be:

Theft – Stealing from the company, from its suppliers or from fellow employees is unacceptable, whatever the value or amount involved, and will be treated as gross misconduct.

Using this style of wording should help to ensure that every employee in the organisation knows the consequences of any dishonest action on his or her part. Ensuring that managers apply the sanction consistently is another problem and one we will deal with later in the chapter.

> How often are the rules in your organisation reviewed, and when were they last updated? Do you know whether different standards apply to the application of the rules?

Theft, whatever standards different organisations might apply, is usually associated in the public mind with gross misconduct, notwithstanding the problems of definition that we have just discussed. The distinction between gross misconduct and other serious infractions of the rules can often be harder to identify. The first thing we have to acknowledge is that no clear distinction exists, but that it is possible to apply some common sense to the issue. For example, it is possible to understand that a serious assault on another person ought to be treated as gross misconduct, but that poor time-keeping would not be. While a consistent failure to observe time-keeping standards might ultimately lead to dismissal, the two offences will clearly provoke different outcomes initially: immediate dismissal in the first case and probably a verbal warning in the second. Perhaps one way in which a distinction might be drawn, therefore, is by a reference to the expected outcome of the disciplinary process and to the relationship of trust that needs to exist between employer and employee. Without detailing the wider range of terms contained in the contract of employment, it is implied in every contract that for an employment relationship to be maintained there has to be mutual trust and confidence between employer and employee. When issues of discipline arise, that relationship is damaged. As we will discuss in more detail later in the chapter, one of the purposes of disciplinary action is to bring about a change in behaviour, and if the offence is one of poor time-keeping there is usually no question of a total breakdown of trust and the expected outcome of disciplinary action is of improved time-keeping and a re-building of the relationship. If the cause of the disciplinary action was a serious assault on another employee, perhaps a manager, a disciplinary sanction might bring about a change in behaviour or ensure that the offence is not repeated, but there is a high probability that the relationship of mutual trust and confidence might be damaged beyond repair and it might be impossible for the employment relationship to be maintained.

HANDLING DISCIPLINARY ISSUES

The way in which managers and employee relations specialists need to approach disciplinary issues will be subtly different depending on the nature of the problem. We have acknowledged that most organisations will have some form of disciplinary procedure, and probably some company rules, but we have also highlighted that the use and application of the procedure may vary from company to company and from manager to manager. In some organisations disciplinary action is very rarely taken, either because standards are clear and accepted by employees or because standards are vague and applied haphazardly. In others, standards are maintained by an over-reliance on mechanistic procedures, which usually act as a de-motivating influence on the workforce. The purpose of any disciplinary procedure should be 'to help and encourage all employees to achieve and maintain standards of conduct, attendance and job performance' (ACAS Code). This is what 'best practice' means, and the aim of all managers should be to handle disciplinary issues in as fair and equitable way as is possible. They should do this because it represents 'good practice' in terms of management skill, but they must also do so because of the influence of the law.

The law on unfair dismissal is now so ingrained into the fabric of the workplace that only by maintaining standards of 'best practice' does it cease to become an issue. It is not unreasonable to say that good managers have nothing to fear from the laws relating to individual employment rights. That is not to say that the law should be ignored, but neither should it be feared. In an ideal world managers would act in such a way that they avoided accusations of unfair treatment – but this is not an ideal world, and even the best managers can find themselves defending their actions before an industrial tribunal, which is why it is important for the concept of 'best practice' to become part of the organisation's ethos. Not only does this allow them to demonstrate 'consistent and fair treatment for all' (ACAS Code) but it ensures that they meet their absolute duty to act reasonably, as is set out in section 98(4)(a) of the Employment Rights Act (1996). Furthermore, such an approach not only makes good business sense, it fits the concept of natural justice that is so important in handling disciplinary issues. The reasons for fairly dismissing an employee are set out in section 98(2) of the statute, and earlier in the chapter we identified conduct, capability and 'some other substantial reason' as matters that were likely to have been dealt with by using the disciplinary process. Although we will look at each of these in turn, a good manager will consider whether some other route will be more appropriate before becoming embroiled in the disciplinary process. Maintaining good standards of discipline within an organisation is not just about applying the rules or operating the procedure – it is about the ability to achieve standards of performance and behaviour without using the 'big stick'. One example of this might be counselling, which might provide the required change in behaviour without making the individual concerned feel that he or she was some kind of dissident.

Counselling

Counselling is more than simply offering help and advice: it is helping, in a non-threatening way, an individual to come to terms with a particular problem. The problem may be about performance, it may be about something mundane like time-keeping, it may be potentially serious such as drug or alcohol abuse, or it may involve another employee – an accusation of sexual harassment for example. Counselling an employee, whatever the nature of the difficulty, needs careful preparation. In the case of a drug or alcohol problem the manager needs to ask himself or herself whether he or she has the necessary skills to carry out such a sensitive task, but even if the conclusion is that specialist help is required, he or she can still help to bring the problem out into the open. In other cases, provided the problem is approached in a systematic way, this type of intervention may avoid disciplinary action.

One example of where counselling might be an appropriate first step would be in respect of an allegation of sexual harassment. Provided that the complainant has not suffered any physical assault and, most importantly, that the complainant is happy for the matter to be handled in an informal way, then counselling can be very helpful – not only to the alleged harasser, but also to the victim. Without wishing to minimise or condone what can be a very serious problem in some workplaces, it can often be the case that the alleged harasser does not realise that his or her actions are causing offence. Sitting down with individuals and explaining to them that some of their words or actions are causing distress to another employee can often be very effective. However, it is important not to leave it there but to monitor the situation and ensure both that the behavioural change is permanent and that the complainant is satisfied with the action taken and the eventual outcome.

> Does your organisation's disciplinary code say anything about equal opportunities or discrimination? Is there, for example, a clear rule that says sexual harassment or racial discrimination will not be tolerated? Do you have a code of practice that gives guidance on how to manage these sorts of problems?

Similarly, if the problem concerns poor performance, 'best practice' would be to discuss the problem with the employee concerned rather than go straight into the disciplinary procedure. The first step would be to speak to the employee, in private, explaining what aspects of performance were falling short of the desired standard, and most importantly, what actions were required by the employee to put matters right. The important principle to remember here is to set clear standards. If employees do not know what is expected of them, how can they deliver the performance that is required? Another step in this process might be to consider whether some additional training might be an option.

The formal approach
However, if after following the counselling route there are still complaints of harassment, or the quality of work carried out still falls below standard, then it may be necessary to begin disciplinary proceedings. Again it is important to remember the principle of 'best practice'. The operation of the disciplinary procedure often leads to managerial disenchantment because, as we are often told by line managers, 'it takes too long'. This is where the employee relations specialist has a clear duty to advise and guide management colleagues. Because starting down the disciplinary path can, ultimately, lead to a dismissal, it is important to remember the requirement that in taking a decision to dismiss somebody you should act reasonably and in accordance with natural justice.

It is easy to understand the frustration a line manager might feel if the disciplinary process takes too long, but it is the employer who is in control of the process and can determine the timings. The question of fairness relates not to how long the process takes but to the quality of the procedures followed. For example, say you had an experienced employee who was responsible for carrying out a very important task within the organisation and which had serious cost implications if it were not carried out efficiently. If the task was not being performed to your satisfaction, the amount of time you could allow the employee to improve his or her performance would be limited. Alternatively, if the employee was inexperienced and performing a task that was less cost-sensitive and important, it could be argued that the time allowed for improvement should be longer. It is also necessary to consider how long the sub-standard performance has been allowed to continue unchallenged, because it may be the case that a previous manager was prepared to accept a lower standard of performance. What is important in both of these scenarios is that the employee is made aware of the standard that is required and understands the importance of achieving that standard in whatever time-scale is agreed. Under the ACAS Code it is perfectly acceptable to miss out stages in the disciplinary procedure and this may be the most obvious solution if the consequences of the poor performance are so serious.

USING THE DISCIPLINARY PROCEDURE

Whatever the nature of the problem, once the decision has been taken to invoke the formal disciplinary procedures it is important to ensure that the application of that procedure cannot be challenged. The following guidelines, which are broken down into two stages, should help to ensure a consistent and fair approach. Firstly, there are the steps that need to be taken in preparing to conduct a disciplinary interview. There are 12 points to consider:

- Prepare carefully, and ensure that the person to conduct the disciplinary hearing has all the facts. This sounds straightforward, but it is not always possible to get all the facts. Very often the evidence of alleged misconduct is no more than circumstantial, particularly in cases involving theft. However, the important principle is to ensure that a thorough investigation takes place, and that whatever facts are available are presented.

- Ensure that the employee knows what the nature of the complaint is. Again this sounds straightforward, but it can be the point at which things begin to go wrong. For example, it would not be sufficient to simply tell an employee that he or she is to attend a disciplinary hearing in respect of poor performance. The employee would need to be provided with sufficient detail to prepare an adequate defence.

- Ensure that the employee knows the procedure to be followed. Simply because individuals are provided with a copy of the disciplinary code when they commence employment does not imply that they know the procedure to be followed. It is always wise to provide them with a new copy of the disciplinary procedure – not least because there may have been amendments since they received their original version.

- Advise the employee of his or her right to be accompanied. Where individuals work in a unionised environment this tends to be automatic: an invitation to attend the meeting is sent directly to the appropriate union official. However, in non-unionised environments people are not always sure who would be an appropriate person to accompany them or whether they want to be accompanied at all. As a matter of best practice it is always wise to encourage somebody to be accompanied, but if he or she refuses you must respect that. When it does happen, you need to ensure that the fact that the employee wishes to attend a disciplinary interview alone is recorded.

- Enquire if there are any mitigating circumstances. What is or is not a mitigating circumstance will be dictated by each case. It is not for the employer to identify matters of mitigation, but it is important to ask the employee who is facing a disciplinary sanction whether there are any particular circumstances that might account for his or her actions. Whether an individual manager will accept what may seem to be no more than excuses is a question determined by individual circumstances. For example, an employee with a bad time-keeping record might be excused if he or she was having to care for a sick relative before attending work, whereas another employee might put forward a less acceptable excuse, such as a broken alarm clock.

- Are you being consistent? This is where the employee relations specialist can provide invaluable assistance to the line manager. Most line managers deal with disciplinary issues very rarely and may not be aware of previous actions or approaches that have been taken in respect of disciplinary issues. The employee relations specialist can provide the advice and information that ensures a consistent approach.

- Consider explanations. This is not the same as mitigating circumstances or excuses. This is the opportunity that you must give to an employee to explain acts or omissions. For example, if the hearing was about poor performance, the employee might want to point out factors that have inhibited performance but which might not be immediately apparent to the line manager conducting the hearing; these may be issues around the quality of training received or the quality of instructions given.

- Allow the employee time to prepare a case. The question here is how much time? It is important that issues of discipline are dealt with speedily once an employee has been advised of the complaint against him or her, but it is important for the employee not to feel unfairly pressured in putting together any defence that he or she has.

- Arrange a suitable place for the interview. This would seem to be obvious, but as with so many things in employee relations, what may seem obvious to the specialist is not always apparent to the busy line manager. There can be a tendency for managers to arrange meetings within their own offices where the potential for being interrupted is more pronounced and privacy is less easily guaranteed.

- Ensure that personnel records etc, are available. This means more than basic information about the individual, and must also include records relating to any previous disciplinary warnings, attendance, performance appraisals, etc.

- Where possible, be accompanied. It is very unwise for a manager to conduct a disciplinary interview alone because of the possible need at some future time to corroborate what was said. It also helps to rebut any allegations of bullying or intimidation that may be made by a disgruntled employee.

- Try to ensure the attendance of witnesses. This should not be a problem if the people concerned are in your employment but can prove difficult when they are outsiders.

We cannot stress too strongly the importance of careful preparation, for it is at this stage that things often go wrong. Also, good preparation helps the second part of the process: conducting the actual disciplinary interview. There are six points to remember at this stage:

- Introduce those present – not just on the grounds of courtesy but because an employee facing a possible sanction is entitled to know who is going to be involved in any decision. In a small workplace this may be unnecessary, but it can be very important in larger establishments.

- Explain the purpose of the interview and how it will be conducted. This builds on the need to ensure that the employee fully understands the nature of the complaint against him or her and the procedure to be followed. As with any hearing, however informal, openness about what it is for, what the possible outcomes are, and the method by which it is to be conducted is an important prerequisite for demonstrating that natural justice has been adhered to.

• Set out precisely the nature of the complaint and outline the management's case by briefly going through the evidence. This may seem like overkill but it is important to ensure that there are no misunderstandings.

• Give the employee the right to reply. Put simply: no right of reply – no natural justice.

• Allow time for general questioning, cross-examination of witnesses, etc. If this did not happen, it would be difficult to persuade a tribunal that the test of reasonableness had been achieved.

• Sum up. There is a need to be clear about what conclusions have been reached and what decisions are to be made, and for this reason it is better to adjourn, if only briefly, so that a properly considered final decision can be made.

Careful preparation and a well-conducted interview are not guarantees that individuals will not complain of unfairness, but they are essential if the test of reasonableness is to be satisfied.

MISCONDUCT DURING EMPLOYMENT

As we have already noted, there are two distinct types of misconduct: those perpetrated by the persistent rule-breaker and those by the individual who commits an act of gross misconduct. In most instances, dealing with the persistent rule-breaker should be relatively straightforward, provided that the disciplinary code is applied in a sensible and equitable manner. Assuming that it has been possible to go through some form of counselling with the employee but that the required change in behaviour has not been forthcoming, then it is likely that the only alternative is to begin the disciplinary process. As we noted above, the likely first step would be a verbal or written warning followed, if necessary, by the subsequent stages in the procedure, leading ultimately to dismissal.

While the dismissal of an employee is never an easy task for a manager, it can, if the steps outlined above are followed, be a relatively straightforward process. Furthermore, individuals who are dismissed for persistent infringements of the rules, infringements for which they have had a series of warnings and, as we will see later, the opportunity to appeal, rarely go to industrial tribunals. It is very difficult for an individual to claim that the employer acted unreasonably when he or she has been given a number of opportunities to modify his or her actions. The only complaint that an individual might have in such circumstances is that the procedure itself was unfair or had been applied contrary to the rules of natural justice. This could happen if some people were disciplined for breaches of the rules and others were not.

> Imagine that your organisation has dismissed somebody for bad time-keeping and unauthorised absences, and the employee has challenged this at an industrial tribunal. What evidence would you need to present in support of your organisation's action?

Gross misconduct, on the other hand, presents totally different problems for the manager. Earlier in the chapter we examined some of the issues surrounding the concept of gross misconduct and the need to be absolutely clear what breaches of the rules 'will' mean as opposed to 'might' mean. For the manager who is called upon to deal with a case of alleged gross misconduct it is vitally important that all procedural steps are strictly adhered to, for mistakes can be costly. For obvious reasons managers are often under extreme pressure to resolve matters quickly – not just because it is much fairer to the accused individual that the matter is resolved, but because other colleagues may have already prejudged the outcome. Pressure cannot always be avoided, but it is necessary that in such circumstances the requirement to prepare properly and conduct a fair hearing is not forgotten.

Some cases of gross misconduct are very clear-cut: the employee concerned either admits the offence or there are sufficient witnesses to confirm that the alleged offence was committed by the employee in question. In such cases the first decision for the employer is to decide whether to treat the matter as gross misconduct – for which the penalty is summary dismissal without notice or pay in lieu of notice – or to take a more lenient line Such decisions are made easier if, as we saw above, the company rules are clear and unambiguous about what constitutes gross misconduct. But in our experience, many cases of gross misconduct are not clear-cut and managers are very unsure about how to deal with them. Some of the cases we have been asked to assist with include suspected theft of goods or money, suspected tampering with time-recording devices, suspected false expense claims, and seeking payment of sick pay while fit for work. One of the reasons why managers can be unsure about this type of offence is that some of them could lead to criminal charges being laid against the employee or employees concerned.

One way to approach this very sensitive issue is by ensuring that the Burchell Rules are adhered to. These rules relate to a case dating back to 1978 involving an incident of alleged theft (British Home Stores *v* Burchell (1978) IRLR 379). The specific facts of the case are not particularly important, but it is significant because of the test of reasonableness that flowed from it. The Burchell test states that where an employee is suspected of a dismissable offence, an employer needs to show

• that the dismissal was *bona fide* for that reason and not on a pretext

• that the belief that the employee committed the offence was based on reasonable grounds – ie that on the evidence before him, the employer was entitled to say that it was more probable that the employee did, in fact, commit the offence than that he or she did not

- that the belief was based on a reasonable investigation in the circumstances – that the employer's investigation took place before the employee was dismissed and included an opportunity for the employee to offer an explanation.

Let us look at this test in a little more detail and try and relate to events as they might take place in the working environment. Take the example of a suspected fraudulent expense claim. The first part of Burchell says that the dismissal must be *bona fide* and not on a pretext – this means not using the alleged offence as a convenient means of dismissing an employee whose face no longer fits or who has a history of misconduct for which no previous action has been taken. The second and third parts of Burchell relate to the employer's belief in the employee's guilt and to the standard of the investigation carried out. As Lewis states (1997; p171), 'The question to be determined is not whether, by an objective standard, the employer's belief that the employee was guilty of the misconduct was well founded but whether the employer believed that the employee was guilty and was entitled so to believe, having regard to the investigation conducted.' Using the Burchell test in the case of a suspected fraudulent expense claim, the employer would need to be very diligent in assembling the evidence. What guidelines were laid down for the benefit of those allowed to claim expenses? What expenses had been accepted in the past? Were the same standards applied consistently to all staff? Had any other employee made a similar claim in the past without challenge? Assembling such an array of evidence is only likely to happen if there is a thorough investigation – but this is only the first part of the process: the employee is also entitled to offer an explanation. What do you do if the explanation is linked to the lack of guidelines about what is and is not claimable? While the findings in the Parsons case (see above) – that some things are so obvious that they do not need a rule – are relevant, the seniority of the employee concerned might also be relevant. A 'reasonable' belief that a senior employee, who regularly claimed expenses, was acting dishonestly might be easier to demonstrate than in a situation in which a junior employee was claiming expenses for the first time. We acknowledged, above, the uncertainties we sometimes encounter when the possibility of criminal proceedings is on the agenda. The question we are asked is, Can we dismiss somebody if we have asked the police to investigate with a view to prosecution? The short answer is yes, provided that the Burchell test is followed. Quite properly, the burden of proof placed on an employer in such circumstances is totally different from the burden of proof imposed by the criminal justice system. In a criminal trial the prosecution must prove 'beyond all reasonable doubt' that an offence was committed. This is entirely reasonable when an individual's liberty is at risk and it is why, under the Burchell test, you can dismiss somebody 'fairly' for dishonesty, who may be found 'not guilty' in a criminal trial.

LACK OF CAPABILITY

This is the second of the fair reasons for dismissing an employee, and we need to consider it under two subcategories: firstly, capability that is linked to an employee's ability to do his or her job because of poor performance, and secondly, capability that relates to an individual's ability to do a job because of poor health or sickness.

Performance

Advising a line manager who has a member of his or her team delivering less than adequate performance is very common for the employee relations specialist. Very often the initial step in this advisory role is persuading the line manager not to take precipitate action. It is not unusual for the personnel professional to be told by a manager that a particular employee is 'useless' and that he or she needs help to 'get rid of them'. Persuading a line manager not to launch into a formal disciplinary process without considering what other options are open to him or her is very important. Earlier in the chapter we looked at the question of counselling – and in the event of an ultimate dismissal, an industrial tribunal would want to satisfy itself that such a step had, at the very least, been considered before formal disciplinary procedures began. Another option might be the provision of alternative work for the employee concerned if he or she had demonstrated an incapability of the present tasks.

Whatever options are taken, the employee is entitled, on grounds of fairness, to be told exactly what is required of him or her, what standards are being set, and the time-scale in which he or she is expected to achieve them. During the period of time that an individual is being given to reach the desired standards, a good manager will ensure that he or she is kept informed of any progress – back to the principle of 'best practice'.

Managing absence

This can be one of the most emotive issues that any manager has to face and has to be handled with sensitivity, particularly where there is no dispute about the genuineness of any illness.

Absences from work can occur for a number of reasons. Some, like holiday, bereavement or paternity leave, will normally be arranged in advance and cause minimum disruption to the employing organisation. The absences that cause disruption within any organisation are those that are unplanned – either because the employee concerned is sick or has simply failed to turn up for work. In so far as the second reason, it would be normal to treat this as a breach of the rules on unauthorised absence and deal with it as a case of misconduct.

One reason for unauthorised absence could be that an employee has failed to return from an authorised absence – say, a holiday – at the due time. For individuals to return late from holiday has become a much more widespread problem in recent years due to the increase in overseas travel, and most individuals who return to work late in such circumstances do so because of delayed air flights or other travel problems. For some employers the disruption caused by a late return from holiday will be minimal and they may treat it as no more than an irritation, but for others, particularly at a time of the year when large numbers of people are on holiday, the disruption caused can be very serious. Notwithstanding the fact that the cause of the problem (a late flight) was outside the employee's control, the employer might take the view that steps could have been taken to minimise the disruption: a telephone call, for example. Whether disciplinary action is taken in such circumstances will clearly rest on the facts of each individual case, but in any event action should follow the guidance given above for preparing and conducting a disciplinary interview, particularly in respect of mitigating circumstances and other explanations.

However, in most establishments, the most widespread cause of absence from work is sickness or alleged sickness and, while it would be wholly unreasonable to treat a case of genuine sickness as a disciplinary matter, incapacity for work on health grounds can be a fair reason for dismissing an employee. Because of this, the way in which an employer deals with health-related absences is very important, and some analogies with a disciplinary process can be identified. Dealing with sickness absence can be a minefield for any manager, but for the employee relation specialist who is expected to give clear and timely advice, it is even more so. As we have already pointed out, unauthorised absence is usually a disciplinary matter, but most absences do not fall into this category: they will be recorded as sickness. Without wishing to suggest that any employee deliberately seeks to be untruthful, notifying the employer of 'sickness' remains the most common reason for absence from work. Absence, therefore, needs to be managed effectively, but with due regard to 'best practice'.

The starting-point is adequate record-keeping. ACAS advises that 'records showing lateness and the duration of and reason for all spells of absence should be kept to help monitor absence levels'. Such records enable the manager to substantiate whether a problem of persistent absence is real or imagined. All too often the employee relations specialist who is asked for advice is expected to work with insufficient data. Managing absence is not just about applying rules or following procedure, it is about addressing problems of persistent absence quickly and acting consistently. This sends out a clear and unambiguous message to all employees that absence is regarded as a serious matter. But how do you act rigorously and at the same time retain fairness and consistency? ACAS has set out the following guidelines for handling frequent and persistent short-term absences, which should prove helpful in most cases.

• Absences should be investigated promptly and the employee asked to give an explanation.

• Where there is no medical advice to support frequent self-certified absences, the employee should be asked to consult a doctor to establish whether medical treatment is necessary and whether the underlying reason for absence is work-related.

• If after investigation it appears that there were no good reasons for the absences, the matter should be dealt with under the disciplinary procedure.

• Where absences arise from temporary domestic problems, the employer in deciding appropriate action should consider whether an improvement in attendance is likely.

- In all cases the employee should be told what improvement is expected and warned of the likely consequences if this does not happen.

- If there is no improvement, the employee's age, length of service, performance, the likelihood of a change in attendance, the availability of suitable alternative work, and the effect of past and future absences on the business should all be taken into account on deciding appropriate action.

This is very helpful and useful advice in respect of absences that are deemed not to be genuine or sickness-related, but what happens if the reason for the absences is illness or injury supported by medical certificates? If doubt still remains about the nature of the illness or injury, the employee can be asked if he or she is prepared to be examined by an independent doctor to be appointed by the company. Normally, unless there is some form of contractual provision which allows for this, an employee cannot normally be compelled to attend. However, with the growth of occupational sick pay schemes, many organisations have overcome this problem by building compulsion into their scheme rules. Very often, advising an employee that such an examination will be required if attendance does not improve is sufficient to resolve the problem. Complications can arise when the injury or illness which necessitates persistent short-term absences is genuine, because it could never be reasonable to discipline in such circumstances. It can be fair to dismiss the employee concerned, but only after a careful process of assessment and examination has been carried out. A similar problem arises in respect of employees whose absence is long-term, and again ACAS provides guidance in recommending a procedure to be followed:

- The employee should be contacted periodically and should himself or herself maintain regular contact with the employer.

- The employee should be advised if employment is at risk.

- The employee should be asked if he or she will consent to their own doctor's being contacted (the employee's right to refuse consent, to see the report, and to request amendments to it, must be clearly spelt out to him or her).

- The employee's doctor should be asked if the employee will be able to return to work and the nature of the work he or she will be capable of carrying out.

- On the basis of the report received, the employer should consider whether alternative work is available.

- Employers are not expected to create special jobs, nor are they expected to be medical experts. They should simply take action on the basis of the medical evidence.

- As with other absences, the possibility of an independent medical examination should be considered.

- Where an employee refuses to co-operate in providing medical evidence, he or she should be told, in writing, that a decision will have to be taken on the basis of what information is available, and that the decision may result in dismissal.

- Where the employee's job can no longer be kept open and no suitable alternative is available, the employee should be informed of the likelihood of dismissal.

All of the above makes good sense and fits in with the principle of managing absence with a 'best practice' ethos. However, dealing with employees who have a recurring health problem or whose capacity has been impaired by accident or sickness has now been complicated by the Disability Discrimination Act (1995). This Act, which came into force in December 1996, has added a further dimension to the management of absence.

The principal purpose of the Act is to protect disabled people from discrimination in the field of employment. As part of this protection, employers may have to make 'reasonable adjustments' to employment arrangements: in the context of managing absence, Section 4(2)(d) of the Disability Act states that 'It is unlawful for an employer to discriminate against a disabled person by dismissing them or subjecting them to any other detriment.' Because the Act applies equally to existing employees as well as to new recruits, it will no longer be possible for employers to initiate action in respect of employees with a permanent health problem without paying due regard to the new legislation. Section 6(1) of the Act states that an employer has a duty to make 'reasonable adjustments' if any employee is disadvantaged either by the physical features of the workplace or by the arrangements for the work itself. The Code of Practice which accompanies the Act lists a number of 'reasonable adjustments' that an employer might have to consider, including

- making adjustments to premises
- allocating some of the disabled person's duties to another person
- transferring the person to fill an existing vacancy
- altering the person's working hours
- assigning the person to a different place of work
- allowing the person to be absent during working hours for rehabilitation, assessment or treatment
- giving the person, or arranging for the person to be given, training
- acquiring or modifying equipment
- modifying instructions or reference manuals
- modifying procedures for testing or assessment
- providing a reader or interpreter
- providing supervision.

Clearly, employers will not have to make 'reasonable adjustments' in respect of all 'sick' employees, only those who fit the Act's definition of disability. A disabled person is a person with 'a physical or mental impairment which has a substantial and long-term adverse effect on his or her ability to carry out normal day-to-day activities' (Section 1). This chapter is about discipline and not disability, but employee relations specialists must be aware that the disability legislation imposes challenges which must be taken into account when managing absence.

Some other substantial reason
It would not be right to leave a chapter on discipline without taking a brief look at one of the other fair reasons for dismissal set out by Section 99 of the Employment Rights Act (1996): 'some other substantial reason'. This concept was introduced into the legislation 'so as to give tribunals the discretion to accept as a fair reason for dismissal something that would not conveniently fit into any of the other categories' (Lewis, 1997; p177). Dismissals for 'some other substantial reason' have, as Lewis points out, been upheld in respect of employees who have been sentenced to a term of imprisonment, employees who cannot get on with each other, or where there are problems between an individual and one of the organisation's customers. Interestingly, the cases which Lewis quotes all relate to the 1970s and 1980s, which might indicate that businesses are less reliant on this rather vague concept. It is certainly the case that the more professional employee relations specialists, recognising that such issues and conflicts do arise, have amended their disciplinary procedures accordingly, and many organisations will have a rule relating to general conduct which may be worded in the following way:

> Any conduct detrimental to the interests of the company, its relations with the public, its customers and its suppliers, damaging to its public image or offensive to other employees in the company, shall be a disciplinary offence.

It is easy to see how such a rule could be used to deal with any of the examples cited by Lewis, and, in the context of managing discipline, it is a much more systematic route. Some other substantial reason can, to the non-lawyer, be a rather vague concept: by being able to proceed against an individual for a breach of a specific rule is much clearer to everybody involved.

APPEALS

Every disciplinary procedure must contain an appeals process; otherwise, it is almost impossible to demonstrate that you have acted reasonably within the law. In common with every other aspect of the disciplinary process, it is important to ensure fairness and consistency within an appeals procedure, and this should provide for appeals to be dealt with as quickly as possible. An employee should be able to appeal at every stage of the disciplinary process. Common sense dictates that any appeal should be heard by someone who is senior to the person imposing the disciplinary sanction. This will not always be possible, particularly in smaller organisations, but if the person hearing the appeal is the same as the person who imposed the original sanction,

ACAS advises that the person should hear the appeal and act as impartially as possible. In essence, an appeal in these circumstances is going to be no more than a review of the original decision, but perhaps in a calmer and more objective manner.

As with the original disciplinary hearing, an appeal falls into two parts – action prior to the appeal and the actual hearing itself. Before any appeal hearing the employee should be told what the arrangements are and what his or her rights under the procedure are. At the same time it is important to obtain, and read, any relevant documentation. At the appeal hearing it is important first to explain its purpose, how it will be conducted, and what decisions the person or persons hearing the appeal are able to come to. It is important too to consider any new evidence and ensure that all relevant issues have been properly examined. While it is important that appeals are not seen as the opportunity to seek a more sympathetic assessment of the issue in question, it is equally important that appeals are not routinely dismissed. Overturning a bad or unjust decision is just as important as confirming a fair decision. It is an effective way of signalling to employees that all disciplinary issues will be dealt with consistently and objectively.

Many organisations fall into the trap of using their grievance procedure in place of a proper appeals process. This is to be avoided wherever possible. The grievance procedure should be reserved for resolving problems that arise from employment and will be covered in the next chapter. Finally, it is important to note that not only should appeals be dealt with in a timely fashion, the procedure should specify time-limits within which appeals should be lodged.

CONCLUSION

In this chapter we have tried to explain discipline in a systematic way, starting with the origins of disciplinary procedures and then explaining the current legal position. We have discussed the importance of procedures and the need to follow as closely as possible to the guidelines set out by ACAS. We put great stress on the need for clear and unambiguous rules within the workplace, and recommended that both procedures and rules be regularly monitored.

In the final part of the chapter we concentrated on the handling of disciplinary issues, looking at counselling, preparing for and conducting a disciplinary interview, misconduct and capability. Finally, we explained the need for a fair appeals procedure.

It is because poor management of discipline can create employee relations problems that we make no apology for the stress we have placed on the importance of best practice and the need to act professionally. We have tried to reflect the realities of managing discipline within an organisational context because discussions that we have had with managers from a whole range of organisations show that disciplinary issues can cause major employee relations problems.

There is also an overwhelming business case for the effective management of discipline. More and more organisations are actively seeking to gain employee commitment by involving employees in the business, as Marchington (1995) indicates. Assuming that this is a trend that most organisations would wish to see continue, an employee relations climate that recognises the rights and responsibilities of both parties to the employment relationship is absolutely vital. One factor in establishing this climate is the need to manage discipline fairly and consistently. This will not happen unless the following principles are adhered to. There must always be a just cause for disciplinary action, whether misconduct, inability to perform the job in a satisfactory manner, or some other reason. Employers have to act reasonably as demonstrated by the operation of a procedure that conforms to the principles of 'natural justice'. Finally, employees are entitled to know the cause of the complaint against them, entitled to representation, entitled to challenge evidence, and entitled to a right of appeal.

None of this guarantees success in the handling of a disciplinary issue, but it is more likely to ensure good personnel management practice – and that in itself aids the establishment of a positive climate for employee relations.

FURTHER READING

LEWIS D. *Essentials of Employment Law*. 5th edn, London, Institute of Personnel and Development, 1997.

8 Grievance-handling

INTRODUCTION

Grievance-handling involves an element of negotiation in which the conclusion is jointly agreed. It requires distinct procedures and is primarily a line management responsibility. Employee relations managers oversee the effectiveness of grievance procedures and the training of managers to operate those procedures. However, a grievance procedure tends to follow the line management structure: eg supervisor, departmental manager, unit-wide manager, managing director, etc. Grievances can, if not handled properly, escalate into collective disputes. This why grievances and disputes are normally considered together and why they often have the one procedure. Most grievances are handled by supervisors and managers, but the employee relations manager has the important role of overseeing the effectiveness of the procedures and advising line managers.

After you have read this chapter, you will be able to

- understand the business case for resolving grievances

- explain why grievances are or are not taken up

- understand the principles that underpin grievance procedures

- describe the steps involved in managing employee grievances

- understand why some grievances are best dealt with by a specific procedure

- explain the importance of reviewing and monitoring the operation of grievance procedures.

THE BUSINESS CASE FOR RESOLVING GRIEVANCES

An employee grievance is an individual expression of dissatisfaction with management behaviour. However, a grievance may be felt by a group of employees which, if left unresolved, may develop into a collective dispute involving a trade union. But whether individual or collective, all employee grievances have the potential to damage the quality of the organisation's employee relations and thereby its competitive advantage. All grievances are important to those who express them, and must be treated seriously by management.

Employee grievances are an outward expression of worker

dissatisfaction which, if not resolved, can result in unsatisfactory work behaviour that has adverse consequences for the organisation's competitive position. Unresolved dissatisfaction gives rise to employee frustration, deteriorating inter-personal relationships, low morale, low productivity, poor quality of output or service provision, increased labour turnover, increased employee absenteeism, and increased sabotage by employees. Collective dissatisfaction may accelerate into industrial action, with all the associated increased costs stemming from such action. If an organisation has a reputation for having a high level of employee dissatisfaction, it is a disincentive for individuals or organisations to purchase goods and/or services from the organisation, fearing that they are likely to be of poor quality. A reputation for employee dissatisfaction also gives the organisation a 'poor employer' image in the labour market. Such an image accentuates the organisation's problems of recruiting and retaining the appropriate quantity and quality of labour services necessary to achieve its corporate objectives.

The presence of employee dissatisfaction results in an increase in the cost structures of an organisation relative to a competitor who has lower absolute and relative levels of employee dissatisfaction. This means the organisation loses competitive advantage, and with it, customers, sales and revenue. There is a clear business case for the effective and professional management of employee grievances. If a management knows employee dissatisfaction exists, it cannot afford to ignore this fact. The business consequences will include permanent damage to the organisation's competitiveness.

WHAT IS A GRIEVANCE?

A grievance is a complaint by an employee against management behaviour. It usually arises because an aggrieved individual regards some management decision (or act of indecision) as 'unfair'. However, not all employee complaints are justified: the management's action may be permissible – for example, within the terms of a collective agreement between the employees and the management, or within a company rule contained in the company's staff handbook. In managing employee grievances it is important that management acquires the ability to distinguish real grievances from unfounded ones, and to explain clearly and openly to the employee why a complaint may merit management's taking no action.

All grievances, however, whether real or unfounded, are important to the individual concerned and have to be treated on their merits. If management receives a complaint which it considers frivolous, it is not good practice to reject it out of hand. Management investigates why and how it has arisen, and if the complaint is not justified explains to the individual employee concerned the reasons. By behaving in this way management sets the record straight and demonstrates to its employees that both unfounded and genuine complaints are being handled effectively.

Complaints from individual employees can centre on many aspects of management behaviour. Employees may, for example, complain that the employer has acted in breach of a collective agreement (ie management is not applying it as the parties intended), the canteen facilities are poor and inadequate, the workplace is unsafe and/or unhealthy, and the disciplinary penalty imposed upon them is too harsh. Other areas of individual employees' complaints against management behaviour can include that they have been passed over for promotion, they have been denied access to a training and development opportunity, their holiday allocation does not meet their family circumstances, and their job is graded at an inappropriate level. Increasingly, many employee complaints are falling into what are broadly described as 'equality' issues. Individual women employees, for example, now complain more frequently to management that their job is undervalued and paid less than a comparable job which is of equal value to the organisation but is paid more than the job that the woman employee is currently doing. Complaints of sexual harassment also constitute employee grievances, although they usually constitute a complaint about the behaviour of an individual who may happen to be a manager rather than against a management decision. In addition, an increasing number of individual employee complaints against management behaviour are based on claims of injustice in that the behaviour complained of was motivated by a dislike of the employee on the grounds of race, creed, colour or disability.

Nevertheless, employee grievances can be collective in that a group of employees may all have the same complaint. All the employees in an office, for example, may complain that the temperature is too high or too low, while employees collectively in the workroom may complain that their level of pay or bonuses seems unfair compared with that of other groups of employees in the organisation. Whether individual or collective, real or unfounded, all grievances are important to those making the complaint, and management must deal with them quickly and in a fair and reasonable manner to prevent adverse effects on the organisation's competitiveness.

THE TAKE-UP OF GRIEVANCES

The main vehicle through which employees express their complaint is the organisation's grievance procedures (see below). Management should have a knowledge and understanding of the operation of these procedures. However, it is best practice to ensure that the organisation has the appropriate mechanisms to guarantee employee dissatisfaction is identified quickly and is dealt with to mutual satisfaction before an individual's complaint is put formally into the grievance procedure. Activating the grievance procedure is time-consuming and costly in terms of time for management.

Most employees' complaints against management behaviour do not get put into the formal grievance procedure. Few employee grievances are actually raised formally with management. There are many reasons for this. First, something may happen to make it unnecessary. As Torrington and Hall (1992) point out, the employee's dissatisfaction can disappear after a good night's sleep and/or after a cup of tea with a colleague. Second, the employee may merely want to get a dissatisfaction off his or her chest and the grievance is resolved simply by the appropriate manager's listening to the employee: 'a shoulder to cry on' provides release for the employee from disapproval of management's behaviour. Third, in times of high levels of unemployment individuals are reluctant to raise their grievances formally with the company because they fear management may hold this against them and retaliate by denying them promotion, access to training and development programmes and merit award payments. Fourth, employees may see little point in formally raising their grievance since they have no confidence that the management will do anything about it. Some individuals are unwilling to raise formally their dissatisfaction with management because they are fearful of offending their immediate superior who may regard their complaint as a criticism of their skills. To pursue the complaint will merely worsen an already unconstructive relationship between the supervisor and the individual employee, who has no desire to make his or her life at work any more unpleasant by questioning an immediate superior's judgement. Further, many individual employee grievances do not get informally raised because the basis of the complaint is the supervisor's management style (or lack of it). The employee believes that senior management will back the supervisor's case in preference to his or her own.

A lack of employee grievances formally entered into the grievance procedure does not necessarily mean that employee relations in the organisation are in good shape. It is good practice for management to identify employee dissatisfaction at an early stage and deal with it in a fair and reasonable manner. To do so will considerably reduce the probability of the employees' level of dissatisfaction reaching the point where they are prepared to make a formal complaint against management behaviour.

Management cannot allow a situation to continue where complaints are being suppressed because employees feel that senior management will not act against a supervisor whose style of management is the cause of the grievance. Management must take some action. It might, for example, counsel the supervisor on why his or her management style must change or provide him or her with formal training after which the style should change for the better. If such action fails to produce a more constructive management style, management should either redeploy the supervisor elsewhere or consider dispensing with his or her services. If employee complaints are shown, following proper investigation, to be the result of a personality clash between a supervisor and an individual employee, the grievance may best be resolved by redeploying one individual to a new area of employment.

> What are the sources of employee dissatisfaction in your organisation? Are these well-founded? If yes, why is this the case? If no, why is this the case? How many formal grievance complaints have been formally raised in the last three years?

GRIEVANCE PROCEDURES

A grievance procedure provides a means whereby an individual employee can process a complaint about management behaviour and embodies the steps he or she must go through in doing this. A procedure for dealing with grievances is found both in companies and organisations which recognise trade unions and in most which do not. In the latter case, the procedure itself involves informing the individual of the action to be taken to raise the grievance and the steps which management must take in giving it consideration. Where there is established negotiating machinery, the arrangements for handling grievances are normally set up by joint agreement and the joint negotiating machinery may be involved as part of the procedure, if the grievance is not resolved in the earlier stages of the prescribed arrangements.

Purpose and form

In managing employee complaints, management has to be guided by the principle of behaving in a visibly fair and reasonable manner. The grievance procedure ensures standards. Under the procedure, employees can raise a complaint which is then dealt with quickly. In raising a just complaint, the employee is entitled under the procedure to representation, at every stage in the process; to appeal to a higher level of management (via an appeals procedure) involving individuals different from those at earlier stages; and to appeal, in some cases, to an independent external body. The procedure provides employees with adequate time to prepare their cases and to cross-examine management representatives. It also prevents management from dismissing employee grievances on the grounds they are trivial, too time-consuming, or too costly to be considered seriously.

The grievance procedure ensures that management must listen to justified employee complaints and treat them in a fair and reasonable manner by acting in accordance with procedural rules which conform with the principles of natural justice. The individual employee is assured of dignity and respect of treatment. A grievance procedure provides 'order and stability' in the workplace by establishing standards of behaviour and due processes to resolve employee grievances in a peaceful and constructive manner.

The form of grievance procedures varies immensely. In a small non-union establishment, the procedure is likely to be found in the employee's contract of employment and expressed in a statement of which the following would be typical:

> 'If you have a grievance relating to your employment, you should raise it with your immediate supervisor.'

In larger and unionised organisations, a comprehensive grievance procedure is likely to exist as part of a collective agreement. However, individual employees in such organisations are likely to find the grievance procedure reproduced in the further particulars of their employment, where a typical wording would be:

> 'If you have any grievance relating to your employment, you should raise it with your immediate supervisor. If the matter is not settled at this level

you may pursue it through the grievance procedure agreed between the company and the trade union representatives. Further details of such procedural agreements are maintained separately in writing and may be consulted on request to management.'

In many organisations, procedures for managing grievances in such areas as health and safety provision, job-grading (a job evaluation scheme), sexual harassment, and discrimination on the basis of race, colour or creed have a separate existence from the general grievance/disputes procedure. There are advantages to both management and unions in recognising that specific issues call for specific treatment. Grievances about job-grading, sexual harassment, etc, are thus normally dealt with through a purpose-built procedure. The degree of differentiation from the general grievance procedure depends on the volume of business and on any improvements in speed, efficacy and acceptability which can be looked for from specialised procedures.

Stages

There are set stages in a typical grievance procedure (see Table 12). Common factors in the stages fall in four areas. First, they spell out the details of who is involved and present at each stage in the process, including who can represent the individual. Second, they explain the appeal mechanisms available to employees. Third, they define the time-limits in which the stage must be completed. Fourth, grievance procedures explain what will happen when the grievance is resolved or if it remains unsettled.

The aim of grievance procedures is to reach a resolution as quickly as

Table 12 Managing employee grievances

- Employee makes complaint.
- Manager carries out grievance interview.
- Outcomes of grievance interview:
  - grievance is unfounded: management behaviour complained of is legitimate
  - employee decides to drop grievance
  - management decides the grievance is genuine and can deal with the problem immediately (miscalculated pay is corrected, holiday allocation changed)
  - management needs to consider its response.
- Preparation for meeting with employee and representative:
  - analysis – what are the issues?
    - on what will management be prepared to compromise?
    - on what will employee and representative be prepared to compromise?
  - aims – ideal, realistic, fall-back
  - strategy and tactics.
- Resolution of grievance:
  - common ground
  - write up resolution.

possible but without undue haste. A grievance procedure usually specifies how and to whom employees can raise a grievance. The procedures spell out the stages through which the grievance will progress. To ensure that grievances are settled quickly, it is essential that time-limits be specified by which each stage will be completed. The first stage of a grievance procedure invariably states that any employee who wishes to discuss a complaint with management must, in the first instance, raise it with his or her immediate supervisor. If the supervisor is unable to resolve the matter, the procedure moves to its second stage which usually involves the employee's consulting with his or her representatives and then the representatives, accompanied by the employee, taking up the complaint with the employee's immediate manager. If the matter still remains unresolved, the third stage is entered into, in which the employee's representative appeals to a higher level of management (usually the departmental manager). If there is no resolution to the grievance at this stage, the complaint is normally considered by the employee's representative and the general manager. In unionised establishments at this fourth stage the local union branch secretary usually becomes involved. If a resolution still eludes the parties, a fifth stage of procedures which normally involves external bodies – like an independent arbitrator or conciliator, a representative of an employers' association and a district/regional trade union officer – comes into action.

Management's objective in managing grievances is to settle each grievance as near as possible to the point of its source. If employee complaints are allowed to progress to a higher level than necessary, this principle is undermined. A professional employee relations manager must ensure that his or her managerial colleagues (particularly line managers) understand the limits of their authority when acting within the constraints of the procedure. If the preventative character of the procedure is to be fully realised and the significance of the different procedural stages established and maintained, grievances have to be settled as near as possible to the point of origin.

Clearly defined stages up the management line through which the grievance can pass if not resolved at a previous stage are essential. There is no ideal number of stages. The number is influenced by many factors – for example, the size of the organisation – but there should be at least two in order to provide a minimum of one level of appeal from the immediate decision. But there should not be too many stages either.

Many grievance procedures are purely 'domestic', being concerned essentially with laying down a recognised method of bringing a grievance to the attention of management and securing further consideration of the employee complaint if it is not settled when first raised. This is normally achieved through a staged procedure of progressive reference to higher management authority.

> Do you have a grievance procedure in your organisation? If you do not, why not? If you do, how many stages does it have? Why does it have that number?

Time-limits

An employee with a complaint wants his or her grievance settled as soon as possible. He or she may well regard it as a great deal more important than anything else which the manager to whom they present it may currently have on hand. The manager, conversely, needs time to gather the facts, consult with other managers and consider what action to take, all of which have to be fitted in with the other daily duties. The idea behind a time-limit is that it provides managers with an opportunity to consider the problem whilst also committing them to providing an answer within a fixed period of time. This relaxes the pressures on the employee or the representative, both of whom now know that if a satisfactory answer has not been provided by the end of the time-limit, the grievance can be taken to the next stage in the procedure.

The usual practice is to allow progressively longer time-limits between stages as a grievance passes up through the procedure. Internal stages time-limits, for example, range from 24 hours to five days, but such limits tend to be longer for external stages. Time-limits alone will not ensure the expeditious handling of grievances but they serve a useful purpose in establishing agreed standards of what is considered to be reasonable behaviour by the parties. In external stages, when the initiative for resolving the employee complaint passes to some extent out of the hands of the parties directly involved, time-limits provide a useful reassurance against fears of indefinite delay. Most of the doubts and criticisms (for example, loss of flexibility, undermining of mutual trust, issues not dealt with properly at the lower levels) of time-limits can be overcome if there is a proviso in the procedure which permits their extension by mutual agreement.

Each stage of a grievance procedure should have a clearly defined time-limit. The objective is to ensure that the employee's complaint progresses quickly to the level needed to find a resolution to the problem, and that managers do not 'sit on' the individual's grievance in the intervening stages.

Employee representation

In devising and implementing a grievance procedure, management must recognise the employee's right to representation in pursuing a complaint against it. As well as this basic right to representation, there are also the issues of when during the procedure should the representational rights be triggered and what the role of the employee's representative is.

The procedure clarifies the individual employee's right to be represented by a union representative or, as is the case in non-unionised firms, by a work colleague or friend. Representation assists the individual employee who lacks confidence and experience to negotiate with the supervisor or senior managers, especially those operating at the executive level (eg the managing director). It is normally the case in a grievance procedure that the role of the employee's representative is that of an advocate speaking and arguing on behalf of the employee. However, some organisations operate a grievance procedure which restricts the role of the employee's representative to one of an observer who is present only to ensure that fair play takes place.

Natural justice requires employee representation, and a grievance procedure should state at which stage the employee is entitled to representation. In many procedures, it starts at the second stage – after the individual has raised the complaint with his or her immediate superior. In these circumstances, representation only becomes available if the employee is dissatisfied with the response from the immediate superior and wishes to appeal to a higher level of management. The argument is that a grievance is not really a grievance if the individual employee's immediate superior is able to resolve the problem. Many unions also favour this approach and will not finally raise their member's complaint with management unless it has been taken first to his or her immediate manager.

However, there are employee relations managers (and indeed trade union officials) who consider that the employee should have the right to representation from the very start of the complaint. In these circumstances the employee's first step is to take the grievance to the workplace union representative, rather than to the immediate superior, in order to seek the union's support for raising the complaint against management's behaviour. In these cases, the union representative acts as a useful filter, sorting out the genuine grievance from the unfounded complaints. The stage at which the employee's right to representation is activated depends on the situation and the relationship which exists between management and unions in that establishment.

In the internal stages of the procedure, the individual employee's representative is also an employee of the organisation. In their roles of employee and employee representative, their relationship with management in status terms is very different. As employees they are in a subordinate position to management who can give them instructions, supervise them, check the quality of their work, warn them about their time-keeping and ultimately dismiss them. As employees they are contracted to supply work to the employer.

However, when they are wearing an employee representative's hat they interact with management as equal partners. This equality is expressed in the grievance procedure which is the formal outward acceptance by management of the equal status with them of the employee representative as employee relations players. When management and the employee's representative meet at different stages, they do so on the basis of equality. If at the third stage of procedure it states the employee's representative and the chief executive/managing director will meet to try and resolve the grievance and the meeting is held in the MD's office, they meet there as employee relations players of equal status. The MD treats the employee's representative as such, and provides him or her with adequate facilities (seating, appropriate space for documents, etc) to conduct a presentation in a professional manner.

The procedure, by recognising the right of employees to representation, also prevents the supervisor/team leader from refusing to allow an employee representative to leave his or her own job to represent the 'client's' interests. The grievance procedure is management's acceptance that in certain circumstances the individual employee's role as an employee relations player takes preference over the role of employee. In managing grievances, management representatives and the employee's representative are equal partners and have a joint responsibility for settling grievances. This equality relationship in grievance-handling is difficult for some line managers to accept. Most find it hard because they tend to relate to employee representatives as employees of the company who are managed members of the organisation. Some managers never come to terms with the distinction between the individual as an employee representative and the individual as an employee under their own supervision and direction. Such managers often feel their authority is undermined when senior managers treat employees wearing their representative's hat as equal. They find it difficult to understand how their senior managers can behave in this way towards individuals who are for most of the time 'merely' employees of the organisation.

Operation of the procedure

Grievance procedures are an integral part of the whole way in which an organisation is managed. They directly affect line management at all levels, and line managers have the main responsibility to operate the procedure. It is the role of the employee relations manager to assist the line managers in this task by the provision of training programmes which take account of the need for all managers to have a clear understanding of the way in which the procedures are intended to operate. The employee relations manager also ensures that the grievance procedure conforms with best practice (ie that management's behaviour in managing employee grievances is fair and reasonable) and that all employees are aware of their rights under the procedure.

The employee relations manager also has an important role to play in monitoring and reviewing the operation of the grievance procedure and for making recommendations for revisions to its design and/or operation. This involves reviewing what have been the outcomes of the grievances taken through the procedure, and whether these outcomes have been such that management's interests have been protected. This review-and-monitor function also requires the employee relations manager to analyse the subject matter of individual employee grievances, to discern why the outcomes have been what they have, and to check that the procedure has been applied in all cases fairly and consistently (ie that management has behaved reasonably in processing employee grievances).

A key player in the operation of the grievance procedure is the first line manager. Because it is easy to see a grievance as a criticism, first line managers may feel that a formal grievance, or more than one grievance, reflects badly on their managerial skills. If grievance procedures are to operate effectively, senior management must reassure first line managers that they do not see this as the case. Line managers should be encouraged to hear grievances. It is important that they are aware of employee dissatisfaction as early as possible. It is usually easier to resolve grievances if they are handled as quickly and as close to the source of the complaint as possible.

The first line manager is the least powerful manager, and his or her authority to make decisions without reference to more senior management is restricted. If a supervisor has to pass grievances continuously up to a superior, an employee may gain the impression that the best way to have a problem resolved is to short-circuit the first line manager and go directly to the next superior. This undermines the supervisor's legitimate authority. It causes the procedure to break down and the number of stages to be reduced. The effect is to remove the grievance from its source of origin, to slow down the process by having to go back through the correct stages, and to cause confusion and bad feeling. To avoid this, three things need to be clearly understood and accepted by management: everyone knows within the procedure the limits of their own and others' authority; the procedures are adhered to consistently; and first line managers have authority to settle grievances.

In situations where union representatives believe line managers are unable to take a decision at the appropriate level, good practice requires management to insist that the protocol of the procedures are followed. By doing this, management demonstrates that it applies the procedure consistently and that its operation is understood by those managers who have a part to play in its operation. It is important that first line managers have authority to deal with as many types of grievance as possible. The first line supervisor must be able to say 'yes' as well as 'no'. If an employee's immediate supervisor is continually saying 'no' because he or she lacks scope and authority, then employees and/or their representatives will find ways of bypassing first line management. They will justify this on the grounds that it is pointless to raise a grievance with a member of management who has no authority to settle without the permission of a higher-level management. They see it as a classic case of 'Why talk to the monkey when you can speak to the organ grinder?'

It is equally important that first line managers continue to be involved in the settling of grievances, even if they pass beyond them, either by being at meetings or at the very least by being informed of the outcome of the grievance process. It is bad management practice for a first line manager to hear the outcome of employees' complaints from the employees themselves and/or their representative.

Grievance records
When a grievance passes to a higher stage in the procedure, a certain amount of documentation is necessary for the benefit of those managers who are not familiar with the complaint of the individual employee and his or her supporting arguments and evidence. It provides a record of information and events to be passed up through the procedure. In practice, the extent to which records of grievances are kept varies widely. In some organisations the completion of grievance records is a required activity for line management. In others, only the personnel/HR management department keeps any records. In yet others, no documentation of any kind is kept except when an employee complaint progresses to the external stage of the procedure.

Grievance records serve several useful purposes for management. If there is a failure to agree at any stage, a written record clarifies the facts and the contentions of the individual employee and will be helpful to those managers involved in the next stage of the procedure. If the record is agreed by both parties – commonly completed by the manager concerned and countersigned by the employee and/or the representative – it is even more valuable. Grievance record forms assist the personnel/HR management function to keep in touch with the progress of unresolved grievances.

Grievance records are also useful because the resolution of the grievance may provide a significant interpretation or perhaps an important precedent. They are also particularly useful for analysing trends in the causes of grievances. Analysis will show where and why delays in the procedure most frequently occur. When a resolution to an individual's grievance has been reached, a written and agreed statement helps to ensure that there are no misunderstandings about what has been agreed. In the absence of an agreed statement, the parties may find they have different versions of the terms of the agreement. A written statement is also useful for communicating the outcome of the employee's complaint. However, systems which require line management to keep records of grievances are not easy to keep going unless management keeps a watchful eye on matters. Some first line managers who handle grievances often complain that having to keep grievance records is an extra, irksome administrative chore. Without a watchful eye from more senior management, grievance record systems may not operate effectively at the first line level.

The law
The basic statutory requirement covering employees' grievances is that the employer has to specify, by description or otherwise, a person to whom an employee can take a grievance. This information is to be given to the individual employee in the statement of particulars of their terms of employment. A formal grievance procedure is not legally required, but almost every organisation finds it useful to adopt one. When they do, the statement of particulars specifies any further steps available to the employee beyond the first point of contact. This, as we have seen, is often in a separate document setting out a full grievance procedure.

However, employees who do not have a formal grievance procedure can fall foul of the law. In W. A. Goold (Pearmack) Ltd v McConnell (1995), an industrial tribunal held that the employer's failure to provide and supply a grievance procedure amounted to a breach of the employment contract, which entitled the employees to resign and therefore claim constructive dismissal. The two employees concerned were also held to be unfairly dismissed. The facts of this case were simple. Mr McConnell and Mr Richmond were jewellery salesmen and were paid a basic salary plus commission. In 1992 their employer changed sales methods and, as a result, the commission suffered. The employees wished to complain about this issue but there was no established grievance procedure and the employer had not issued them with a written statement of main terms and conditions of employment. In July 1992 a new managing director joined the firm and the employees tried to complain to him. He told them he was unable to deal with their complaint immediately. The two employees then decided to seek an interview with the chairman but were fobbed off by his secretary. The employees resigned and claimed constructive dismissal. The Employment Appeals Tribunal agreed with the industrial tribunal's view that it was an implied term in any employment contract that employers should reasonably and promptly give employees an opportunity to obtain redress of any grievance.

The benefits of having procedures for handling employee grievances, even though the law does not require them, are also clear from the case of Chris Metcalf Ltd *v* Maddocks (1985). In this case the company had no formal grievance procedure for its 90 employees and had failed to issue statements of particulars to its employees. The crux of the issue was that an employee had refused to carry out a particular instruction and had been dismissed. In the tribunal hearing the argument was that the omissions by the management had caused a breakdown in communications between management and the employees, to the point where the employee's reasons for refusing the instruction had no means of being expressed or heard properly. The industrial tribunal ruled that a grievance procedure would have enabled employees to articulate their worries and anxieties, and would thus have prevented the problem's occurring. An appeal by the firm against the decision failed.

MANAGING GRIEVANCES

Much of an employee relations manager's work can be occupied in dealing with individual employee's problems or complaints. However, most employee grievances are dealt with satisfactorily before they reach the formal grievance procedure. For example, take the case of an employee who claims to have received an incorrect amount of pay. On checking, management accepts this fact and rectifies the matter immediately. The employee grievance has been resolved. Again, take the case of an employee who claims that the official factory clock is five minutes slow relative to the other clocks located in the factory. In investigating this claim, management concedes this to be the case, alters the clock, and the individual grievance has been resolved. However, not all grievances are of as simple a nature and so quickly resolved.

Management has to deal with all grievances in a competent and systematic manner. This systematic approach can be broken down into a number of stages:

- hearing the grievance
- preparing for meeting with the employee and/or his or her representative
- meeting with the employee and/or his or her representative
- confirming the common ground between the employee and the management
- resolving the grievance
- reporting the outcome.

Hearing the grievance

The purpose of the grievance interview is to enable an individual to air his or her grievance and for management, if possible, to discover and remove the cause of the employee's complaint. The interview is to enable management to obtain the facts of the situation, analyse the problem and, if appropriate, suggest action to resolve the grievance. It is good management practice in preparation for a grievance interview to check the employee's employment record with the organisation. This may not be possible for some managers because of time pressures. It is as well to bear in mind that an employee with a grievance against management may be angry and adopt an aggressive attitude towards management. The first management task may be to help calm down the aggrieved individual. If the individual is angry, care is required that the manager does not respond in a similarly aggressive way. Few people can think rationally when they are angry. The manager should not be provoked into losing his or her temper by being faced with an aggressive employee critical of management's behaviour.

Gathering information about an employee's grievance is extremely important. If incorrect information or insufficient information is collected, the result may be a wrong analysis and an incorrect decision. Information-gathering via interviewing techniques is vital to the effective management of grievances, as is listening carefully to what is said by the individual employee. Once the employee begins to outline the grievance, the manager should start thinking ahead about how he or she might resolve the employee's problem. However, if the manager starts to do this before the employee has finished outlining the grievance, the manager may miss vital points through lack of concentration. It is important during the grievance interview that the manager concentrates on what the individual employee is saying and does so until the employee has finished. In conducting the interview, the manager keeps an open mind and does not hear only what he or she expects to hear or wants to hear. Once the employee or the representative has finished presenting the grievance, the manager conducting the interview should ask questions for clarification of the employee's view. During the interview, the manager will be taking notes.

For the whole of the grievance interview, the manager must strike a balance between being sympathetic towards the employee but sufficiently businesslike to obtain the necessary information he or she requires. The employee needs to be put at ease and have explained to him or her that the purpose of the interview is for management to gain all the facts on the individual's grievance so a decision can be made whether the claim is genuine or ill-founded. If the former, management will explain the steps it will take to investigate the matter. The employee should feel the manager is genuinely concerned about his or her grievance and is capable of dealing with it fairly and competently.

During the interview, the manager collects the basic facts using the 5Ws technique:

• What is the grievance about?

• When did the grievance happen? (dates, times, etc)

- Where did the grievance happen? (warehouse, office, factory floor, etc)

- Who was involved in the grievance issue? (other employees, other managers, etc)

- Why does what happened create a grievance for the individual employee and what does the individual want management to do about the grievance?

At the end of the interview, the manager will have an understanding of how the employee would like the complaint resolved. If the employee is claiming to have been denied access to a training opportunity, then the employee will explain why he or she believes he or she has been denied the opportunity and how management should resolve the situation by sending him or her on the next available appropriate training opportunity. The why question is likely to be the most difficult. An individual always gives a favourable view of his or her case, withholding information which weakens the case. But the manager needs to get all the facts, including those that might make the individual's case against management less clear-cut. The manager will probe the employee's case, and this will involve seeking additional information from the employee to gain a full picture of the case.

Once the manager decides he or she has collected all the information possible from the individual concerning the grievance, he or she 'plays-back' to the employee, using the employee's own words, what management understand the individual's grievance to be. The 'play-back' gives the employee the opportunity to correct any misunderstanding the manager may have, allows the manager to assess whether the employee's story is consistent and complete, and enables the employee to see that management is treating the grievance seriously. If the individual's story is not logical and clear, it usually means that a vital piece of information is missing, on which the employee will be questioned further. It is natural for individuals to give a favourable account of their case. They often hold back information deliberately or unconsciously, or they do not realise the significance of some information when it comes to management's making sense of their complaint.

The manager requires all the facts. Management is seeking to reach a decision on whether the employee's grievance is genuine, is well-founded, and if so what action to take. If the grievance interview fails to bring out vital information, the manager may conclude – wrongly, with adverse consequences – that the employee does not have a genuine complaint. On the basis of the information gained from the grievance interview the manager makes an assessment of the situation. He or she decides upon an appropriate course of action, explaining to the individual employee, to his or her representative and to managerial colleagues why he or she has decided upon that action.

At the end of the interview, management may conclude that the individual's complaint is not justified on the grounds that

- it is not a grievance but a clash of personalities between the individual employee and the immediate manager

- the employee has misunderstood the works rule and the management's behaviour is legitimate

- the employee does not want to take the matter further, and is content enough that management has listened sympathetically to the case.

On the other hand, the manager may conclude that further information is required about the grievance before management's attitude to the issue can be established. (For example, what does the agreement say? Are there any witnesses or other people with relevant information that also need to be interviewed?) In this case, the manager makes definite arrangements with the employee and the representative about when a further meeting will take place. Another possibility is that in the light of the grievance interview management will decide that the employee's grievance is genuine and be prepared to seek a resolution to the matter but will require time to prepare its response and case. In this situation, management will also make arrangements for when and where it will meet with the employee and/or the representative to resolve the issue.

Planning to meet with the employee and their representatives
There are three stages of preparing for a meeting with the individual employee and his or her representative to negotiate a settlement to the individual's grievance. These are:

- analysis

- establishing the aims to be achieved in the forthcoming meeting

- planning the strategy and tactics to be used in the meeting.

The analysis stage involves management in collecting and analysing relevant information to substantiate its proposals for resolving the individual employee's grievance. It also includes developing the argument to be put to the employee and his or her representative to support management's case. In managing grievances the main source of relevant information will be colleagues and employees who are known to have information relevant to the issue at stake (for example, they witnessed the incident about which the employee is complaining).

This analysis stage also involves management's checking whether the subject of the grievance has been complained of previously by employees, and if so, what was the outcome. Knowledge of outcomes of the grievance procedure enables management to establish whether any precedent exists for dealing with the employee's grievance in the way management proposes.

Other important management activities in the analysis stage include checking whether any company rules, collective or individual agreements, other arrangements and 'custom and practice' are relevant to the employee's complaint. In preparing to meet with the employee and his or her representative, the manager concerned needs to understand the limits of his or her authority under the grievance procedure. Should the grievance not be resolved at this stage, the employee will need to be advised of the right to take the case to the next stage in the procedure.

The most important activity for management in the preparation stage of handling a grievance is the identification of its details and which of these details it is prepared to trade. You will recall from Chapter 6 that the resolution of one individual's grievance is never achieved at the expense of dropping another individual's grievance. In managing grievances the parties concentrate on resolving one grievance before preceding to resolve the next grievance. However, in handling grievances which cannot be resolved simply, agreement may be reached if the parties trade the details of the issues surrounding the grievance. In making a decision about which details to trade, management assesses their significance to the individual concerned. Having decided which details of the grievance to trade, management turns to anticipating which details it believes the employee would be prepared to trade.

Let us assume that for swearing in the presence of a supervisor management has suspended an employee for three working days without pay. The individual concerned considers the penalty to be too harsh and (in this case) he and his representative approach management to have the penalty revoked. Management will quickly see there are three issues involved: suspension, the length of the suspension, and pay or no pay during the period of suspension. Given the offence, for the employee not to be disciplined at all would be totally unacceptable to management. It is not a matter on which management would normally entertain a constructive compromise. However, before finally deciding so, management has to make a judgement on how strongly the individual's fellow employees feel about the disciplinary penalty. Would they be prepared to impose industrial sanctions against the company, and if they would, how successful might such action be? Management, if it persists with retaining the initial penalty against the employee, has to weigh up whether the grievance will escalate into a collective dispute with all its associated costs. If management concludes that the employees would not take the issue to a collective dispute, it can be confident that its view of no constructive compromise on some disciplinary action is sustainable.

Management now turns to consider the issues of the length of the suspension and possible loss of pay. Again, the management would not see payment of wages during the suspension period as a detail upon which a constructive compromise can be made. If management assesses that to sustain this stance will not provoke a collective dispute, then no payment during a period of suspension will be a non-tradable issue. This would leave the length of the suspension. If management's assessment is that the employees feel strongly about this issue, then it will conclude that a constructive compromise to the individual's grievance of too harsh a penalty may lie in making concessions on the length of the suspension (ie is management prepared to reduce the period from three days?) in return for retaining the loss of pay and some penalty. If management's assessment is that a penalty and loss of pay can be retained in return for some compromise on the length of suspension, it would anticipate a mutually acceptable solution to the complaint of too harsh a disciplinary penalty. Management has decided which details it is prepared to trade in the light of assessing its bargaining power relative to the group of workers concerned should the individual complaint develop into a collective dispute. Management has anticipated that the employee will accept the principle of suspension but will trade the length of the suspension and the loss of pay.

Having completed its analysis, management moves on to establish objectives for the forthcoming meeting with the individual employee and his representative. Management asks itself three questions:

- How would it ideally like the grievance to be resolved?

- How does it realistically think the grievance can be resolved?

- What is the least for which management will settle (the fall-back position)?

Management establishes responses to these three questions for each of the issues involved in the employee's grievance. Having established its own aims and objectives, management turns its attention to anticipate the aims and objectives of the employee making the complaint – ie what is the individual employee ideally, realistically and minimally, expecting to achieve as a resolution to his grievance?

Management can now construct an aspiration grid which sets out the parameters for the expected outcome from the forthcoming grievance-handling negotiations. The aspiration grid enables management to identify the expected common ground between itself and the individual. In the grid (see Table 13) an X means that the party is not prepared to trade that detail while an O means it is willing to do so. The aspiration grid demonstrates whether a basis for an acceptable joint agreement exists. In the example, the grid shows that management ideally would like to trade no details surrounding the grievance with the employee. However, management knows this is unrealistic and has established on the basis of its analysis of the situation a realistic position of wishing to trade a retention of the suspension and no pay for the period of the suspension in return for a reduction in the period of the suspension from three days to two days. Its fall-back position is to retain the suspension and lost pay for a further reduction in the length of the suspension (to one day).

Table 13 Aspiration grid: three days' suspension without pay grievance

Possible Resolution to Grievance	Management			Employee		
	Ideal	Real	Fall-back	Fall-back	Real	Ideal
3 days' suspension and pay restored	X	X	X	O	O	X
2 days' suspension and pay restored	X	X	X	O	O	X
1 day's suspension and pay restored	X	X	X	O	X	X
2 days' suspension – no pay	X	X	O	O	O	X
1 day's suspension – no pay	X	O	O	O	O	X

The grid shows that management anticipates the employee will understand that management will be reluctant to make concessions on suspension and the lost pay accompanying it. It also demonstrates how management anticipates the employee will accept a reduction in the length of suspension and that the basis for resolving the complaint of too harsh a punishment lies in making compromises on the length of the suspension. It also reveals that no problems are anticipated over the loss of pay issue because although management is not prepared to make compromises on this aspect of the grievance, the employee is.

The aspiration grid shows there is a basis for a resolution to the employee's complaint that management has imposed too harsh a discipline penalty on him. This is shown by the fact that the fall-back positions of the two parties on each of the issues do not have two Xs against them. In the fall-back position, management is not prepared to compromise on the suspension issue but the employee is. The management is prepared to make compromises on the length of the suspension but not on pay during suspension. The employee is also prepared to make compromises on these issues. Management now has a picture of how the resolution of the grievance might be achieved. It will now use the forthcoming meeting with the individual employee and his representative to test whether its expectation as to the common ground between itself and the employee is correct or needs to be reassessed in the light of information ascertained during that and any subsequent meetings. It will also use the forthcoming meeting to ensure that the employee and his representative receive information concerning management's attitude towards trading details of the grievance.

Having established its negotiating aims, management now moves to planning its strategy and tactics to realise its objectives. There are a number of issues for management to decide here. These include the size of team to meet with the employee and his representative, deciding who will speak on behalf of management, agreeing a method of communication within the management team, anticipating the arguments to be used by the other side, and 'playing the devil's advocate'.

There is no hard and fast rule on the size of a management team in a grievance-handling negotiation. It is the quality of preparation rather than the numbers on each side that is important. Lung power should not be confused with quality of preparation. The management team in a grievance-handling situation is likely to have a leader, a note-taker and an observer (who listens and watches but does not speak). The anticipation of the most likely arguments to be used by the other side and how these might be countered is particularly important. The role of the manager 'playing the devil's advocate' is to probe management's case for weaknesses. In the light of this, management can strengthen its case.

The preparation stage is the most important stage in grievance-handling negotiations. Why this is so was explained in Chapter 6, where it was also pointed out that the golden rule for management when preparing for negotiation is:

Failure to prepare

is

preparing to fail.

It was also stressed in Chapter 6 that if management prepares inadequately, it does not mean that the grievance-handling situation cannot be rescued. It can be corrected by management's reassessing its analysis, aims and strategy in the light of new information it did not have, for whatever reason, while preparing its case for presentation to the individual employee.

Meeting with the employee and his or her representative

If management is making the initial presentation, it gives a summary of its proposals. It informs the employee and his or her representative of the matters it intends to raise and then substantiates its case with facts and information. Management details its proposals and the rationale for them.

In grievance-handling negotiations management proposes solutions to the employee's complaint and does not just say it rejects the complaint. The employee is informed of how it sees a resolution to the complaint but at this stage management does not spell out the details. The presentation stage of grievance negotiations involves management's informing the employee how it prefers the grievance to be resolved. The employee will have stated his or her case in the grievance interview.

If management were receiving proposals from the employee for the first time, it would listen to what the grievance is and not interrupt the presentation. When the presentation has been completed, it would be unwise of management to make an ill-considered response to the employee's complaint. Management should confine itself to asking questions of the employee and/or the representative to seek clarification of the case and of the arguments. Management only makes counterproposals if they have been agreed after detailed analysis and discussion by the management.

After management's meeting with the employee and his or her representative, both parties will have informed each other of what their ideal positions are for the resolution of the grievance. The employee would have done this during the grievance interview. There is unlikely, at this stage, to be much common ground between them. However, the issues to be resolved will be out in the open. The parties now have to start the task of seeking confirmation of their expected common ground and anticipated trading of details.

Confirming the common ground

Management has anticipated possible areas of common ground and made a judgement about the compromises it considers the employee will be prepared to make. Management now needs to gain information from the employee, and/or his or her representative, to confirm whether these expectations are correct. The information is obtained through face-to-face contact with the individual employee who is pursuing the grievance. We saw in Chapter 6 that there are a number of techniques available to management whereby identification of the common ground can be achieved. These included listening, questioning for clarification, the if and then method, and watching skills.

However, such information will not be obtained if the negotiation sessions are unconstructive. This can happen because one or both parties seek to 'blame' each other for the origination of the grievance. The parties then interrupt each other during presentation, they talk too much and do not listen to what each other is saying, and they verbally attack personalities on the other side. In grievance negotiating sessions management will not gain the necessary information it requires to confirm its expected common ground if it seeks to score points off the other side, to shout down the other side, or becomes hostile or sarcastic towards the other side.

However, if the use of these techniques leads to new information of which management was not aware when preparing for the grievance negotiations, an adjournment can be called to consider its implications, including whether management needs to reassess its negotiating aims, analysis and strategy and tactics. In most grievance-handling situations, however, adjournments are only likely to be called to obtain information to confirm facts or to find a witness who can confirm facts. It is unlikely to involve the provision of significantly new information which requires either party to reconsider its strategy and tactics.

RESOLVING THE GRIEVANCE

If a manager is unable, after meaningful negotiations, to resolve the grievance, he or she can refer the issue to the next stage in the procedure, where a higher-level manager will have to prepare, present and negotiate a solution. If the grievance remains unresolved and the matter is taken to the next stage, the manager concerned in the first stage should check that the grievance really has passed on to the next stage of the procedure.

If the grievance can be resolved, however, management needs to consider a number of things. The most important of these is that management must be convinced that the employee and his or her representative fully understand management's proposals. If management feels there is some uncertainty on the part of the employee about its proposals, it should go over its case again with him or her. It is good practice for management to develop the habit of 'playing-back' to the other side what its proposals or points mean. This identifies any differences between what management actually proposed and what the other party thinks management proposed.

Once management has an oral agreement for the resolution of the employee's grievance, it should be written up. In many grievances this may take the form of an internal memo to another manager recording what has been agreed with the employee. For example, in the case of a complaint of denial of access to a training opportunity, the manager dealing with the matter and who has been convinced that the denial complaint is justified will write to the personnel department reporting that it has been agreed that the individual concerned will attend the next available appropriate training course. On the other hand, it may take the form of a signed agreement by the manager concerned, the individual employee and his or her representative. The outcome is then reported to the relevant interested parties. Clarity is important and the manner by which points are recorded should leave no one who refers to the record later in any doubt about what is meant.

Outline the skills required of managers in successfully handling grievances. Which do you consider to be the most important, and why?

Specific issues/specific procedures

Job evaluation – Some employee complaints are best dealt with by specific procedures for specific subjects. Job-grading disputes are an example. A grievance centred on this issue concerns the claim of an individual that his or her job has increased in value in that it now, for example, carries greater responsibility for people (supervision, training), for financial resources (budget size and control procedures) and/or for physical resources (modern hi-tech machinery) and therefore warrants a higher grading and a higher level of remuneration. On the other hand management may argue that the value of the job has not increased but the volume of tasks the individual now undertakes relative to some post-reference point that has increased. Moreover, this increased range of tasks is regarded by management as being of the same level of responsibility as all other tasks involved in undertaking the job. There has not, therefore, been an increase in the responsibility of tasks performed, so the job is appropriately graded and remunerated. The employee has a grievance in that he or she claims the job is undervalued and underpaid.

In the case of job-grading disputes, there are advantages to management in having specific procedures tailor-made to deal with such disputes. The first stage of a job-grading dispute procedure normally involves the individual employee's discussing the basis of his or her appeal against the grading with the immediate line manager/supervisor. The second stage usually involves the individual's completing a formal Job Appeal Form which would then go before a meeting of the job evaluation panel. The aggrieved individual, accompanied by his or her representative, present their case to the appeal panel. The panel considers the basis of the appeal and makes a decision either to upgrade the job or to reject the appeal. This decision is usually communicated to the individual through his or her manager/line supervisor. If the appeal is upheld, the decision will be implemented from the date of the decision.

If the job holder or management is dissatisfied with the decision of the appeal panel, they may request that the case be heard by an independent panel body. At this stage the job holder (assisted by his or her representative) would present the basis of the appeal. A member of the appeal panel would present justification for their decision and the independent appeal body, which is usually chaired by an independent chairperson acceptable to both parties, would make a decision which is final and binding. The independent appeal body, like the appeal panel, can only make one of two decisions – namely, the job is wrongly graded and should be upgraded, or the grade of the job is correct. Individual grievances over job evaluation are, at the end of the day, decided by arbitration.

Sexual harassment – Harassment is an important area and is becoming subject to increasing attention. Many organisations now have policies and procedures which link the complaints procedure on harassment with the existing grievance procedure rather than establishing separate arrangements for such complaints. Others have tackled it as a specific issue. Both can work.

When an employee complains that he or she has suffered sexual harassment (the victim) from another employee, manager or not (the accused), he or she has a grievance and is making a complaint to management. In dealing with such an accusation the manager first conducts a thorough investigation to see whether there is a *prima facie* case of sexual harassment to answer. This involves interviewing and listening to those directly involved (the victim and the accused), and to any witnesses to the alleged incident, and ascertaining the employment record of those directly involved. If the manager decides, on the basis of investigation, that there is a case to answer, disciplinary proceedings will be instigated against the accused. However, this has to be conditional on the 'victim's' agreeing that the issue can be taken further. If the victim does not want to take the matter any further, management cannot proceed with disciplinary hearings.

If the disciplinary proceedings go ahead and the charge of sexual harassment is upheld, an appropriate penalty will be imposed – including, often as a last resort, dismissal. If on the other hand the manager decides the sexual harassment allegation has no foundation, he or she must explain fully to the 'victim' and his or her representative why this is the case (for example, the lack of or poor quality of the evidence). Different organisations define their acceptable standards of behaviour differently, particularly with respect to gross misconduct. In some organisations sexual harassment is regarded as gross misconduct, carrying instant dismissal if proved. This, however, is not the case in all organisations.

If a manager is sitting in his or her office and a woman employee comes in claiming she has been sexually harassed, that she has witnesses and wants action taken against the individual concerned, then it is clear what the manager should do. First, he or she must investigate the complaint thoroughly, including interviewing the witness, to decide whether there is a case to answer. Second, if there is a case and the matter cannot be settled amicably between the parties, and the 'victim' insists on continuing with the complaint, the manager will initiate disciplinary proceedings. However, if the manager feels there is no justification for the claim, it must be explained carefully and sensitively to the woman employee concerned.

Other Areas – Other complex areas of employee complaint which justify having separate grievance procedures include discrimination in promotion and advancement, and alleged unequal treatment in terms of pay, overtime, travel, etc. Each case is unique and requires thorough investigation before a decision is made on whether the grievance is real or imagined, whether the offence if proven can be considered gross misconduct, and whether informal or formal action through procedures is appropriate. All cases of grievance have to be handled with equal care: procedures offer the means by which management can behave fairly and reasonably in managing grievances.

FURTHER READING

FOWLER A. *Effective Negotiation*. London, Institute of Personnel and Development, 1996.
KENNEDY G., BENSON, J. *and* McMILLAN, J. *Managing Negotiations*. London, Hutchinson, 3rd ed., 1987.

9 Bargaining with employees

WHAT IS BARGAINING?

In Chapter 6, you were presented with an overview of the negotiation process. This chapter looks in more detail at what is involved in bargaining with the workforce. After you have read this chapter, you will be able to

- define bargaining

- understand what is involved in preparation for bargaining

- explain what is involved in conducting and concluding negotiations

- understand what is involved in writing up a collective agreement.

Bargaining is one of a number of different forms of *negotiation*, which we defined in Chapter 6 as the coming together of two parties to make an agreement by purposeful persuasion and constructive compromise. It is in a bargaining situation that the buyers and sellers of labour services are in their more adversarial relationship because their representatives are seeking to protect and advance the economic interests of their constituents. Bargaining is a situation in which the parties involved have a 'shopping list' of demands of each other.

One party (usually the employees collectively) proposes a list of improvements to pay and to other conditions of employment, while the other (normally the employer) responds with a set of counterproposals covering changes in working practices. For example, in the 1996 national agreement negotiations between the Graphical, Paper and Media Union (GPMU) and the British Printing Industries Federation (BPIF), the former had the following 'shopping list':

- a substantial pay increase

- a shorter working week

- maternity/paternity arrangements

- child-care facilities

- a harassment and bullying protection clause

- a sick pay scheme

- consultation on redundancies and transfer of businesses.

The BPIF presented the following 'shopping list':

- the abolition of call money
- an increase in the skilled/non-skilled pay differential
- the right to transfer employees temporarily to other tasks
- the ending of balancing time
- any additional costs arising from the 1996 national settlement to be recovered by efficiency and productivity.

A bargaining situation involves issues of collective interest to the workforce, unlike an employee grievance which normally involves an issue of interest only to one individual. Bargaining, unlike grievance-handling, involves 'trading' of items in the relative 'shopping lists' with the use of such language as 'If you drop that part of your claim, we shall drop this part of ours.' The parties to collective bargaining thus come to an agreement by trading items in their respective shopping lists (ie the demands of each other).

Bargaining is thus about trading with the other party and not about conceding to the other party. In the 1996 national agreement, the BPIF traded

- increases in pay ranging from £6.21 to £6.90 per week for adult workers
- increases in the pay of learners from £2.83 to £6.21 per week
- increases in the pay of apprentices
- a guarantee for people working in small firms of the right to be consulted on any plans for redundancy and the transfer of the business
- the establishing of two pilot out-of-school-holiday play schemes
- protection of employees against harassment and bullying at work

in return for

- an increase in the skilled/non-skilled differential
- full cost recovery by efficiency and productivity improvements at the workplace, such improvements to be wide-ranging in scope
- the establishment of a joint working party to provide a new national agreement to meet the changing requirements of the industry and its employees, to improve profitability and job security, and to embrace the increasing demands of the industry's customers.

Such something-for-something agreements have been traditional in large parts of the manufacturing sector. However, they are bargaining outcomes, especially in the public and private services sector where the employer gives a pay increase to the workforce, perhaps to compensate for an increase in the index of retail prices, without receiving anything in return. In bargaining situations, the parties involved are normally seeking to defend and enhance their economic interests, and the tenor and style of negotiations is likely to be adversarial, the bargaining ritual described in Chapter 6 to the fore.

> Has there recently been bargaining in your organisation? If there has, what was the outcome? What was traded for what?

PREPARATION FOR BARGAINING

Selection of the bargaining team

The size of the management team will vary, but there are advantages in its being small and of an uneven number. If the team is small, it is easier to retain team discipline. An odd number means that if the bargaining team has to take a vote to determine its position, there will always be a majority view to prevail. A team of three will always at most split two to one while one of five will at most divide three and two. The management bargaining team should represent all major parts of the business.

There are a minimum of three functions to be covered by a bargaining team. There is a need for a leader who will be the main spokesperson, the principal negotiator, and who will conduct the negotiations. In addition, the leader will call for an adjournment if management considers one to be necessary, and will hold the ring in adjournments. It is the team leader who will enter corridor (private) discussions with the leader of the other side. The leader will also be responsible for finalising the agreement on behalf of management. He or she requires a number of attributes: good inter-personal skills to build the team as a coherent whole, a knowledge of the employees' attitudes and, if appropriate, a knowledge of the policies and problems of the trade unions who represent the employees. It is imperative that the leader can give leadership and is respected by the other members of the team. In addition, the leader must be firm, be capable of exercising good judgement, be patient, be a good listener and be skilful in communicating ideas and getting points across.

The bargaining team also requires a note-taker who records what is actually said on crucial issues. He or she notes the key arguments and records movement of position between and within the bargaining parties, partial commitments made by one or both parties, and the items that have been traded. The note-taker records and then drafts the final agreements for signature by the relevant parties.

The team also requires a strategist whose role is to monitor the strategies of both sides and to identify, and seek to confirm, the anticipated basis of common ground and constructive compromise for both sides. The strategist also provides any additional information or details that may be required by the team. In addition, he or she monitors and assesses any proposal made by the other party.

Some bargaining teams also find it is useful to have a member whose sole purpose is to listen to what is being said and to make no spoken contribution in the bargaining sessions, perhaps also a person whose role is to watch the body and facial reactions of the members of the other side when they are receiving proposals from management or making proposals to management. These reactions can convey useful information and reveal the extent to which the other party is committed to its own proposals and to countering proposals from the other side.

Regardless of the size of the management bargaining team and the division of labour amongst them, it is imperative – prior to the first meeting with the other side and to meeting again after an adjournment – that each member of the management team be given the opportunity to contribute to the discussion and agree on the bargaining objectives, strategy and tactics. Ideally, the bargaining team should determine these issues. This provides each team member with an insight into the overall plan and strategy and thereby generates commitment amongst the whole team to its objectives. So while the role of the team leader is most important during negotiations, the role of the whole team is very important in determining policies and strategies.

Team discipline

Members of the management team should conduct themselves during the negotiations in line with the agreed position(s) established in the preparation stage so that the team in the actual negotiations is united and purposeful. It is important before meeting with the other side that the team agrees that only one member should speak at a time in the negotiation sessions and that the team leader not be interrupted unless it is absolutely necessary. However, all members of the team should be prepared to speak when called upon to do so by the team leader. If members of the team other than the leader are to make a spoken contribution during the bargaining sessions, it should be part of a predetermined strategy and the leader should have indicated to the other party that the new speaker is speaking by invitation of the leader.

It is also important before meeting with the other party that the team reminds itself of the importance of not disagreeing as a team in front of the other side, and that if team discipline begins to break down, the leader should seek an adjournment so that the necessary action to re-establish discipline can be taken – even to the extent, if necessary, of excluding a member of the team from participating any further in the face-to-face bargaining sessions. The maintenance of team discipline is easier where all members are fully acquainted with the bargaining objectives, the necessary arguments and the tradable items seen as essential to achieving those objectives, and if before meeting with the other side the management team has agreed a non-verbal method of communicating among itself (eg signals, passing notes, etc) during the negotiation session.

The arguments from the management bargaining team need to be consistent. No matter how unprofessionally the other side behaves, it should not influence the management's behaviour as individuals or as a team. If during negotiations the other side attempts to disrupt the discipline of the management team by trying to bring in another speaker from the management side against the planned sequence of contributors, the team leader must intervene immediately. Management should tell the other side to address all its remarks to the team leader. If a member of the management bargaining team begins to talk out of turn, the leader will restrain him or her by the use of appropriate language in the right tone of voice. It may, for example, be necessary only to tell the team member to keep quiet or to calm down for discipline to be restored, but if this does not work an adjournment may be necessary during which discipline can be restored.

The members of the bargaining team must remain within their agreed roles and speak only when invited to do so unless a change of plan is agreed during adjournments in the negotiations. However, the team members should help each other out of any difficulty and avoid assuming a 'nothing to do with me' expression when the team comes under pressure. This transmits to the other side a clear message that management is not united in its commitment to its case, and that unexpected gains may be made by playing to these perceived differences.

> What considerations do management need to take into account in selecting its team for bargaining with its employees' representatives? Justify your answer.

The analysis stage

As we saw in Chapter 8, the analysis stage of preparing for bargaining involves management in collecting and analysing relevant information to substantiate its claims and/or its proposals to be put to its employees' representatives. In preparing for bargaining situations, management is likely to have to analyse information derived from sources internal and external to the organisation. Internal sources are likely to cover issues such as the labour productivity trends, profitability, labour turnover, absenteeism, total sales, investment, pay changes granted to other employees, orders pending, and cash-flow position, etc. External sources of information for bargaining purposes will include employers' associations, the employee relations trade press and UK Government departments. These external sources contain mainly national average data, and as a result the pay data they contain may not be over-useful in local pay negotiations. For local pay negotiations, of much more value is likely to be data from local pay and salary surveys which the organisation is likely to collect for itself.

Employers' associations are an important external source of information. They have records about the types of agreement that exist in an industry and collect data on the size of pay increase settlements being granted by member companies. Many employers' associations are also trade associations and as such collect information on an industry basis on a number of subjects – eg total sales figures, the balance of foreign trade (export/import trends) and unit labour costs.

An important source of pay information available to those engaged in preparing for bargaining is Industrial Relations Services. Its twice-monthly *Employment Review* provides information on employment trends and special features based on a survey of organisations, covering their employment policies and practices. It also contains a Pay and

Benefits Bulletin which reviews trends in the general level of pay settlement and reports on pay deals concluded in private and public organisations as well as those involving a whole industry. It also summarises the latest pay awards, showing the name and size of the group of workers covered, the effective date and length of the agreement and brief details of the main changes. Its datafile contains information on price changes (the retail price index), on changes in average earnings (the average earnings index) and on future forecasts of annual rates of change in prices and earnings. In addition, it contains a useful summary of the main bargaining statistics (inflation, average earnings, productivity/labour costs, hours worked, unemployment and employment). The *Employment Review* also contains an Industrial Relations Law Bulletin which covers European Union directives, case notes on significant employment law cases and up-to-date news items. Its final section, entitled Health and Safety Bulletin, contains briefings on health and safety issues.

Industrial Relations Services also publishes a monthly Pay Intelligence updating service. It features key facts and statistics from its pay databank, including settlement levels for the public, private manual, private non-manual, manufacturing and services sectors as well as the whole economy and other analysts' settlement figures. It also contains a summary of the IRS monthly pay analysis and settlement chart, and a 'state of play' table detailing news and deals in key negotiations as well as the latest official inflation and earnings figures, together with the predictions of ten leading forecasting organisations. The IRS pay databank is the only regularly published source of pay statistics independent of employers, trade unions and the UK Government. Each year it records the details of pay settlements for some 1,500 bargaining groups covering more than 9 million employees across all sectors of the economy.

Another important independent source of pay statistics for bargainers is Incomes Data Services Ltd. Its *Report*, published twice monthly, describes the changes to pay and conditions that are being agreed at company and industry level, and reports current developments in collective bargaining quickly and simply. Pay settlements are given in detail, and the latest statistics on wages, earnings and prices are reported and interpreted. The IDS *Pay Directory* is published three times a year. It lists the wage rates, holidays, shift premiums, etc, of a wide range of occupations in a variety of companies. It also records the wage rates that apply in selected industries and the public sector. It also publishes studies twice monthly, which report on the results of research into single topics such as the pay of a particular group of workers, paid holiday entitlement, sick pay, pensions provisions, shift premium pay, redundancy and absenteeism. Changes to practice are described and explained. Its *Top Pay Review*, published monthly, monitors the changes to the pay and benefits of executives and professionals, and provides a comprehensive briefing on remuneration trends in companies and in the public sector. Its *Focus* publication is published every quarter and puts forward views on a wide range of issues that influence pay and collective bargaining.

Two important UK Government sources of information for bargainers are *Labour Market Trends*, which incorporates the former *Employment Gazette*, and the New Earnings Survey. *Labour Market Trends* provides statistical information on the labour market, of which the most significant are employment, unemployment, unfilled vacancies, labour disputes, earnings and UK Government-supported training schemes. It also provides regular statistical information on inflation trends, being the official outlet for the index of retail prices, and provides information on changes in unit wage costs for all employees in manufacturing, energy and water supply, production industries, construction, and the economy as a whole.

The richest source of pay data for bargainers is the New Earnings Survey. It is the most comprehensive source of earnings information in Great Britain. An annual survey of 1 per cent of employees in different businesses and organisations, it has been in operation since 1970 and produces, on average, 170,000 individual records to build up a picture for the country as a whole. It provides an annual snapshot of earnings and hours worked analysed by industry, occupation, age group, region and country, and collective agreement.

The New Earnings Survey is conducted during April each year, and its results are published in six parts. Part A is a streamlined analysis giving selected results for full-time employees in particular wage negotiation groups, industries, occupations, age groups, regions and sub-regions. Part B provides analyses of earnings and hours for particular wage negotiation groups, while Part C analyses hours and earnings for particular industries. Part D provides the same analysis for particular occupations, and Part E for region and county. Part F provides an analysis of the distribution of hours, joint distributions of earnings and hours, and an analysis of hours and earnings for part-time women employees. The earnings data covers the level of earnings, the make-up of total earnings (basic pay, overtime pay, shift premiums, incentive payments, etc) and the distribution of total earnings (by decile, quartile and median).

> Go and look at the New Earnings Survey. Write a report on how pay and conditions in your organisation compare with the national average. How would you account for any differences you have found?

However, the most important activity for management in preparing for bargaining, as in grievance-handling, is the identification of the key issues involved in the forthcoming negotiations and of which of these management is prepared to trade. In making this decision, management weighs up the significance of the issues at stake for its economic interests. In a bargaining situation, for example, the management team may decide that changes in paid holidays and a reduction in the working week are not tradable items, but that it is prepared to trade improvements in pay levels and improved child-care facilities in return for greater flexibility between work tasks, the right to recruit part-time labour, and the tightening of the operational rules surrounding the sick pay scheme.

Having decided which items it is prepared to trade, the management team starts the task of anticipating which issues it believes the employees (the union) will be willing to trade. In doing this it assesses the strength of feeling of the employees about the issues in their shopping list, including whether they feel sufficiently strongly that at the end of the day they would be willing to impose industrial sanctions against the organisation. Taking the above example, the management team might anticipate that its employees do not feel particularly strongly about increased holidays and a shorter working week. However, it knows they feel strongly about a pay increase and improved child-care facilities, and will be reluctant to trade these items. The judgement for the management team then rests on 'Will the employees be prepared to trade changes in working practices and changes in the sick pay scheme to achieve improved pay and child-care facilities?' If management decides, after due consideration and analysis, that this is the case, it will see a basis for agreement around increases in pay and child-care provisions in return for changes in working practices and the operation of the sick pay scheme in directions which are more favourable to management.

Establishment of aims

As in grievance-handling, so in bargaining: when management has completed its analysis of the forthcoming negotiating situation it is about to enter, it moves to establish its objectives in terms of what it would ideally like to achieve, what it realistically expects to achieve, and what is the minimum it must achieve. Management's bargaining team will establish these three positions for each of the items in the respective shopping lists of both parties. Having established its negotiating aims and objectives, management's next step is to anticipate the aims and objectives of the representatives of the employees – for example, what do they idealistically and realistically want, and what is the minimum for which they would settle?

As in a grievance-handling situation, the management bargaining team can now construct an aspiration grid which sets out the parameters for the expected outcome of the bargaining (see Table 14). The grid shows that ideally management would like to trade no items with the employees. However, it knows this is unrealistic and has established a realistic position of wishing to trade increases in pay and child-care facilities for changes in working practices and tightening of the conditions surrounding the sick pay scheme. Management's fall-back position is to improve its pay offer, to provide child-care facilities and reduce the restrictions surrounding the sick pay scheme in return for obtaining changes in working practices. The bottom line for the management negotiating team is to trade pay, child-care facilities and aspects of the sick pay scheme in return for no change in holidays and working hours but alterations to working practices.

The aspiration grid also shows what management expects are the negotiating objectives of its employees' representatives. It expects ideally the employees' representatives will want to change every item on the list. Management knows that the employees' representatives will view this as unrealistic. The grid therefore shows that management expects the employees' realistic position to be one of seeking a deal

Table 14 Aspiration grid: bargaining situation

Possible Resolution to Grievance	Management			Employees and their representative organisation		
	Ideal	Real	Fall–back	Fall–back	Real	Ideal
Increased holidays	X	X	X	O	O	X
Reduced working week	X	X	X	O	O	X
Increased pay	X	O	O	X	X	X
Improved child-care facilities	X	O	O	X	X	X
Greater task flexibility	X	X	X	O	O	X
Tightening the sick pay scheme	X	X	O	O	X	X

around increases in pay and child-care facilities, and lesser restrictions on the sick pay scheme, in return for no changes in holidays and working hours and some changes to existing working practices. The grid shows that management anticipates that the bottom line for the employees' representatives is likely be to trade increases in pay and child-care facilities in return for no changes in holidays and hours of work but acceptance of management's desire for changes in working practices and in the details of the sick pay scheme.

The grid shows there is a basis for agreement between the parties. This is indicated in that the fall-back positions of the two parties do not have two Xs against the same issue. Management is not prepared to trade holidays, working hours and changes in working practices, but anticipates the employees' representatives are prepared to trade these issues. The employees are expecting management not to be prepared to concede some pay increases and increased child facilities. However, management has evaluated that it can live with trading these issues. The management negotiating team now has a structure of how the bargaining can be expected to develop and evolve. In the face-to-face sessions with the employees' representatives it will have to pass information to them on what issues management is prepared to trade and at the same time seek to gain information from the employees' side which confirms management's expectations of what the employees are prepared to trade.

Before establishing its aims for the forthcoming bargaining, management will have assessed its bargaining power relative to the group or groups with which it is to negotiate. The outcome of this assessment will be a significant factor in determining its bargaining objectives. In making an assessment of its relative bargaining power, management gives consideration to such questions as:

• Are the employees at the end of the day willing to impose industrial action?

• What is the degree of organisation and solidarity amongst the employees?

• What is the quality of the leadership of the union/group employees?

- Have the employees imposed industrial sanctions previously, and if so, what was the result?

- What type of industrial sanctions did they use? What tactics did they use?

- What is the degree of substitutability of product/service produced by the employees concerned?

- Can an alternative supply of labour be obtained?

- How crucial is the group of employees in the production/service supply process?

- How long will it take for industrial sanctions, if imposed, to have an adverse effect on the operation of the organisation?

The management bargaining team must take all these factors into account. They were discussed in greater detail in Chapter 1. If the balance of bargaining power favours the employer, the aspiration grid will be different from the situation of the bargaining power lying with the employees and their representative organisation.

Planning strategy and tactics

Having established its negotiating aims on the basis of its analysis of the situation, management now moves to planning its strategy and tactics to deliver its objectives. This covers some of the issues raised above when discussing the selection of the bargaining team and discipline within the team and the issues raised under this aspect of preparation in the managing grievances chapter. In bargaining, as in grievance-handling, the preparation stage is the longest and most important stage in the process. The golden rule to remember when preparing for bargaining is:

Failure to prepare

is

preparing to fail.

As in grievance-handling, so in bargaining: management should keep under regular review its bargaining objectives in the light of the information it gains from the face-to-face negotiating sessions with the other party. Any information received that was not known or anticipated during the original preparation stage must be analysed for its implications for the established bargaining aims and strategy and tactics.

'Failure to prepare is preparing to fail.' Explain the importance of this statement for managers who are involved in bargaining.

PRESENTATION OF PROPOSALS

In presenting its proposals for the first time, the management team will begin by presenting a general summary of the proposals by the use of such language as:

> We want to put to you today proposals in six areas – increased holidays, reduced working hours, increased pay, child care facilities, changes in working practices and conditions surrounding the operation of the sick pay scheme ...

After stating what it is going to tell them, the management team then moves on and outlines in detail, supported by facts and other appropriate evidence, its proposals in each of the six areas. The team will stress the rationale behind its proposals and give some indication of its strength of feeling on the issues. At the presentational stage management puts its ideal position on the table. The importance of putting all the proposals out on the table has been discussed in both Chapter 6 and Chapter 8.

However, the opening statement is important because it sets the parameters for the bargain, determines the amount of room available for movement, and can be used to structure the expectations of the other party. There can be advantages from opening with an extreme position. It provides more scope for movement in the bargaining sessions, allows extra time to identify the position of the other party, and avoids the problem of opening too low and passing up an opportunity of maximising possible outcomes. However, these possible advantages have to be weighed up against possible disadvantages. First, extreme demands might be given no credibility by the other side and be ignored. Second, the other party might perceive it as totally unreasonable and question the seriousness with which management is treating the negotiations. There is also the danger that the other side might respond with an equally extreme position. In deciding on the level at which to pitch its opening demand, the management team would be influenced by what it knows to be the style of the other side. Knowing and understanding the other party is very important for bargainers in that it contributes to the process of predicting how they might react to your proposals and to understanding their style of negotiations so that 'ritual' can be distinguished from the real position.

As in a grievance-handling situation, if management is receiving proposals from its employees' representatives it listens carefully to what is being said and does not interrupt the presentation. After the conclusion of the presentation, the management team should avoid an unthought-out response to the proposals that have just been put before it. Management should limit its response to questions to seek clarification of the employees' proposals so that it can be confident it understands what the other party's proposals actually mean.

CONFIRMATION OF COMMON GROUND

At the completion of the original presentation of proposals by the two parties, all issues/demands/proposals will be out in the open. At this stage, there will be little common ground between the two parties. The bargaining sessions now move to confirm the anticipated common ground from which a basis for a mutually beneficial agreement can be built. The tone of the meetings switches from concentrating on differences between the parties to confirming points of common interest and possible agreement. The management bargaining team acknowledges the point has been reached at which both it and the employees' representatives identify the common ground within and between their positions.

As we have already noted, management's objective is to gain information from the negotiating sessions to confirm its expectations about the areas of common ground between the parties. The implication is that the bargaining sessions must be used constructively by both parties. This is more likely to be the case where management seeks to ascertain relevant information from the other party by

- listening to the other side no matter how outrageous the statements of the employees' representatives might be: management must hear them carefully

- questioning for clarification of the other side's position

- summarising issues neutrally (eg 'So what you have been telling us is . . .')

- seeking and giving information

- suggesting solutions as to how problems of implementing the proposals might be overcome.

Bargaining sessions taken up with pointless arguments which go nowhere (eg It is your fault. No it is not, it is your fault. We tell you again, it is your fault), constant interruptions, point-scoring, attacking personalities on the other side, failing to listen to the other side (eg talking too much) and shouting down the other side are unconstructive and a waste of time. In such bargaining sessions it is likely that one side will fail to take up a proposal or agreement by the other side that is compatible with one or more of its own proposals. It can be difficult then to get the offer repeated, although in a subsequent adjournment the note-taker should point out what has happened and the negotiating team will consider how it can get the other side to repeat its offer or agreement. A golden rule of bargaining is that once the other party makes an offer to one of the items in your shopping list which is acceptable, it should be agreed immediately. The team having gained its point should stop talking and move the negotiations to the next issue(s).

It was demonstrated in both Chapters 6 and 8 that there are a number of techniques a management bargaining team can use to help confirm, or otherwise, the expected basis for an agreement as outlined in the aspiration grid. The most important of these are the 'if and then' technique, interviewing techniques, watching and listening techniques and linking of issues. If you are not familiar with these techniques you should re-read the appropriate sections of Chapters 6 and 8. In seeking to identify the common ground, management can also make progress by seeking agreement in principle to trade an item before discussing the details of the trade. For example, it is pointless discussing the details of how a new incentive payment scheme would work if one side is totally opposed to the idea of incentive schemes in the first place. It is also advantageous in seeking to confirm the common ground if the management negotiating team adopts the policy of being firm on principles. For example, management might say, 'If we are to agree to this, then we must be given greater flexibility in the utilisation of labour.' Management then proceeds to propose particular changes to working practices which can be the basis of discussion and negotiation.

In bargaining situations, listening skills enable the team to decode the hidden language of signals. Let's look at some examples.

- 'At this stage, we are not prepared to consider that' means 'That is a tradable item but at this stage it is not thought necessary to trade it'.

- 'We would find it extremely difficult to meet that demand' means 'It is not impossible'.

- 'I am not empowered to negotiate on that' means 'See my boss'.

- 'We can discuss that point' means 'It is negotiable'.

- 'These are company standard terms' means 'They are negotiable'.

- 'It is not our policy to make bonus payments, and even if we did they would not be as large as 10 per cent' means 'I'll give you 2 per cent'.

- 'It is not our normal practice to' means 'But we might if you make it worth our while'.

There is significant information to confirm tradable items in these statements. If management does not consider the meaning of these statements very carefully, it will miss important information.

In Chapter 6 we saw that the confirmation of the common ground between the two parties enables the bargaining sessions to have momentum. If the negotiations get bogged down on a particular item, they can be kept going by switching to a new issue. The difficult issue can be returned to later, and if it is then the only outstanding issue to an agreement's being secured, the parties are likely to readjust their attitudes towards the issue.

Concluding the agreement

In pay bargaining where increases in pay and other conditions are being given in return for changes in working practices, etc, the last item to be decided is what will be the amount of the increase in pay. There are a number of reasons for this. First, the management wants to know exactly what it is getting in terms of increased work effort for the pay increase. It is only when an amount is on offer that the employer can make a considered judgement over whether the 'price' for the changes in practices gained is worth while. The same applies to the employees. It is only when they know the things they have to give up (ie the price to be paid) that they can make a considered decision on whether the proposed pay increase offer is adequate compensation.

Second, if the pay issue is put on the table early in the negotiations, the negotiations are likely to become deadlocked. The momentum to the negotiations will come to a halt. Neither of the parties could accommodate each other's interests because they would not, at that stage, be able to assess whether the 'price' was worth while. The management would not have a complete picture of what it was receiving in return for the proposed pay improvement. The employees, by the same token, would be unable to judge whether they were being asked to pay a fair price in return for their pay improvement.

Third, by bargaining over pay after all other issues have been agreed, the bargainers are faced with a stark choice. If they cannot accommodate each other over pay, the whole agreement collapses. What has been agreed on the other items in the respective shopping lists is withdrawn. The parties have to weigh up whether they want 'to throw out the baby with the bath water'. The agreement must cover all the issues raised by both parties unless one or both have agreed to take an issue off the table. The attitude of the parties to accommodate each other over a difficult and basic issue, but which is the only outstanding item of non-agreement, will be favourable and not antagonistic. Neither party will want to see all its previous hard work go to waste. Attitudes are thus more compromising than if there were more than one outstanding issue. Both sides also have to weigh up whether, if an agreement fails to materialise over the one outstanding issue of pay improvement, they are prepared to bear the costs that go with the other party's imposing industrial sanctions against them.

Chapters 6 and 8 drew attention to some of the considerations a management team needs to take into account in concluding a collective agreement with its employees – for example, making sure that the other party really understands the management proposals to which it has agreed, 'playing-back' to the other party what management believes has been agreed, and the avoidance of a series of 'final' offers, etc. If you are not familiar with these possible pitfalls in concluding an agreement you should re-read the relevant sections of Chapters 6 and 8.

Writing up the agreement
Once management has an oral agreement, it should summarise to the employees' representatives what has been agreed and secure agreement that what has been summarised was agreed. It should then be written up in draft form. The written agreement should state:

- who the parties to the agreement are

- the date on which the agreement was concluded

- the date upon which the agreement will become operative

- which groups/grades are covered by the agreement

- what are the exceptions (if any) to the agreement

- the contents (clauses) of the agreement

- the duration of the agreement

- whether the agreement can be changed before this finish date, and if so, in what circumstances

- whether the agreement can be terminated if it has no end date, and if so, how

- how disputes over its interpretation and application will be settled (will it be through the existing grievance/disputes procedure?)

- which, if any, other agreements it replaces

and should contain the signatures of representatives of the parties covered by the agreement.

> Explain why recording of the negotiating process is vital. Outline what techniques can be used for this purpose and what the advantages are of each of them.

The agreement is usually drafted by management and then sent to the other side who will usually initial the clauses the wording of which it accepts. Only when both sides are happy with its wording will the agreement be printed and formally signed. There are some pitfalls that management should avoid when writing up the agreement. First, it should check the wording very carefully. One word can make a big difference to the meaning of a clause in the agreement. There is a big difference in meaning between a clause which states 'the management *may* provide' and one which states 'the management *will* provide'. The first implies that in certain circumstances management may not provide. The second leaves no room for doubt.

Second, management should retain full concentration in the latter stages of the bargaining. It is likely that the negotiations will have gone on for some time. There is a danger that the management bargaining team will relax once they have an oral agreement thinking that the hard work is over. However, management should bear in mind that, in a very short time, what was said in negotiations will be forgotten. The agreement will be what is down in black and white on the signed agreement.

Third, the agreement must be clear and easy to understand. Unless the agreement is fully understood by both parties and its wording and intent clear, its operation will cause endless disputes over its interpretation and application.

Fourth, it is important for management to keep an accurate record of what was agreed. This may be management's only protection against the other party's attempting to insert into the agreement something that was not agreed during the negotiations. Fortunately, attempts to cheat when writing up an agreement are extremely rare amongst management, employees and employees' representatives. To behave in this way would be to try and pull a fast one over the other side. A party may get away with this type of behaviour once but the cost could be high in terms of lost professionalism and of lost trust with the other party.

FURTHER READING

FOWLER A. *Effective Negotiations*. London, Institute of Personnel and Development, 1996.

KENNEDY G., BENSON J. *and* MCMILLAN J. *Managing Negotiations*. London, Hutchinson, 3rd ed., 1987.

CAIRNS, L. *Negotiating Skills in the Workplace*. Pluto Press, 1996.

10 Handling redundancy situations

INTRODUCTION

Since the 1960s British business has been exposed to ever-increasing competition in its own markets. In the 1960s, 1970s and early 1980s this tended to impact more heavily on manufacturing industry, which therefore experienced the greatest job losses, but in the last 15 years this increase in competition has spread to the public and service sectors. For example, banking – once considered one of the safest of occupations in terms of job security – has seen a steady rise in job losses over the past ten years. In declaring their 1996 results, National Westminster Bank made it clear that their policy of branch reduction, with the consequent loss of jobs, would continue over the next five years. Notwithstanding the great strides forward in competitiveness made by many businesses, we pointed out in Chapter 2 that Britain has not always been successful in competing in overseas markets nor in defending home markets. We also discussed how the supposed weakness of the British economy has variously been blamed on trade union resistance to change, poor and badly trained management, a financial system that is geared to shareholder reward rather than capital investment, too much or too little UK Government spending, and a whole range of other economic and social factors.

It is probably fair to say that no single cause is to blame, but whatever problems there have been with our economic and competitive performance there is no doubting one of the most significant outcomes in recent years has been an increase in the number of redundancies. Between 1945 and 1970 unemployment in Britain never rose above 3 per cent. Following oil price rises and other economic setbacks during the mid-1970s the average level of unemployment rose to just over 5 per cent by 1979. Following a climb during the 1980s to around 13 per cent, levels of unemployment at the end of 1996 were averaging about 8 per cent. However, as Blyton and Turnbull (1994) and other commentators have pointed out, comparisons are hindered by the many changes in the way that unemployment figures are compiled. Running parallel with the steadily increasing numbers of unemployed has been a large increase in the number of redundancies. It is for this reason that we are devoting a whole chapter to redundancy issues, which 'can mean different things to different people. Even as a specific legal concept, it has been the subject of differences and errors of interpretation' (Fowler, 1993; p3). When you have completed this chapter you will be able to

- understand the connection between redundancy and the management of change

- be able to produce a redundancy policy and associated procedures

- explain the legal framework in respect of redundancy, in particular the requirements on consultation

- understand the need to have clear policies for managing the 'survivors' of a redundancy exercise.

For personnel professionals, job security policies and the avoidance of redundancy are an increasingly important part of the employee relations framework of the 1990s. In Chapter 4 we discussed the fact that organisations have a continuing need to evolve – to constantly search for their distinctive capabilities (Kay, 1993). This in turn means a continuing process of change and leads to the inevitable weakening of employees' confidence in their employer's ability to maintain job security. Where redundancy is unavoidable, 'best practice' dictates that organisations have in place policies and procedures that enable them to deal with a difficult situation with sensitivity and equity. The employee relations specialist has a key role to play in this process in advising managerial colleagues on the scope and extent of any policies. Such policies and procedures are important not only because the law dictates certain minimum requirements but because, like most activities connected with employee relations, there is a good business case for doing so. An important part of any policy is the need to provide effective counselling and support for the redundant employee in terms of job seeking, outplacement etc. But it is also important to ensure that those who are to remain in employment, and may be fearful for their future, are not ignored. Ignoring the 'survivors' is likely to produce a de-motivated workforce that is prone to conflict with management.

REDUNDANCY AND THE MANAGEMENT OF CHANGE

In the context of redundancy we need to look at what it is that causes firms to need to change and ask whether job losses have to be the inevitable result. In many cases, organisations have had no option but to declare redundancies. An urgent need to cut costs, or the failure to win an important contract – these are just two examples of where immediate action needs to be taken. But redundancies could sometimes have been avoided if organisations had invested more time in manpower planning, training or skills development.

During the last 20 years, the world in which organisations have had to operate has seen many changes. In particular, they are under continuing pressure to improve their effectiveness, increase profitability and reduce costs. Changes in markets have created a need for organisations to be much more responsive to their customers' requirements. In manufacturing, for example, consumers demand higher and higher quality standards combined with better value for money. Motor cars are a good example of this where we, the customers, want enhanced safety features and more options, but at a lower cost. In the service sector, former public utilities have discovered that while privatisation may have freed them from the shackles of UK Government interference, customers with choice can exercise a tremendous influence. Even in what remains of the public sector, the concept of the customer is growing. The Benefits Agency does not have clients any more: it has customers; the National Health Service has its patients' charter; and the world of education, with its accent on parental choice, is much more accountable than ever it was.

In Chapter 4 we looked in detail at the need for businesses to develop clear business strategies which would, in turn, help them to identify what their people strategies ought to be and how they should manage change. For many the answer has been – to use the language of the 1990s – to downsize the organisation. The growth in unemployment over the past two decades has had a number of causes, but there is some evidence to suggest that had alternatives to redundancy been at the top of everybody's agenda, some jobs might have been saved. For many senior managers the need to deliver very large productivity increases and cost savings made redundancy the only option (Lewis, 1993). While this lack of choice needs to be acknowledged, there are two reasons why employers need to be considering the alternatives to redundancy. One is that every organisation needs to maintain some form of competitive advantage; the other is that it is a reasonable presumption to say that competitive advantage is unlikely to be achieved and maintained without a committed and motivated workforce. Redundancy can create the entirely opposite effect by engendering a mood of disillusionment and cynicism which, if allowed to fester, can destroy any of the short-term financial gains of a redundancy exercise, together with any hope of gaining employee commitment to the future.

If employee commitment is to be obtained, together with high levels of motivation, then employees need to feel secure in their employment, not afraid for their future. In 1983, when unemployment was running at over 3 million, Ron Todd, then General Secretary of the Transport Workers Union (T&GWU), commented that there were 3 million people on the dole, and another 23 million who were scared to death (Blyton and Turnbull, 1994). There is very little evidence to suggest that the fear factor has gone away. In a 1996 report the IPD stated that 'insecurity has damaged people's commitment', a state of affairs that if not remedied has the potential to damage competitive performance. While we can acknowledge that all businesses have to worry about competition, about retaining their competitive edge, about growth and even survival, these worries can be eased if they know they have a committed and loyal workforce. The challenge is how to overcome the fear factor and achieve the necessary commitment which we argue is so important.

There is no magic formula for achieving commitment, but a 1995 survey by the IPD and Templeton College, Oxford, identifies some important elements which can help management achieve this objective. One of these is trust, on which, says the survey, the 'psychological contract' that the employer has with employees must rest. The employees will have trust if they are confident that the employer will continue to search for new customers and new markets, thus making it possible for their talents to be employed. Clearly, as the survey points out, 'trust is vulnerable to the incidence of redundancy in an organisation' and serious questions are now being raised about some of the cost reduction, redundancy and downsizing policies that have been prevalent in recent years. This, says the survey, has caused some employers to declare that they will offer continual employment unless the most exceptional circumstances arise. Where businesses find it impossible to underwrite job security, they should commit to consulting on those strategic issues that can affect security of employment.

> Whether or not there have been redundancies in your own organisation, what do think is the current position in respect of employee security? Do you and your colleagues feel secure, or is there some concern about the future?

This type of approach has been taken up by the Bristol & West Building Society, one of whose strategic objectives was to protect jobs in the communities that it served. But such words by themselves do not deliver results. Much depends on the interaction that can be created between managers and the workforce as a means of fostering the levels of commitment and loyalty that are being sought. Such imperatives are the major reason that there has been such a concerted push by human resource specialists to integrate people-management issues into strategic management. As Pettigrew and Whipp (1993) argue, one of the central contributors to competitive performance is the way in which people within a firm are managed. In employee relations terms this means creating a partnership between workers and their managers which is collaborative, not adversarial.

We can perhaps explain this more effectively by looking at the example of Rover Cars. After years of decline characterised by poor industrial relations, poor productivity and, some would say, poor management, the reputation of Rover had, by the mid-1980s, reached an all-time low. The range of vehicles was regarded as poor, the workforce was demoralised, the company was loss-making and the balance sheet was weak. Rover, now owned by BMW, is still making a loss, but it is a totally different company from what it was in 1986. This is due in no small part to the initiative of the then chairman, Graham Day. He argued that profit would be the result of people, and that people therefore came first. This philosophy became the driving force behind their employee relations policies, and over a period of six years Rover worked hard to develop a partnership between managers and workers. The outcome of this was the launch, in 1992, of the company's far-reaching 'Rover Tomorrow – The New Deal', which included a company undertaking not to make compulsory redundancies in return for a commitment from employees to continuous improvement and flexibility. Clearly, there was much more to the Rover New Deal than an undertaking not to impose redundancies on individuals, and the accounts by Blakstad and Cooper (1995) and Burnes (1996) give a fuller understanding of all the actions that were taken to improve employee relations. However, the Rover experience, which was not totally unique, does provide evidence that employees, and their trade unions (where representation exists), are prepared to trade benefits for job security, and in Rover's case this has given them ten years free of serious industrial conflict. How long this trade-off between job security and flexibility can be sustained is questionable, and by the beginning of 1997 tensions, in the form of a positive vote for industrial action, were beginning to surface. Despite this, the Rover experience shows what can be done when employer and employees are prepared to trade over job security. Trade-offs can take a number of forms, one of which is 'worksharing'. At the end of 1993 a pioneering agreement on worksharing, cutting hours and pay to save jobs, was negotiated by Volkswagen, the German car manufacturer. Since then such arrangements have gained an increasing profile in German industrial relations (*European Industrial Relations Review* 254, March 1995), and in the UK, Sheffield City Council employees voted for a worksharing deal intended to avoid around 1,400 redundancies (*Personnel Management Plus*, January 1994). Another example of a job security agreement, although not worksharing, can be found in the deal negotiated in January 1997 between Blue Circle, the cement manufacturer, and the GMB and T&GWU unions. This agreement traded job security for a degree of pay restraint over a five-year period.

Are you aware of any other arrangements of this kind? Is it something your organisation has considered?

POLICIES AND PROCEDURES

No matter what sort of strategic vision an organisation employs, there will sometimes be no alternative to reducing the numbers employed. Because the possibility of this occurring is much higher now than it was 20 years ago, good employee relations practice dictates a need for clear policies and procedures which allow redundancy situations to be dealt with in a professional and equitable manner – not only because there are legal regulations to be taken into account, but in order to maintain the 'psychological contract' we discussed above.

Policy

A statement of policy on redundancy might, in some ways, be better classified as an organisation's statement of intent in respect of maintaining employment. For example, a policy statement on redundancy might be set out as follows:

> The company intends to develop and expand its business activities in order to maintain its competitive advantage within our existing marketplace. It is also our intention to seek new products and markets provided they have a strategic fit with the rest of the business. To achieve these objectives we need the active co-operation and commitment of the

whole workforce. In return our aim is to provide a stable work environment and a high level of job security. However, we also need to ensure the economic viability of the business in the competitive world in which we now have to operate. In such a world changes in markets, technology or the corporate environment may cause us to consider the need for reductions in staffing levels. In order to mitigate the impact of any reductions in staff the following procedure will be adopted.

You will note that such a policy statement does not make any commitment to no compulsory redundancies, but it is an important first step in recognising people as an important asset. Evidence, as the IPD/Templeton survey found, is already beginning to suggest that the downsizing, re-engineering culture of the late 1980s/early 1990s is having a detrimental effect on businesses that are seeking to grow. A study by International Survey Research cites a survey of senior HR managers which found that downsizing has gone too far and the overall effect has been negative (*People Management* No. 22, November 1996; p15). Many organisations are now beginning to recognise that they have lost valuable experiences and skills which are proving difficult to replace. Local UK Government, which has seen its share of downsizing in recent years, has been accused by the Audit Commission of knee-jerk restructuring and de-layering which has exposed it to fraud and poor management (*People Management* No. 23, November 1996; p11). Mumford and Hendricks in charting the rapid rise and fall of the re-engineering concept (*People Management,* May 1996) argue that it has failed as a technique because many of its followers did not understand people- and change-management techniques; they point to evidence that re-engineering always took longer than expected, involved more resources than were available, and presented unforeseen problems. Developing a redundancy policy, or statement of intent, as described above should be driven by an organisation's overall business strategy and can be an important first step in building that very important management-workforce partnership. But even in the most strategically aware organisations not everything is predictable and there may be situations in which job losses cannot be avoided. This is where the procedure, mentioned in our example of a policy statement, comes into play.

Procedure
The first thing to say about a redundancy procedure, as with any other procedure, is that it needs to fit the business. That is, it needs to be written and designed to cater for the individuality of each organisation. Draft procedures can be obtained from professional bodies like the IPD or from commercial organisations like Croner's, but they should always be treated as guidelines or templates and be amended to meet individual organisations' requirements. As a basic minimum, there are a number of things that a redundancy procedure should cover, starting with alternative courses of action. Where the possibility of a reduction in employee numbers arises, management should begin a process of consultation (there are a number of legal rules relating to consultation which we will consider in the section 'The Legal Framework') with either trade unions or elected workplace representatives. The purpose of this consultation would be to establish whether any potential job

losses can be achieved by means other than compulsory redundancies. Some of the factors that would normally be considered at this juncture would be a ban on recruitment (unless unavoidable) and the possible re-training or re-deployment of surplus staff. It would be normal to restrict the use of subcontract labour, temporary and casual staff, and to reduce the amount of overtime working. Depending on the nature of the business, other considerations might include temporary lay-off, short-time working or even job sharing. If there were any employees who were over normal retirement age, it might be necessary to insist on their immediate retirement and, at the same time, it might be appropriate to ask for volunteers for early retirement. This last point does, however, need careful consideration. Early retirement, if it is to be a serious option, needs to carry some form of financial inducement. As an absolute minimum the pension scheme must allow for the payment of pensions early on the grounds of redundancy. In effect, the potential retiree is credited with more years of pensionable service than he or she has actually worked. The question of how many extra years to credit will depend on how near to normal retirement age a particular employee is. It is possible that the employer might have to make a payment into the pension fund to ensure there is no detriment to the early-retired employee or to provide a lump sum that will take the employee up to an agreed date for receiving the pension. It is important that these financial considerations are taken into account by employee relations specialists when they are asked, as they often are, to cost the available options for reducing the workforce. A further point to remember in considering early retirement is the position of pension trustees. Following the Maxwell scandal, trustees now have much more responsibility for the management of individual schemes. Whether to allow early retirement on redundancy grounds or to enhance the value of an individual's pension is not just a management decision, the trustees have a role to play. For the employee relations specialist all of this means that the question of early retirement as an alternative to compulsory redundancy needs to be carefully costed and researched.

When management has given very careful consideration to the alternatives discussed above but concludes that the need for redundancies still remains, the next step in the procedure would be for them to give employees, or their representatives, written details of their proposals. This would include details of the methodology that management proposes to use for selecting individuals. They may indicate at this stage that they are prepared to accept volunteers, but this must be subject to the company's need to retain a balanced workforce, with the appropriate mix of skills and knowledge. As Lewis (1993) and others have indicated, the concept of voluntary redundancy has become the most widely acceptable method of dealing with redundancy, and there are obviously a number of advantages in adopting the voluntary approach. Firstly, it can help to avoid some of the de-motivating effects that redundancy inevitably has on an organisation, and secondly, it can be cost-effective. While persuading people to go, rather than forcing them to leave, will probably require higher individual payments (possibly in pension costs), the financial benefits of a redundancy exercise can begin to impact much earlier if a costly and time-consuming consultation exercise can be avoided. It may be possible to reduce the workforce by a higher number than was originally envisaged if a voluntary approach is adopted, as British Telecom found with their 'Release 92' scheme which was considerably over-subscribed. Accepting more people in this way obviously has unbudgeted cost implications and it is important, before paying extra costs in this way, that a comprehensive manpower planning exercise has been carried out in order to assess future labour requirements.

If the voluntary option was not feasible, because the wrong people were volunteering or insufficient numbers came forward, the next step would have to be compulsory redundancy. At this point in the procedure there would be an acknowledgement that the organisation would, as far in advance of any proposed termination date as possible, notify all employees that compulsory redundancies are proposed, and that a provisional selection has been made. As we will see, this part of the procedure fulfils a statutory requirement. The easiest and most non-contentious method of selection is last-in first-out (LIFO), but this can have significant downside effects. Using LIFO can, for many organisations, mean that they lose their youngest employees or those with the most up-to-date skills. For this reason many organisations have adopted a selection system that is based on a number of criteria, such as attendance records, range of work experience, disciplinary records, etc. Such criteria, which need to be as objective as possible, and be based on a system of points scores, tend to be looked on very favourably by tribunals. It would be important to stress that any selection was provisional and subject to change following consultation with the employees affected. Once the selection of individuals has been confirmed it is important – particularly if the procedure is to be consistent with the policy – that an acknowledgement is made in respect of alternative employment. Of course, alternative employment is not always possible, nor is it always desired by those to be made redundant. Nevertheless, it is incumbent on the employer to make every effort to look for alternatives and where they exist, consider redundant employees for suitable vacancies. Where the organisation, or the number of jobs to be reduced, is very small, options in respect of alternatives are very rare. Nevertheless, the procedure needs to set out the basis on which employees will be interviewed for any vacancies, and the terms and conditions on which alternative jobs will be offered. Terms and conditions may be the standard terms for the job in question, they may be the terms previously enjoyed by the individual concerned, or there may be some form of transition. These are all issues that the employee relations specialist needs to consider. Naturally, as we will see when we look at the legal framework, the procedure needs to say something about trial periods.

It would be normal practice for a redundancy procedure to set out what steps the organisation proposed to take in assisting the redundant employee who could not be found alternative employment within the business. Such steps should include provisions for paid time off to attend interviews, to seek re-training opportunities or to attend counselling sessions. This latter point will be dealt with in more detail later in the chapter.

Finally the procedure might set out the basis on which employees will be compensated for the loss of their employment. There is a statutory entitlement laid down in the current legislation, but some organisations are prepared to make enhanced payments in order to ease the trauma that redundancy can cause or, as we have seen, to encourage volunteers to come forward. Employee relations specialists who are charged with drawing up a procedure should be warned of the pitfalls of setting out too much detail on compensation. It is important to ensure that the organisation retain some flexibility on the issue of enhanced payments. Whatever motives lie behind paying more than the statutory amount, no organisation can predict the future or the circumstances in which redundancies may occur. It is important therefore, to ensure that any payments set out in a procedure document are not considered to be contractual.

Now that you have had an opportunity to consider these guidelines on policy and procedure, how do they compare with your own? Does your organisation even have a policy and procedure, and if it has, is it up-to-date?

THE LEGAL FRAMEWORK

Prior to 1965 employees had no statutory protection in respect of redundancy. The 'right' of organisations to hire and fire at will was seen as one of those inalienable 'management rights' that were necessary if organisations were to compete successfully in a commercial world. However, by the beginning of the 1960s there was a widespread belief that economic growth was being held back because of a lack of labour mobility. The Redundancy Payments Act of 1965 was part of the answer to this problem and enjoyed the support of both major political parties as well as both sides of industry – a classic example of the post-war consensus that we discussed in Chapter 2! The Act laid down for the first time that a worker with a minimum period of service was entitled to compensation for the loss of his or her job through redundancy. Compensation was decided on the basis of age and length of service and was subject to both a maximum and a minimum amount. The basic law in relation to redundancy compensation has not changed much in the intervening years, but there have been significant developments in respect of consultation, selection and the transfer of undertakings.

In order to properly understand the way in which the law seeks to offer protection to those facing the loss of their employment there are a number of factors which need to be considered. The first of these concerns the definition of redundancy, which is set out in Section 139 of the Employment Rights Act (1996). Principally, there are two ways in which a redundancy can occur, and these are set out in 139(1) as follows:

(a) The fact that [the] employer has ceased or intends to cease –

    1) to carry on the business for the purposes of which the employee was employed by him, or

    ii) to carry on that business in the place where the employee was so employed, or

(b) The fact that the requirements of that business –

    i) for employees to carry out work of a particular kind, or

    ii) for employees to carry out work of a particular kind in the place where the employee was employed by the employer, have ceased or diminished or are expected to cease or diminish.

To put that in everyday language: redundancy occurs when the employer closes down completely, moves premises, requires fewer people for particular jobs or requires no people for particular jobs. Redundancy can also occur when an individual has been laid off or kept on short-time for a period that is defined in Sections 147 to 152 of the 1996 Act. Assuming that the reason an individual's employment comes to an end is within one of the statutory definitions, or that he or she has been laid off or kept on short-time and, assuming that he or she has a minimum period of qualifying employment, then he or she is entitled to a statutory redundancy payment. The amount of payment that an individual is entitled to is set out in Section 162 (2) of the 1996 Act as follows:

• one and a half weeks' pay for each year of employment in which the employee was not below the age of 41

• one week's pay for each year of employment that the employee was between the ages of 22 and 40

• half a week's pay for each year of employment under the age of 22.

No more than 20 years' service can be taken into account in calculating an individual's redundancy payment and there is also a maximum weekly amount that an individual can receive irrespective of how much he or she earns. This maximum amount is usually, but not always, reviewed by the UK Government on an annual basis.

There are a number of exceptions to these basic payments. For example, an individual who was in his 64th year would have his payment reduced proportionately, depending on how close he was to his 65th birthday. Certain holders of public office and some domestic servants are also excluded. On the other hand, the scale of payments set out above represents only a statutory minimum; organisations can, and as we acknowledged earlier, do enhance them. They can also pay for more than 20 years' service if they so wish, but it is important to remember that any enhancements, to either amounts or length of service, are entirely at the employer's discretion, unless there is a specific contractual arrangement. In the context of redundancy payments, the definitions of redundancy can be of particular and significant importance. Before 1990, an employer had certain rights to reclaim part of any redundancy payment made to an individual employee, and while this rebate only applied to the statutory part of a redundancy payment, it was an important factor for an employer to take into consideration when considering an enhanced payment. With the ending of the rebate, employers now have to meet the total cost of all redundancy payments and as a consequence have become much more concerned with ensuring that any loss, or diminution of work, does actually justify a payment.

There are three sets of circumstances which an employer might argue create no entitlement to a redundancy payment. An employer might say that the events which led to an individual's leaving employment had nothing to do with redundancy but was simply the consequences of a legitimate and lawful business reorganisation which were unacceptable to the employee concerned. In such circumstances it is likely that the employee will argue that the 'work of a particular kind' which he or she had been carrying out had 'ceased or diminished' and that he or she is entitled to the statutory rights. This would then need to be resolved by a tribunal, which D. Lewis (1997) describes as one of their more difficult tasks. In the case of Lesney Products v Nolan (1977) IRLR 77, Nolan and some of his colleagues argued that the change from a long day shift with overtime to a double-day shift was a diminution in the employer's requirements for work of a particular kind, and that they should have received a redundancy payment. The Court of Appeal held that such a change was a legitimate reorganisation, based on efficiency, and that therefore no payment was due.

The second set of circumstances in which an employer might refuse to make a redundancy payment concerns the words 'in the place where the employee was so employed'. This raises the whole question of mobility clauses in the contract of employment, and how much the employer can rely on them. For example, if the contract required that an employee could be required to work anywhere, a refusal to do so could lead to a dismissal for misconduct, but not to redundancy. For the employer to rely on the terms of a mobility clause to rebut a claim for a redundancy payment there must be an express clause in the contract which allows the employer to ask an employee to work at a different location or locations. Even then it is by no means certain that the employer will win the argument.

In 1995, the Court of Appeal held that a clause contained in a contract of employment requiring an employee to work in such parts of the UK as her employers might dictate, constituted unlawful sex discrimination within the Sex Discrimination Act (1975). The case in question, Meade-Hill and Another v British Council, revolved around the British Council's decision to require Ms Meade-Hill to accept the incorporation of a mobility clause into her contract as a consequence of a promotion. While this particular case, which was decided in Ms Meade-Hill's favour, was more concerned with sex discrimination than redundancy payments, it is important because of statements made by the Court of Appeal in respect of mobility clauses generally. It commented that even if [this particular mobility clause] could not be justified in its present form, the objectionable aspects would disappear if it were modified in a relatively minor respect. In the court's view there was no great cause for celebration by employees as a result of this particular decision.

For most employee relations practitioners the question of mobility is more likely to arise when the whole, or part, of a business is moving – either to a new geographical location some distance from the present workplace or to new premises broadly within the existing geographical location. In order that an organisation can retain a degree of flexibility in terms of its location it is important to be clear about an employee's place of work. For the same reason it is important to be very clear about it when drawing up the employee's 'Statement of Terms and Particulars of Employment' as required by the Employment Rights Act (1996). The statement must identify whether 'the employee is required or permitted to work at various places' 1 (4)(h).

> What does your contract say about mobility? Are there any circumstances in which the current wording could bring you into conflict with an employee?

The third set of circumstances that might lead to refusal to make a redundancy payment is when the employee refuses an offer of 'suitable alternative employment'. When the employee is offered a new contract of employment, to begin immediately or within four weeks of the termination of the old contract, and the offer is unreasonably refused, there is no entitlement to a redundancy payment. However, the burden of proving that an offer is suitable lies with the employer. If the employee were to express the view that the proposed new job was inferior to the old one, it would be for the employer to demonstrate that it was not – and how an employer can do this has been the subject of many industrial tribunal cases. In Hindes v Supersine Ltd (1979) IRLR 343, it was argued that whether the proposed employment was 'substantially equivalent' to the former job was an objective assessment as any. In Cambridge and District Co-op v Ruse (1993) IRLR 156, the Employment Appeal Tribunal held that 'It is possible for an employee reasonably to refuse an objectively suitable offer of alternative employment on the ground of his personal perception of the job offered.' In this case Mr Ruse had refused an alternative job because he considered it represented a demotion and a loss of status.

It is very difficult to give absolute advice on such matters as alternative employment. The sensible employee relations specialist will deal with each case individually and on its merits. It may be that what is suitable for one employee may be totally unsuitable for another. One alternative is the provision within Section 138(3) of the legislation that allows for a 'trial period'. This gives the redundant employee an opportunity to try a new job for a period of four weeks, or such longer (specified) period as may be agreed, to allow for re-training. If, having opted for a trial period, the employee decides at the end of it that the job is not suitable, then a redundancy payment is still payable.

The law and consultation

Since the mid-1970s all member states of the European Union have been required to enact legislation which would oblige employers to consult with workers' representatives about redundancy. This was generally assumed to mean consultation with recognised trade unions and was first implemented into our legal framework by Sections 99 to 107 of the Employment Protection Act (1975). The relevant provisions are now contained in Sections 188 to 198 of the Trade Union and Labour Relations (Consolidation) Act (1992).

During 1992, the European Commission claimed that there were imperfections within the UK legislation because

• there was no provision for consulting with employees in the absence of a recognised trade union

• the scope of the UK legislation was more limited than was envisaged by the original European Directive (75/129/EEC)

• there was no requirement that an employer considering collective redundancies had to consult workers' representatives with a view to reaching agreement in relation to the matters specified in the directive.

The Commission's complaints were considered to be well-founded and amendments made by the 1993 Trade Union Reform and Employment Rights Act (1993) made it a requirement that consultations about proposed redundancies must include discussion and consultation about ways of avoiding dismissals altogether. This change to the legislation was considered to be insufficient, and in 1994 the European Court of Justice ruled that the UK could not limit the right to be consulted to representatives of recognised trade unions. As a response to this, additional regulations – the Collective Redundancies and Transfer of Undertakings (Protection of Employment) (Amendment) Regulations (1995) – were introduced and took effect from March 1996.

What, then, does this plethora of Directives, legislation and regulation mean in practical terms for the employee relations specialist? What is an employer required to do if there is a possibility that employees will be made redundant? The question needs to be considered from two angles: collective redundancies and individual redundancies.

Collective redundancies

The 1992 Trade Union and Labour Relations (Consolidation) Act (TULR(C)A) together with the 1995 regulations oblige any employer wishing to make 20 or more redundancies to consult with 'appropriate representatives'. These appropriate representatives do not have to be union representatives, even where there is a recognised union in the workplace, but may, if the employer so decides, be employee-elected representatives. The regulations are silent on how many representatives can be elected or how they are to be selected, but the DTI has published guidelines on the issues an employer should consider, such as whether

- the arrangements adequately cover all the categories of employees who are to be, or might be, made redundant and provide a reasonable balance between the interests of different groups

- the employees have sufficient time to nominate and consider candidates

- the employees (including any who were absent from work for any reason) can freely choose who to vote for

- there is any normal company practice for similar elections, and if so, whether there any good reasons for departing from it.

The guidelines also cover the position where an elected body already exists. This must be a committee or council that is suitable – a social committee will not be appropriate. In so far as the timing of any elections is concerned, the employer will not be in breach of the regulations if the invitation to elect representatives was issued in sufficient time for an election to take place before consultation was required to begin. The whole purpose of the legislation is to make certain that where a collective redundancy situation exists, there is genuine and meaningful consultation. It does this in four ways. One, it sets out a timetable for consultation; two, it sets out when the process of consultation has begun; three, it sets out the matters to be discussed during the consultation process; and four, it sets out penalties which will be imposed on employers who fail to adhere to the requirements.

Section 188(2) of TULR(C)A (1992) requires consultation about proposed redundancies to begin at the earliest opportunity, but in cases involving 20 or more people minimum time periods are a necessity. If the employer is proposing to dismiss over 100 employees, the consultation process must begin at least 90 days before the first dismissal takes effect. If the proposal is to dismiss less than 100 but 20 or more, the consultation process must begin no later than 30 days before the first dismissal. Some commentators have expressed doubt about how the phrase 'proposes redundancies' should be interpreted, particularly as the Collective Redundancies Directive uses the phrase 'contemplating redundancies'. There is a degree of agreement that the Directive requires consultation at an earlier stage than TULR(C)A, but at the time of writing there is no case law which helps to clarify the problem. The safest course for any employer is to start the consultation as soon as possible.

The timetable described above can only start to run once employees or their representatives have been provided with certain information. One, they have to be told the reasons for the employer's proposals; two, they have to be told the numbers and descriptions of the employees the employer is going to dismiss; three, they have to be told what method of selection the employer proposes for dismissal; four, they must be told what method of carrying out the dismissals the employer proposes, having due regard to any procedure agreement that might be in existence and the period of time over which the programme of redundancies is to be carried out; and five, they must be told what method the employer intends to use in calculating redundancy payments unless the statutory formula is being applied. Should an employer fail to provide any or all of the information required, or the information that is provided is insufficient, the consultation period will be deemed not to have started. In such circumstances the employer faces the risk of a penalty being imposed (see below) for failing to consult at the earliest opportunity. It is difficult to give precise guidance on what, and how much, detail must be provided, but vague and open-ended statements will not be acceptable. For the employee relations specialist there has to be an acceptance that every case must be decided on its merits and will need to be researched. It is no good relying on 'what happened last time'; that may not be good enough. In MSF *v* GEC Ferranti (Defence Systems) Ltd (1994) IRLR 113, the Employment Appeal Tribunal held that 'Whether a union has been provided with information which is adequate to permit meaningful consultation to commence is a question of facts and circumstances. There is no rule that full and specific information under each of the heads [of the legislation] must be provided before the consultation period can begin.' It went on to confirm an earlier judgement which held that a failure to give information on one of the heads may be a serious default, but that there is nothing to say that it must be treated as a serious default.

For consultation to be deemed genuine it has to be undertaken with a 'view to reaching agreement' with employees' representatives. Three things have to happen. An examination has to take place into ways of avoiding dismissals. If this is impossible, ways of reducing the numbers to be dismissed should be looked at. Finally, ways must be found of mitigating the consequences of any dismissals. How tribunals will measure whether these obligations have been fulfilled is open to question. It would be strange if the legislation, as amended, meant that the employer and the representatives have to reach an agreement. What is more likely is that employers must approach the discussions with an open mind and where possible take account of any proposals put to them by the representatives.

If there has been a failure to follow the proper consultation process, an application can be made to an industrial tribunal for a declaration to this effect and for a 'protective award' to be paid. This is an award requiring the employer to pay the employee remuneration for a protected period. The legislation relating to protective awards is quite complex, but some of the important elements are:

- the affected employee receives payment at the rate of one week's gross pay for each week of the 'protected' period

- unlike some compensatory awards there are no statutory limits on a week's pay

- subject to certain maximums, the length of a protected period is at the industrial tribunal's discretion; the test is what is just and equitable, having regard to the seriousness of the employer's default

• the maximum periods are 90 days when 90 days should have been the consultation period, and 30 days when 30 days should have been the consultation period; in any other case the maximum is 28 days.

As P. Lewis points out (1993), the financial implications of protective awards can be quite significant as there are often substantial numbers of employees involved – and yet, according to a report commissioned by law firm Nabarro Nathanson, around one in five companies were unsure about the requirements of the legislation (*People Management* No. 25, December 1996; p7).

Employers with well-established redundancy procedures are unlikely to come into conflict with the law over a failure to consult. Notwithstanding this, the prudent employee relations specialist will keep the procedure under review in the light of any relevant tribunal decisions. The real problems arise for those organisations that do not have a procedure or who try to put together a procedure in a hurried and casual manner when redundancies are imminent. Such organisations might find that the price they pay for a lack of preparedness is extremely high. Tribunals have shown an increasing tendency to take a very narrow view of any special pleading by employers that there was no time to consult. To be acceptable, non-consultation would have to be the result of some event that was quite out of the ordinary.

Individual consultation
Consultation with trade unions and now with the wider constituency of 'employees' representatives' has tended to attract most of the attention in studies of redundancy, and there is certainly a good deal of case law on the subject, but the necessity for individual consultation must not be overlooked. Many managers have fallen into the trap of assuming that when only one or two individuals are to be made redundant there is no obligation to consult. They could not be more wrong, and although there is no statutory framework for individual consultation as there is when collective redundancies are on the agenda, tribunals can still intervene. The Employment Rights Act (1996) identifies redundancy as a fair reason for dismissal (Section 98 (2) (c)), which opens the door for an employee to claim unfair dismissal on the grounds that the employer, by failing to consult, has not acted reasonably. Most claims for unfair dismissal in respect of redundancy are in two areas: unfair selection and lack of consultation. Many employers have argued that because the redundancy only affected one or two individuals, consultation would not have made any difference. This defence has been virtually closed to employers since the decision of the House of Lords in Polkey *v* A. E. Dayton Services Ltd (1987) IRLR 503, but unwise and unprofessional employers still try to use it. In Polkey, the House of Lords did not say that consultation was an absolute requirement but that the onus is on the employer to demonstrate that consultation would have been 'utterly useless'. In the majority of cases it would be difficult to demonstrate the uselessness of something that had not been tried. By far the best option for employers is to recognise that good employee relations would be best served by adopting a systematic approach to

consultation whether the proposed redundancies are going to affect five people or 50 people.

> Are you confident, having read this section that you fully understand the requirements on consultation? Do you need to advise any of your colleagues of their obligations?

Transfers of undertakings

When the ownership of a business transfers there is always the possibility that redundancies will be one of the results that flow from such a transfer. Under the Acquired Rights Directive of the European Union (Directive 77/187/EEC), member states are required to ensure, in broad terms, that all employees who are covered by employment protection legislation should receive additional protection in respect of job security if the identity of their employer changes. This does not mean that an employer who acquires a new business is obliged to retain all the inherited employees irrespective of the commercial realities, but equally the new employer cannot just dispense with those employees without just cause. Should employers find that, on the transfer of a business, there are sound commercial reasons for reducing the headcount, then subject to the normal rules on consultation and the operation of a fair selection procedure, the law will not stand in their way. What the law does insist on, however, is that the transferred employees' rights are retained. This means that if they had the requisite period of service with their old employer to qualify for a redundancy payment, then the new employer cannot avoid making a redundancy payment to them. In the context of consultation, all the issues of representation and the right to information that we have discussed above in respect of collective redundancies apply equally to transfers of undertakings.

POST-REDUNDANCY

The massive rise in unemployment in recent years has meant that more attention is now paid to the needs of redundant employees. In this section we will be looking at the growth in both counselling and outplacement services and, in addition, the position of those employees that remain in employment – the so-called 'survivor syndrome'.

Counselling

We have decided to examine counselling and outplacement separately, notwithstanding that they overlap in many ways. In this section we will be talking about counselling in the sense of helping employees come to terms with the fact that they have lost their job (counselling in respect of personal skills, job search and financial planning will be dealt with under 'outplacement').

Although redundancy has become part of everyday life, the loss of one's job usually comes as a tremendous personal blow. Even when 'the writing is on the wall' and the prospect of job losses in the organisation is inevitable, individuals still hope that they will be unaffected. To paraphrase an advertising slogan made famous by the national lottery, they hope 'it will not be them'.

There can be a tendency for employers to want a redundancy exercise to be forgotten as quickly as possible, and this can manifest itself in a very uncaring attitude. The professional employee relations specialist should be reminding managerial colleagues that they have a continuing responsibility for their redundant employees and, as the IPD guide on redundancy says, be providing displaced employees with a counselling service. Redundant employees can feel anger, resentment and even guilt – emotions which, if not carefully managed, can inhibit an employee from moving forward to the next phase of a career, and this is where effective counselling becomes very important. However, it is important to proceed cautiously, and earlier in this book, in another reference to counselling, we stressed the need for proper training. 'Handling the first stage of redundancy counselling requires considerable skill, and should not be attempted by anyone who does not, as a minimum, understand the general principles of all forms of counselling' (Fowler, 1993).

Not every redundant employee will agree to or want counselling, but nevertheless it is important to understand its key purpose. If you talk to redundant employees, as we have done, you are struck by the violent mood swings that can occur during the initial post-redundancy phase. Depending on the personality of the individual concerned, the mood can swing from pessimism about the future to unfounded optimism – from anger at the former employer to a feeling that they have been given an opportunity to do something different. The objective of counselling is to bring all these emotions out into the open and to help individuals to make decisions about their future. It is not a panacea, it will not stop people being angry or feeling betrayed, but it might help them to view their future constructively.

For the employee relations specialist, there is a further dimension to the provision of counselling. Not only is there a moral imperative but there are sound business reasons. Unless the organisation is closing down completely, there will be other employees left who you will want to build the organisation around. We will discuss these individuals in more detail later in the section, but Richard Baker, director of human resources at Hoechst Roussel, makes a very valid point when he says, 'People ... never forget the way they are treated when they are made redundant, and neither do the friends and colleagues who remain behind' (*People Management* No. 2, January 1996; p31).

Outplacement
Outplacement is a process where an individual or individuals who have been made redundant by their employer are given support and counselling to assist them in achieving the next stage of their career. There are a large number of organisations offering outplacement services, but the range and quality of their services varies greatly and the employee relations specialist needs to carefully research prospective suppliers if a decision to use outplacement is taken.

Broadly, outplacement consultancies offer services on a group or individual basis which fall into the following general categories:

- CV preparation
- researching the job market
- communication techniques
- interview presentation
- managing the job search.

Each organisation operates differently, but in the very best organisations the process would probably start with a personal counselling session with a trained counsellor. Once this has been carried out, the next step would be the preparation of the CV. This involves identifying key skills and past achievements so that the job hunter can self-market from a position of strength. Step three would be to make decisions about job search methods (cold contact, advertisement, recruitment consultants, etc) and contact development (eg networking). Step four would be to ensure that the key communication skills of letter writing, telephone techniques and interview presentation were of a sufficiently high standard to enhance the job search. Where skills need to be improved, the better consultancies will provide the necessary training at no extra cost. The final step is managing the actual job search – setting personal targets, keeping records of letters and phone calls, maintaining notes of interviews, and carrying out a regular job search evaluation.

Running alongside these basic services will be a range of support services, such as secretarial help, free telephone and office space, and financial planning advice. What an individual gets will depend on the particular package that the former employer purchases on his or her behalf.

Does your organisation have any sort of policy on counselling and outplacement? If not, who would make the decisions about what level of support to offer?

Survivor syndrome

When people are forced to leave employment because of redundancy, those that are left behind can be affected just as much as those that have left. Anecdotal evidence we have gathered from the finance sector and local UK Government indicate that disenchantment, pessimism and stress are the likely result of even a small-scale redundancy exercise. Survivor syndrome, as it is called, can be minimised if, as we pointed out above, those who are to be made redundant are treated fairly and equitably and there is a decision made to invest in an effective post-redundancy programme. This usually means a time commitment from senior managers and a good communication process.

The feelings referred to above are the result of two factors. The first is that the remaining employees are often asked to 'pick up' the work of their former colleagues, either directly or indirectly, as the consequence of a re-organisation. In one local authority individuals had to reapply for their own jobs three times in three years following a series of redundancies and reorganisations. The second factor concerns communication. The anecdotal evidence that we have suggests that in many organisations the remaining employees are not always communicated with effectively, thus providing the opportunity for rumour and disenchantment to thrive. Getting the message across about why redundancies were necessary and what happens next is vitally important, and yet most people we have spoken to identify poor communication as one of the principal causes of their dissatisfaction.

Blakstad and Cooper (1995) identify three sets of stimuli which can interfere with communications, one of which is internal stress. Internal stress can be caused by a number of variables, but one of the causes identified is 'group concerns'. The aftermath of a redundancy exercise is a classic example of 'group concerns', and yet many managers do not take this into account when communicating with the survivors. For the professional manager who wishes to minimise the effect of survivor syndrome, communication and communication methodology need to be carefully worked out. 'While it is usually impossible to understand the individual concerns of each member of the [group], structuring the communication around an awareness of group tensions can be used to strengthen retention of messages' (Blakstad and Cooper, 1995).

CONCLUSION

Redundancy is one of the most emotive issues that any manager can be called upon to deal with. Calling an individual into your office and informing him or her that he or she no longer has a job is never easy. For the employee relations specialist who is at the beginning of a career, managing a redundancy exercise can be just as traumatic as for the redundant employee.

No matter how experienced you become, managing redundancy is never straightforward, but in this chapter we have attempted to set the process into some sort of organised framework. Most redundancies occur because organisations need to change, and although we have recognised this, we nevertheless felt it important that employee relations specialists recognise that there should be alternatives to reducing an organisation's headcount. In particular we stressed that in an era of constant change businesses need to retain their competitive advantage. This is unlikely to happen if their employees are constantly looking over their shoulders, fearing for their jobs. One of the challenges that all managers, whether or not they are personnel practitioners, will face in the twenty-first century is how to reconcile the need for organisational change with the individuals' need for contentment and security at work.

Despite our plea for managers, at all levels, to consider the alternatives to redundancy, we do recognise the realities of organisational life. For this reason we have devoted a considerable part of this chapter to the need for effective policies and procedures for dealing with a redundancy situation. We would particularly draw to the attention of employee relations specialists the dangers of not having a policy and procedure.

In the section that dealt with the legal framework, we identified the costs that could accrue to an organisation that did not fulfil its statutory obligations. Evidence from numerous tribunal cases demonstrates that the most expensive failure is that of not consulting. The fact that so many organisations still fall into this trap is a direct consequence of not having an appropriate policy and procedure.

The final section of the chapter dealt with the way in which employers should deal with both redundant employees and those that remain in employment. The words of Richard Baker of Hoechst Roussel which we quoted are very pertinent. People do not forget how a redundancy exercise was handled, and the professional personnel practitioner will take care to ensure that any redundancy exercise considers the needs of all individuals, as well as those of the organisation.

FURTHER READING

FOWLER A. *Redundancy*. London, Institute of Personnel and Development, 1993.

INSTITUTE OF PERSONNEL AND DEVELOPMENT. *IPD Guide on Redundancy*. London, Institute of Personnel and Development, 1997.

LEWIS D. *Essentials of Employment Law*. 5th edn, London, Institute of Personnel and Development, 1997.

LEWIS D. *The Successful Management of Redundancy*. Oxford, Blackwells, 1993.

Part 5
REVIEW

11 Examination questions and advice

INTRODUCTION

The purpose of this final chapter is to review readers' knowledge and understanding of the major issues dealt with in the book. The chapter should prove especially useful for those students preparing for the IPD Professional Standards in the Generalist Module, Employee Relations, in that it provides questions which are similar to those likely to be found on the nationally set examination paper. At the same time, however, it should also prove beneficial to readers who are studying for internally set examinations, since it provides a framework for revision, as well as to those who are interested in posing questions about employee relations in their own organisation.

The chapter comprises two sections which follow the format of the IPD national examination paper in employee relations, and a third section which provides general advice on how to tackle the paper. The first section includes three case-studies similar to the one which is set in the national examination. If students are trying to simulate examination conditions, each of these questions should take about one hour to complete. In the second section of this chapter, there are 32 questions which aim to test knowledge and understanding through short answers, typically one paragraph in length, which can be completed in five to ten minutes. This style of question forms a common element of the IPD assessment portfolio under the Professional Qualification Scheme, not just the Generalist Module, Employee Relations, but throughout the whole set of modules.

SECTION A: CASE-STUDIES

Case 1: Re-location of employment
ABC is an organisation located in the middle of the UK. Although the product market is highly competitive, the organisation is successful.

It is a progressive company which is always looking for new opportunities, but it is also aware of its workforce responsibilities.

ABC employs 85 workers (manual and non-manual), the bulk of whom are full-time and are currently housed in premises which it owns in an expensive part of the city centre. The majority of the workforce live within easy travelling distance to the firm.

ABC is not a member of an employers' organisation. The delivery of the personnel function is line-management-centred. There is only a small personnel department with two personnel officers to advise and assist line managers. There is, however, a personnel director who sits on the highest policy-making body of ABC.

The working hours for manual employees are 36 hours per week but 35 hours for non-manual. Paid holiday entitlement for all employees is four weeks. There is a company pension scheme. Enhanced maternity leave arrangements exist. ABC maintains regular communications with its employees and has grievance, discipline, job-grading and redundancy procedures.

However, ABC is concerned that

a) the city centre location hampers expansion and the ability to invest in the new technology

b) there are problems of recruiting and retaining highly skilled employees

c) suppliers are re-locating outside the city centre assisted by the Government and European Commission Funds.

ABC has, therefore, decided to re-locate its establishment to a new site outside the city centre. The new location is some 50 minutes' travelling distance from its present location. ABC would like to transfer as many of its existing employees as possible to the new site. The employees are understandably concerned, and some of the more skilled employees have already started to look for alternative employment.

> Explain how you think ABC can re-locate its present operation but continue to achieve its employee relations objectives. How might some of the problems that you envisage will arise be overcome, and how might commitment from your managerial colleagues be gained?

Case 2: Threats from the corporate environment

XYZ is an organisation located in south-east England. It employs 400 people; 250 are manual employees, of which half are male and the other half female. There are 100 administrative, clerical, technical and professional staff, and the gender balance between and within these groups is appropriate. The remaining 50 employees are senior, middle and supervisory levels of management. The bulk of employees work full-time, although there are some part-timers amongst the clerical staff.

XYZ is not a member of an employers' organisation. The delivery of the personnel function is highly structured. There is a relatively large personnel department with a number of personnel assistants, officers and managers. There is, however, a personnel director who sits on the highest policy-making body of XYZ.

The working hours for the manual employees are 37 hours per week but 35 hours per week for all other employees. Paid holidays for manual employees are five weeks but six weeks for other employees. There are pay differentials between and within the main occupational categories at XYZ. There is a company pension scheme. XYZ maintains regular communications with its employees. XYZ has the usual procedures to be found in an employing organisation – grievance, discipline, promotion, job-grading and redundancy – and these work satisfactorily. Indeed, relationships with the employees have been good and employees regard employment at XYZ as relatively secure. This has been helped in that the pace of change in the organisation has been slow and evolutionary. It has certainly not been revolutionary.

However, XYZ is becoming anxious about the future. There is no crisis at present but management is giving thought to how the following might affect XYZ's activities in the future:

a) the organisation is becoming exposed to greater product market competition

b) the 'Social Dimension' of the European Union is moving forward at a slow pace but there are pressures from member states for it to be accelerated

c) technology is changing as computers, lasers and telecommunications continue to develop: it is clear that the rate of change at XYZ will accelerate significantly in the future.

> Explain how you think these changes in the external environment in which XYZ operates will impact upon its employee relations strategy and policies. How might some of the problems that you envisage will arise be overcome, and how might commitment be gained from your managerial colleagues and from the workforce?

Case 3: Gaining the confidence of the employees

You are employed as a personnel-HR management specialist with a large multi-plant private-sector company which has just purchased a formerly central-government-owned establishment in the manufacturing sector.

As part of the management, you face many problems at the establishment you have just acquired. The chief ones are:

a) The Government is not promising to guarantee any work to your newly acquired establishment, and the industry in which you operate is depressed. The workforce fears that your first decision will be to declare redundancies.

b) There are pre-privatisation-day grievances, particularly the dismissal of half a dozen employees, which are festering away and if not handled carefully will further alienate the workforce.

c) The workforce feels that the management of the acquiring organisation will have no commitment to its new establishment and will see working in the former government establishment as a staging-post en route to more senior management positions in the main organisation.

d) All trade unions were hostile to the privatisation fearing job insecurity and the abolition of civil service employment conditions. However, they accept the need for improved efficiency. There are two main trade union groups. Three represent administrative employees and five represent the manual workers. Union density is high and each union jealously guards its autonomy and bargaining rights. Although strikes have occurred in the past, they were infrequent and involved small numbers of the employees of one union. There are two nation-wide collective agreements negotiated by the central Government and the civil service unions. One agreement covers manual employees and the other non-manual. There are two separate sets of negotiations and single-table bargaining arrangements operate.

e) The personnel management function is underdeveloped and mainly administrative in operation. Policies merely stem from the acquired establishment's sponsoring ministry. There has also been a rapid turnover of personnel managers at the site.

All these problems mean that your company has taken over a demoralised workforce. You have been asked to produce a personnel-HR management strategy and related policies to gain the confidence of the employees and to demonstrate there is a stake for them in a new privatised establishment which is superior to that of the old civil service world.

> Produce, with justification, the personnel-HR management strategy and policies to achieve this objective.

SECTION B: QUESTIONS REQUIRING SHORT ANSWERS

1 Explain the main components of a grievance procedure.
2 Outline the main services ACAS provides to employing organisations.
3 Why might organisations wish to be members of an employers' association?
4 Outline the main functions of the state in employee relations.
5 How is a Directive agreed via the decision-making machinery of the European Union?
6 Briefly outline the key principles underpinning a disciplinary procedure.
7 Describe three management skills required by an effective employee relations manager-professional.

8 Explain the difference between bargaining and grievance-handling.

9 Explain the difference between qualified majority voting and unanimous decision-making in the European Union.

10 Outline the main roles of the law in regulating the employment relationship.

11 Explain the difference between conciliation, mediation and arbitration.

12 What are the main principles that should underlie employee relations procedural arrangements?

13 List at least four ways in which employee relations negotiating situations are different from commercial negotiations.

14 Explain the importance of interviewing skills in handling employee grievances.

15 Outline at least three pitfalls a management should avoid in disciplining employees.

16 Explain briefly the process you would adopt when dealing with a case of alleged sexual harassment by one employee against another.

17 What factors determine the balance of bargaining power between the buyers and sellers of labour services?

18 What constraints does the Working Time Directive impose on a business wishing to change its pattern of working hours?

19 List at least four reasons either (a) why an organisation may wish to manage with trade unions, or (b) wish to manage in a union-free environment.

20 Explain the differences between joint consultation and collective bargaining.

21 Explain the terms 'substantive agreement' and 'procedure agreement'.

22 Identify and explain a minimum of three 'core skills' required by an employee relations manager when handling employee grievances.

23 Why is the New Earnings Survey a publication with which every employee relations manager should be familiar?

24 In handling disciplinary matters, how does a management demonstrate 'fair' and 'reasonable' behaviour?

25 List at least three pitfalls a management should avoid in managing a redundancy situation.

26 Explain, with examples, how the Social Chapter of the Treaty of Rome has impinged on the day-to-day activities of personnel managers.

27 Explain briefly why 'good practice' behaviour is essential to the professional employee relations manager.

28 List, with justification, the criteria you would use to evaluate whether procedural arrangements were operating satisfactorily from a management perspective.

29 Explain briefly the terms 'quality circles', 'team-briefing' and 'profit-related pay'.

30 In managing a redundancy situation, list the information that the employer concerned must make available to the employees and/or their representatives.

31 List at least four employee relations advantages that might arise from the implementation of employee involvement and commitment schemes.

32 Explain the difference between 'pendulum' arbitration and so-called 'conventional' arbitration.

EXAMINATION GUIDELINES

The purpose of this final section is to provide students with some guidance about the way in which to tackle examination questions on the Employee Relations (Generalist Module) paper. A number of general comments are appropriate, given that students tend to make mistakes on each part of the paper, but these are supplemented with more specific reservations relating to each part of the paper.

Four general points can be made:

1   Many candidates fail to answer all the parts of a multi-part question and this is often the case too on the compulsory case-study. Typically, the majority fail this question because they do not provide costings for their proposals or explain how they would gain the commitment of their managerial colleagues and the workforce to their proposed course of action even though this is usually specified in the question. Students need to remember that they are unlikely to gain more than half the available marks if they answer only half the question.

2   Many candidates fail to address the question that has been set, preferring to tell the examiner all they know about the subject matter of the question. While this can be very interesting, it demonstrates that the student has not read and/or understood the question. Students must read the questions and then answer the question set. Similarly, it is common for students to write an essay rather than a report or draft training programme when this is requested. One of the skills that examiners are trying to assess in the paper is the ability of students to write in a clear, concise and convincing manner. Students are advised to produce a shorter answer which is well planned and reveals knowledge and understanding of the subject matter of the question rather than a longer, unstructured answer which produces the relevant points by accident instead of by design.

3   Many candidates seem to lose sight of the overall objectives when answering a question and provide an unbalanced answer which devotes far too much time to one part of the question to the detriment of others. Clear planning before starting to write an answer can obviously reduce this problem. On some occasions, students seem to believe that making references to well-known academics demonstrates knowledge and understanding of the principal issues surrounding the subject matter of the question. This is all very well if the references are relevant and appropriate, and do not appear to be bolted on to a somewhat peripheral answer.

4   Many students fail to locate their answer in the wider commercial and environmental context, showing little appreciation of national or European-Union-wide trends or longer-term developments in the economy as a whole, the legal framework surrounding management employee relations strategies and policies or in

employee relations in particular. There is often a temptation to assume that current fads and fashions represent a superior solution to organisational problems and little recognition that they may be superficial and trite. Students must demonstrate when discussing current 'new' management practices (sometimes referred to as 'fads') that they are capable of analysing and evaluating whether the success (or alleged success) of the introduction of such practices in one organisation is relevant and capable of being successfully transplanted into another organisation. Students also often fail to recognise the force of existing cultural norms and traditions when putting forward recommendations, somehow assuming that all options are feasible. It is important to demonstrate an awareness of the constraints (financial, resistance from one's managerial colleagues, etc) as well as the opportunities when answering questions. One of the things which the Professional Qualification Scheme aims to develop in students is the ability to persuade line managers of the usefulness of employee relations strategy, policies and practices in solving specific organisational problems.

Taking a more positive stance, there are certain guidelines which students might like to bear in mind when preparing for the examination, some of which build upon what has been said in the previous paragraphs. These are:

1 Make sure that the material in the whole syllabus is understood, at least to the extent of being able to provide a short paragraph-length answer to the questions in Section B of the paper. In addition, when addressing the case-study in Section A, students need to be able to demonstrate a holistic appreciation of employee relations.

2 Provide examples, as appropriate, to support a particular answer and arguments. These may be drawn from any organisation, not only the one for which the student currently works, and it is useful if contemporary examples are provided as these show that the student is up-to-date and is reading the professional journals.

3 Write concisely and clearly, providing signposts to an answer. There is nothing worse for an examiner than having to re-read an answer several times in order to try to identify precisely what the student is trying to say. A clear introduction stating explicitly what will be contained in the answer helps considerably in this respect, as does the use of paragraphs, sections and numbering; the precise technique which is used matters less than the overall impact, and students should therefore use the approach with which they feel most comfortable.

4 Ensure that the examination is timed so that an attempt can be made at all questions. It is worthwhile repeating that approximately one hour should be allocated to each section in the examination paper. This means that in Section B, each question should take between 5 and 10 minutes to answer.

These guidelines should not be seen as some attempt to impose unrealistic academic standards on IPD students. Rather, these skills are central to all aspects of managerial work – *viz* by addressing the question which is posed, choosing from alternatives to formulate a realistic answer, justifying and costing a recommendation, and writing in a clear and well structured manner which manages to persuade the reader.

There are a number of more specific comments relating to each of the sections. When addressing the case-study, students need to ensure they understand the case as a whole and are able to identify the key points within it. In suggesting solutions to the problems posed in the case-study, students must demonstrate

- that they can integrate the different aspects of employee relations

- that they can cost their proposals in ballpark figures – exact costs are not necessary

- that they can explain how they would gain commitment to their proposals from their management colleagues and from the workforce

- that they can discuss policy options, including the pros and cons of each, and which on balance they would select, and why

- that 'new' management practices (fads) are relevant, including why they might be successful in solving an organisation's problem

- how employee relations solutions would contribute to the achievement of an organisation's objectives

- that they understand commercial realities. Students frequently argue that they would reduce an organisation's headcount by early retirement schemes – but without telling the examiners whether the organisation's pension fund scheme could finance such a policy, and without recognising that early retirement is a matter for the fund's trustees and not the chief executive alone. Students have also demonstrated that they do not realise the implementation of technological change takes time as well as money in that the technology has to be ordered, delivered, installed, and the technical problems ironed out, etc.

Section B comprises a number of questions which require short paragraph-length answers. These can be drawn from any part of the syllabus and require students to present fairly basic core information in order to demonstrate their knowledge and understanding of the topics under consideration. The answers in this section need to be concise, but can usefully be supplemented with examples to illustrate the students' understanding of the issue. It is important that all questions in this section are answered.

References

ADVISORY, CONCILIATION, AND ARBITRATION SERVICE. (1997) *Discipline at Work: The ACAS Advisory Handbook.* 20th ed. London, ACAS.

ADVISORY, CONCILIATION, AND ARBITRATION SERVICE. *Annual reports.*

ADVISORY, CONCILIATION, AND ARBITRATION SERVICE. (1995) *Employee Communications and Consultation.* London, ACAS.

ASHTON D. and FELSTEAD A. (1995) 'Training and development', in Storey J. (ed.) *Human Resource Management: A Critical Text.* London, Routledge.

BLAKSTAD M. and COOPER A. (1995) *The Communicating Organisation.* London, Institute of Personnel and Development.

BLYTON P. and TURNBULL P. (1994) *The Dynamics of Employee Relations.* London, Macmillan.

BURNES B. (1996) *Managing Change: A strategic approach to organisational dynamics.* London, Pitman.

CLARK J. and WINCHESTER D. (1994) 'Management and trade unions', in Sisson K. (ed.) *Personnel Management: A Comprehensive Guide to Theory and Practice in Britain.* Oxford, Blackwell.

CLAYDON T. (1989) 'Union derecognition in Britain in the 1980s'. *British Journal of Industrial Relations.* Vol. 27, No. 2; pp214–24.

CLEGG, H.A. (1979) *The Changing System of Industrial Relations in Great Britain.* Oxford, Blackwell.

CONFEDERATION OF BRITISH INDUSTRY. (1996) *Annual Report 1995.* London, CBI.

DONALDSON P. and FARQUHAR J. (1991) *Understanding the British Economy.* London, Penguin.

EDWARDS P. (1994) 'Discipline and the Creation of Order', in Sisson K. (ed.) *Personnel Management: A Comprehensive Guide to Theory and Practice in Britain.* Oxford, Blackwell.

ENGINEERING EMPLOYERS' FEDERATION. (1995) *Developing Employee Relations: Guidance for EEF Associations and Member Companies.* London, EEF.

EVENDON R. and ANDERSON G. (1992) *Making the Most of People.* Wokingham, Addison-Wesley.

FOWLER A. (1996) *Effective Negotiation.* London, Institute of Personnel and Development.

FOWLER A. (1993) *Redundancy.* London, Institute of Personnel and Development.

GALL G. and McKAY S. (1994) 'Trade union derecognition in Britain,

1988–1994'. *British Journal of Industrial Relations*. Vol. 32, No. 3; pp433–48.

GAPPER J. (1990) 'At the end of the honeymoon'. *Financial Times*, 10 January.

GEARY J. F. (1994) 'Task participation: Employees' participation enabled or constrained', in Sisson K. (ed.) *Personnel Management*. 2nd ed., Oxford, Blackwell.

GENNARD J. (1990) *A History of the National Graphical Association*. London, Unwin Hyman.

GUEST D. (1995) 'Human resource management, trade unions and industrial relations'. In Storey J. (ed.) *Human Resource Management: A critical text*. London, Routledge.

HENDRICKS R. *and* MUMFORD E. (1996) 'Business Process Re-engineering RIP'. *People Management*, Vol. 2, No. 9, May; pp22–29.

INCOMES DATA SERVICES. *Report*, published twice-monthly.

INCOMES DATA SERVICES. *Pay Directory*, published three times a year.

INDUSTRIAL RELATIONS SERVICES. *Employment Review*, published twice-monthly.

INDUSTRIAL RELATIONS SERVICES. *Pay Intelligence*, published monthly.

INDUSTRIAL SOCIETY. (1995) *Managing Best Practice: Empowerment*. London, Industrial Society.

INSTITUTE OF PERSONNEL AND DEVELOPMENT. (1996) *Statement on Employment Relations*. London, Institute of Personnel and Development.

JOHNSON G. *and* SCHOLES K. (1997) *Exploring Corporate Strategy*. London, Prentice Hall.

KAHN-FREUND O. (1997) *Labour and the Law*. London, Stevens.

KAY J. (1993) *Foundations of Corporate Success*. Oxford, OUP.

KEEGAN W. (1984) *Mrs Thatcher's Economic Experiment*. London, Penguin.

KENNEDY G., BENSON J., *and* MCMILLAN J. (1989) *Managing Negotiations*. London, Hutchinson.

LEWIS D. (1997) *Essentials of Employment Law*. London, Institute of Personnel and Development.

LEWIS P. (1993) *The Successful Management of Redundancy*. Oxford, Blackwell.

MARCHINGTON M. (1982) *Managing Industrial Relations*. Maidenhead, McGraw-Hill; chapter 7.

MARCHINGTON M. *and* WILKINSON A. (1996) *Core Personnel and Development*. London, Institute of Personnel and Development.

MARCHINGTON M. 'Involvement and participation' in Storey J. (ed.), *Human Resource Management: a critical text*. London, Routledge.

MARCHINGTON M., WILKINSON A. *and* ACKERS P. (1993) 'Waving or drowning in participation'. *Personnel Management*, March, pp 30–33.

MARSH D. (1992) *The New Politics of British Trade Unions*. Basingstoke, Macmillan Press.

MILLWARD N., STEVENS M., SMART D., *and* HAWES W. R. (1992) *Workplace Industrial Relations in Transition*. Dartmouth; chapters 3, 5, 8 and 10.

NOLAN P. *and* WALSH J. (1995) 'The structure of the economy and labour market', in Edwards P. (ed.) *Industrial Relations – Theory and Practice in Britain* Oxford, Blackwell.

OFFICE FOR NATIONAL STATISTICS. *Labour Market Trends*, incorporating *Employment Gazette*, published monthly.

OFFICE FOR NATIONAL STATISTICS, *New Earnings Survey*, 1996, published in six parts.

PETTIGREW A. *and* WHIPP R. (1995) *Managing Change for Competitive Success*. Oxford, Blackwell.

PORTER M. (1985) *Competitive Advantage: Creating and sustaining superior performance*. New York, Free Press.

PURCELL J. (1987) 'Mapping management styles in Employee Relations'. *Journal of Management Studies*. Vol. 24, No. 5; p535.

RAMSAY H. (1996) 'Involvement, empowerment and commitment', in Towers B. (ed.) *The Handbook of Human Resource Management*. 2nd ed. Oxford, Blackwell.

SALAMON M. (1992) *Industrial Relations Theory and Practice*. London, Prentice Hall.

SUMMERFIELD J. (1996) 'Lean firms cannot afford to be mean'. *People Management*, Vol. 2, No. 2, January; pp30–32.

TORRINGTON D. *and* HALL L. (1991) *Personnel Management*, 2nd ed. Prentice Hall.

TRADES UNION CONGRESS. (1994) *Human Resource Management: A trade union response*. London, TUC.

TYSON S. (1995) *Human Resource Strategy: Towards a general theory of human resource management*. London, Pitman.

WADDINGTON J. *and* WHITSTON C. (1995) 'Trade unions: growth, structure and policy', in Edwards P. (ed.) *Industrial Relations: Theory and Practice in Britain*. Oxford, Blackwell.

WEDDERBURN K. *The Worker and the Law*. London, Penguin.

Index

absence management 191–5
abuse of power 5, 37–8
ACAS *see* Advisory, Conciliation and
    Arbitration Service
Acquired Rights Directive 59, 254
    adjournments 151–2, 218,
    224, 225, 226
Advisory, Conciliation and
    Arbitration Service 84–7, 89
    advice on communications 124,
      125, 126
    disciplinary code 175, 177, 178,
      179, 183, 196
    guidelines on absence 192–4
    statistics 22, 25–6, 28
advisory services, employers'
    organisations 72
AEEU *see* Amalgamated Engineering
    and Electrical Union
Agreement on Social Policy 28,
    59–60, 123
agreements 28–31, 143–5
    conclusion of 161–2, 234–5
    documentation of 162, 166,
      235–6
    see also collective agreements
aims *see* objectives
alternatives to redundancy 244
Amalgamated Engineering and
    Electrical Union 78, 83
appeals
    disciplinary procedures 195–6
    grievance procedures 202
arbitration 25–6, 86, 87
    management differences 17
aspiration grids 156, 215–16, 229–30
authoritarian management style
    99–100

Baker, Richard 255
balance of power *see* bargaining power
ballots
    industrial action 55, 64, 111–12

    union membership rights 54–5
banking industry 33, 238
bargaining 148–9, 152–4, 222–37
    confirmation of common ground
      232–6
    definition of 222
    pay bargaining 234–5
    preparations for 224–31
    presentation of proposals 231–2
    team discipline 225–6
    team selection 224–5
    see also agreements; collective
      bargaining
bargaining power 4–5, 12, 13, 31–8,
    43–5, 62–5, 157, 230–1
bargaining units 31
best practice 3, 7–8, 99, 104
    discipline 175, 183, 184, 191,
      194, 196
    grievance-handling 200, 201, 207
    redundancy 239
Blue Circle Cement 242
body language 165, 171, 173, 224
Body Shop 92
bottom-line *see* fall-back positions
BPIF *see* British Printing Industries
    Federation
'brain-pattern' technique 167–8
Bridlington Agreement 83
briefings 127, 128–9
Bristol & West Building Society 241
British Coal 36–7
British Home Stores *v* Burchell
    (1978) 189–90
British Petroleum 93
British Printing Industries Federation
    68–9, 71, 222–3
British Telecom 29, 245
'bubble' technique 167–8
Building Employers' Confederation
    72
Burchell test 189–90
business awareness 116, 117, 123

business-level strategy 95

C. A. Parsons & Co. Ltd v
    McLaughlin (1978) 181
Cambridge and District Co-op v
    Ruse (1993) 249
capability 190–5
car industry 60, 61
    Ford Motor Company 14, 30, 61,
        77, 94, 97, 99
    Nissan 99, 102
    Rover Cars 61, 241–2
    Volkswagen 242
cascading of information 127, 128–9
case-studies 259–62
CBI see Confederation of British
    Industry
CEEP see European Centre of
    Enterprises with Public
    Participation
Central Arbitration Committee 87–8
Certification Officer 68, 88
change 239–42
    cultural change 93, 118
    technological change 33–4, 60–2,
        65
check-off system 105, 110
Chris Metcalf Ltd v Maddocks
    (1985) 210
'chronological' note-taking 168–9
civil service 51, 52
closed shops 56, 110
coal industry 36–7, 63–4
collective agreements 29–31
    national agreements 30, 67–8, 69,
        70–1
    see also agreements
collective bargaining 24
    Conservative Government attitude
        43, 52
    European-wide 84
    role of employers' organisations
        67–8, 70–1, 73
    see also bargaining; collective
        agreements
Collective Redundancies and
    Transfer of Undertakings
    (Protection of Employment)
    (Amendment) Regulations
    1995 250
Collective Redundancies Directive
    250, 251
collectivism 100
commercial negotiations 151–2
Commissioner for the Rights of Trade
    Union Members 55
commitment see employee

commitment; management
    commitment
common ground 159–61, 213–16,
    217–18, 232–4
common interests 20–3
communication skills 39
communications 124–9
company agreements 30
company rules 180–3
comparability 51, 52
competitiveness 46, 47, 48, 238, 240,
    241
conciliation 22, 25, 26, 85–6
conditions of employment see
    employment conditions
conduct see misconduct
Confederation of British Industry 34,
    74, 80
confidentiality 126
Conservative Governments,
    1979–1997 32–3, 49–57
consistency, disciplinary processes
    177, 182, 186–7
constitutional organisations 100
consultation 24, 123, 133–5
    redundancies 250–4
    transfers of undertakings 254
consultative organisations 100
continuous service qualifications 28,
    54
corporate environment 4–5, 7, 12,
    32–4, 41–65
corporate-level strategy 94–5
cost leadership 95
Council of Ministers 57, 58
counselling 184–5, 254–5
craft unions 19, 46, 61, 75–6, 82
criminal charges 189, 190
cultural change 93, 118
custom and practice 30

data collection and analysis 155,
    226–8
Day, Graham 241
de-skilling 61–2
decentralised bargaining 30, 42, 52,
    68, 70, 77–8
demarcation disputes 76
Denco v Joinson (1991) 181
derecognition 33, 106–7, 117
deregulation 50, 51
devolution of personnel function 3
differentials 20, 52
directives 59
    Acquired Rights Directive 59, 254
    Collective Redundancies Directive
        250, 251

Working Time Directive 28, 58
Works Council Directive 60, 123
disability discrimination 96, 194–5
discipline 99–100, 104, 174–97
   appeals 195–6
   company rules 180–3
   handling capability issues 190–5
   handling misconduct 188–90
   interviews 186–8
   legal framework 175–7
   procedures 177–9
discrimination 96–7
   disabled people 96, 194–5
   racial discrimination 96–7
   sex discrimination 59, 96, 200,
      248
dishonesty see theft
dismissal 8, 22, 175–7, 183
   capability reasons 190–5
   for misconduct 188–90
   redundancy reasons 253
   'some other substantial reason'
      195
disputes procedures 30, 71–2, 198
   see also grievance-handling
dissatisfaction 198–201
Donovan Commission 46, 78
downsizing 240, 241, 243

early retirement 244
Economic and Social Committee 58
economic environment 32, 43–53
economic performance see national
   economic performance
employee commitment 101–2,
      115–16, 124, 133, 240–1
employee communications 124–9
employee councils see works councils
employee development 97
employee dissatisfaction 198–201
employee involvement see
      involvement and participation
employee organisations 18–19
   professional associations 18–19,
      84
   staff associations 19, 84
   trade unions see trade unions
employee participation see
      involvement and participation
employee relations
   policies see policies
   processes 23–8
   purpose of 4, 13
   skills 38–40, 102–3
employee resourcing 96–7
employee share ownership plans 133
employees

common interests with employers
   20–3
interests in labour market 17–20
employers
   common interests with employees
      20–3
   interests in labour market 14–17
employers' organisations 42, 66,
      67–75, 88, 226
   see also names of individual bodies
Employment Act 1980 56
Employment Act 1982 56
Employment Act 1988 56
Employment Act 1990 56
employment conditions 14–15,
      17–18, 28–30
Employment Protection Act 1975
      177, 250
Employment Protection
      (Consolidation) Act 1978 176
employment protection rights 54,
      175–7
Employment Review 226–7
Employment Rights Act 1996 176–7,
      183, 246–7, 253
empowerment 103, 114
enabling clauses 70
Engineering Employers' Federation
      67, 68, 69, 70–1, 73
environment see corporate
   environment
equal pay 59, 200
ESOP see employee share ownership
   plans
European Centre of Enterprises with
   Public Participation 57
European Commission 57, 58
European Court of Justice 57, 250
European Monetary Union 44
European Parliament 57, 58
European Trades Union
      Confederation 34, 57, 58,
      83–4
European Union
   directives see directives
   institutions 57
   legislative processes 28, 57–60
   trade union representation 57–8,
      83–4
European Works Councils 60, 123
evaluation skills 39–40, 102–3
examination guidelines 264–6
expense claim fraud 190
eye-contact 165, 171

fall-back positions 156, 161–2, 215,
      216, 229, 230

final offers 161–2
financial participation schemes 115, 123, 132–3
5Ws technique 164, 166, 211–12
Ford Motor Company 14, 30, 61, 77, 94, 97, 99
full employment 44, 45–7
functional-level strategy 95

GCHQ 52
Geary, J. F. 130, 131
general unions 19, 75
globalisation 45
'golden formula' 79
good practice see best practice
government policies 4, 7, 12, 23
    history of 45–57
    influence on bargaining power 32–3, 34, 43–5, 62–5
    in role as employer 51–3, 65
Granada Group 95
Graphical, Paper and Media Union 76, 83, 222
grievance-handling 198–221
    definition of grievance 199–200
    documentation of agreements 162, 218–19
    interviewing skills 155, 163–6, 211–13
    legal framework 209–10
    negotiation of settlements 147–8, 150, 158, 213–18
    procedures 29, 202–10
    records 208–9
    representational rights 205–7
gross misconduct 178, 179, 180, 181–3, 189
group problem-solving 21, 149–50

Hindes v Supersine Ltd (1979) 249
holidays, late return from 191–2
horizontal integration 2, 122
Horton, Robert 93
hours of work 28, 58
human resource managers see personnel/HR managers

IDS see Incomes Data Services Ltd
'if and then' techniques 160, 218, 233
ill-health dismissals 192–5
ILO see International Labour Organisation
immunities of trade unions 55–7, 79
incapability 190–5
Incomes Data Services Ltd 227
incomes policies 46, 47, 48–9, 85
inconsistency see consistency

individualism 100
industrial action see industrial sanctions
Industrial Relations Act 1971 55, 175
Industrial Relations Services 226–7
industrial sanctions 26–8, 36–7
    legal remedies 57, 110–12
industrial tribunals 22, 54, 175, 183, 252
industrial unions 19, 75
industry-wide agreements see national agreements
inflation 32, 47, 49–50, 52, 62
information collection and analysis 155, 226–8
injunctions 56, 110, 112
Institute of Directors 34, 74, 80
Institute of Personnel and Development code on involvement and participation 119
    qualifications and syllabus 6, 9–10
    statement on employment relations 28, 41
inter-union disputes 76–7, 83
International Confederation of Free Trade Unions 83
International Labour Organisation 83
interviews
    disciplinary interviews 186–8
    grievance interviews 155, 211–13
    interviewing skills 39, 141, 163–6
involvement and participation 24, 114–42
    aims and objectives 114–18
    financial participation 132–3
    introduction of schemes 135–42
    mechanisms and techniques 118–35
    representative participation 133–5
IPD see Institute of Personnel and Development
IRS see Industrial Relations Services
issues for negotiation 155, 228–9
    linking of 160, 233

job enlargement 130
job enrichment 130
job evaluation 219–20
job-grading disputes 219–20
job satisfaction 124
job security 239, 240, 241, 242
joint consultative committees 24, 134–5
    see also consultation
judgement 173
just cause 7, 8

Kahn-Freund, Otto 53
Keynesian economics 46–7

labour market
    employees' interests 17–20
    employers' interests 14–17
Labour Market Trends 228
Labour Party 44, 46, 48, 54, 63
    association with unions 79–80
Labour Representation Committee 79
labour turnover 21
last-in first-out 245
late return from holiday 191–2
legal environment 28, 32, 53–60
legal remedies, employers' 110–12
Lesney Products *v* Nolan (1977) 248
LIFO *see* last-in first-out
linking of issues 160, 233
listening skills 39, 141, 171–3, 234
lobbying 4, 34, 73, 74, 79
local bargaining *see* decentralised
    bargaining
London Underground 64, 80, 110,
    145
long-term ill-health 193–5
low pay 14–15
LRC *see* Labour Representation
    Committee

Maastricht Treaty (1993) 28, 58, 59,
    123
management commitment 103, 104,
    116, 131, 132, 137–40
management of change 239–42
management style 99–101, 201
managers
    competing interests 16–17
    negotiations between 145–7
Marchington, M. 34, 35, 69–70, 122,
    138, 139, 197
Marks & Spencer plc 14, 42, 98, 107,
    108
Meade-Hill and Another *v* British
    Council (1995) 248
mediation 25, 26
medical examinations 193
medical profession 84
meetings 127, 137
memory 173
Minford, Patrick 52
misconduct 180, 188–90
    see also gross misconduct
mission 94
mitigating circumstances 186
mobility clauses 248–9
monetarism 49–50, 51–3
monetary union 44

monitoring
    communication systems 128
    involvement and participation
        schemes 141–2
    policies 99, 104
motor industry *see* car industry
MSF *v* GEC Ferranti (Defence
    Systems) Ltd (1994) 252
multi-skilling 97
multinational companies 45

national agreements 30, 67–8, 69,
    70–1, 73
national economic performance 46,
    48, 238
National Graphical Association 71,
    76, 102, 110
National Union of Mineworkers
    36–7, 64
National Westminster Bank 238
natural justice 7, 99, 183, 196, 202,
    206
negotiation 5, 8–9, 21, 143–73
    bargaining *see* bargaining
    between managers 145–7
    commercial negotiations 151–2
    grievance-handling 147–8,
        213–18
    group problem-solving 21, 149–50
    preparations for 154–8
    presentation of proposals 158–9
    purpose of 143–5
    skills 39, 141, 163–73
    stages of 154–62
    types of 145–52
New Earnings Survey 155, 228
New Right 49–50
new technology *see* technological
    change
News International 42, 61, 82, 102
Nissan 99, 102
non-union organisations 6–7, 105,
    107–10
    balance of power 31–2
    collectively-bargained rates and 24
    communication methods 128
non-verbal communication *see* body
    language
note-taking 165, 166–70, 172, 173,
    224
nursing profession 19, 84

objectives
    in bargaining 229–31
    in negotiations 156–7
occupational pension schemes 134,
    244

occupational unions 19
opportunist organisations 100
outplacement 255–6

participation *see* involvement and
     participation
paternalist organisations 98, 100
pay comparability 51, 52
pay data 72, 226–8
pay differentials 20, 52
pay norms *see* income policies
pendulum arbitration 25, 86
pension schemes 134, 244
performance problems *see* poor
     performance
personal contracts 29
personal vision 93
personnel/HR managers, effectiveness
     of 1–3
place of work 248–9
'play-back' technique 161, 165, 212,
     218
pluralism 98
policies 98–104
     communications 124–6, 128
     redundancy 242–3
     trade unions 104–10
political lobbying *see* lobbying
Polkey *v* A.E. Dayton Services Ltd
     (1987) 253
poor performance 126, 180, 184–5,
     187, 191
Porter, M. 95
post-war consensus 45–9, 246
postal services 27, 64, 80
power
     abuse of 5, 37–8
     definition of 31
     see also bargaining power
'presentation' note-taking style 169,
     170
presentation skills 170–1
printing industry 33, 42, 61, 71, 76,
     82, 102, 110, 222–3
private-sector businesses 15–16
problem-solving, group 21, 149–50
procedural agreements 4, 29
product differentiation 95
professional associations 18–19, 84
profit-sharing 132–3
proposals, presentation of 158–9,
     217, 231–2
protective awards 252–3
psychological contract 240–1, 242
public expenditure 44, 52–3, 80
public-sector employment 16, 42–3,
     51–3, 80

Purcell, J. 99–101

qualified majority voting 50
qualifying periods 28, 54
quality circles 130–1
quality management *see* total quality
     management (TQM)

racial discrimination 96–7
Ramsey, H. 116–17, 118, 132
re-engineering 243
reasonableness 8, 29, 183, 188,
     189–90
recognition of trade unions decline in
     23–4
     requests for 109–10
redundancy 238–58
     alternative employment 245,
          249–50
     alternatives to 244
     consultation 134, 250–4
     counselling and outplacement
          254–6
     legal framework 246–54
     payments 246, 247–50
     policies 242–3
     procedures 243–6
     selection methods 244–5
     survivor syndrome 256–7
Redundancy Payments Act 1965 246
relocation *see* mobility clauses; place
     of work
representational rights, grievance
     procedures 205–7
retirement, early 244
reward 14–15, 96, 97
     see also financial participation
          schemes; pay data
Roddick, Anita 92
Rover Cars 61, 241–2
Royal Commission on Trade Unions
     and Employers' Associations 46, 78
Royal Mail 27, 80
rules *see* company rules

safety representatives 134, 176
salary surveys *see* pay data
SCELI investigation 61–2
secondary industrial action 56, 110
selection for redundancy 244–5
sex discrimination 59, 96, 200, 248
Sex Discrimination Act 1975 59, 248
sexual harassment 184, 220
share ownership schemes 133
Sheffield City Council 242
shop stewards 48, 77–8
sickness absence 192–5

single-table bargaining 31
single-union agreements 31
skill changes 61–2
skill shortages 32, 44–5, 68
Social Changes and Economic Life
    Initiative 61–2
Social Chapter 58, 59, 107
Social Charter 59
social partners 57–8
Social Policy Agreement *see*
    Agreement on Social Policy
Social Protocol 28, 59, 123
Society of Graphical and Allied
    Trades 76, 102
'some other substantial reason' 195
staff associations 19, 84
state, role of the *see* government
    policies
stoppages *see* strikes
strategy 91–8
    employment policies and 95–8
    formulation of 92–4
    levels 94–5
strikes 27, 36–7
    see also industrial sanctions
substantive agreements 4, 29
'suitable alternative employment'
    245, 249–50
Sunday Trading Act 1994 176
'super-unions' 42
'supply-side' economics 50
survivor syndrome 256–7
SWOT analysis 93

T&GWU *see* Transport and General
    Workers Union
Taff Vale case (1901) 55, 79
task-based involvement 129–30
team-briefing 129
teamworking 130
technological change 33–4, 60–2, 65
terms of employment *see* employment
    conditions
Thatcherism *see* monetarism
theft 179, 181–2, 189
third-party intervention, 25–6, 84–8
time-keeping 182–3, 186
time-limits
    disciplinary appeals 196
    expiry of warnings 178, 179
    grievance procedures 205
time-scales
    bargaining processes 153–4
    disciplinary processes 185
Todd, Ron 240
total quality management (TQM)
    131–2

Trade Disputes Act 1906 55, 79
Trade Union Act 1984 56
Trade Union and Labour Relations
    Act 1974 55
Trade Union and Labour Relations
    (Amendment) Act 1976 55
Trade Union and Labour Relations
    (Consolidation) Act 1992 56,
    250, 251
Trade Union Reform and
    Employment Rights Act 1993
    57, 176, 250
trade unions 19, 75–84
    Certification Officer 68, 88
    consultation rights 134, 250
    decline in membership 33, 81,
        105
    decline in recognition 23–4
    derecognition 33, 106–7
    in European countries 77
    future prospects 80–2, 89
    immunities 55–7, 79
    involvement and participation
        schemes 116, 117, 128, 129,
        140
    organisation of 77–9
    policies towards 102, 104–10
    and politics 79–80
    post-war power 46, 48–9
    repudiation of members' actions
        57
    restrictions on 52, 53, 54–7
    rights of members 54–5
    role in grievance handling 202,
        204, 206
    and technological change 61
    typology and coverage 75–7
    see also names of individual unions
Trades Union Congress 19, 34, 79,
    82–4
training 48, 97
    for involvement schemes 120,
        140–1
transfers of undertakings 134, 254
Transport and General Workers'
    Union 77, 83, 242
Treaty of Rome (1957) 58, 59
Treaty on European Union *see*
    Maastricht Treaty
trial periods 249–50
trust 124, 240–1
TUC *see* Trades Union Congress
turnover *see* labour turnover

unemployment 32, 49, 50, 51, 52, 53,
    62, 238, 240
unfair dismissal *see* dismissal

UNICE *see* Union of Industrial and Employers' Confederations of Europe
unilateral action 23–4, 144
Union of Industrial and Employers' Confederations of Europe 34, 57, 58, 74–5
unions *see* trade unions
UNISON 42, 81
unitarist organisations 98

vertical integration 2, 122
Volkswagen 242
voluntary redundancy 244–5

W. A. Goold (Pearmack) Ltd *v* McConnell (1995) 209–10
Wages Act 1986 176
wages councils 28

Wapping dispute *see* News International
warnings 177–8, 179
watching skills 173, 224
welfare provision 53
Wilson, Harold 46
'winter of discontent' 20, 48–9
WIRS *see* Workplace Industrial Relations Survey
'work of a particular kind' 247, 248
Working Time Directive 28, 58
Workplace Industrial Relations Survey 23, 24, 29, 106, 108, 117, 128
Works Council Directive 60, 123
works councils 18, 123, 134–5
worksharing 242

zero-hours contracts 38